Gulliver's Travels

Gulliver's Travels

adapted & updated
by

Martin Rowson

Atlantic Books
London

First published in Great Britain in 2012 by Atlantic Books,
an imprint of Atlantic Books Ltd.

This paperback edition published in Great Britain in 2013 by Atlantic Books.

10 9 8 7 6 5 4 3 2 1

A CIP catalogue record for this book is available from the British Library.

Trade Paperback ISBN: 978 1 78239 0 084

Printed in Great Britain by the MPG Printgroup

Atlantic Books
An imprint of Atlantic Books Ltd
Ormond House
26–27 Boswell Street
London
WC1N 3JZ

www.atlantic-books.co.uk

CONTENTS

To the memory of Michael Foot, in gratitude for his company
and appreciation, and in the vain hope that he would accept
that in my poor efforts of fitting homage to his beloved Dean,
I've at least got the politics right...

And, as always, for Anna, Fred and Rose, with love.

'I tell you after all, that I do not hate mankind: it is *vous autres* who hate them, because you would have them reasonable animals, and are angry for being disappointed...'

Jonathan Swift, letter to Alexander Pope

'For what man, in the natural state or course of thinking, did ever conceive it in his power to reduce the notions of all mankind exactly to the same length, and breadth, and height of his own?'

Jonathan Swift, "A Digression on Madness", *Tale of a Tub*

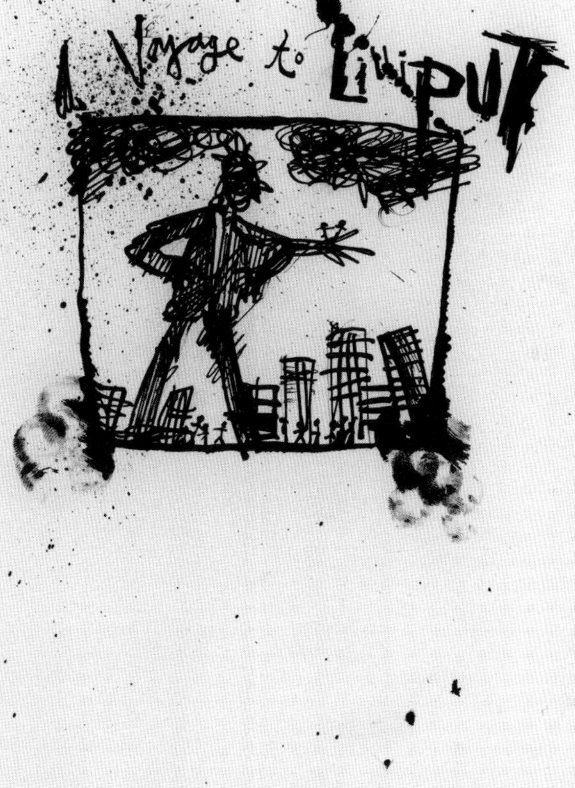
A Voyage to Lilliput

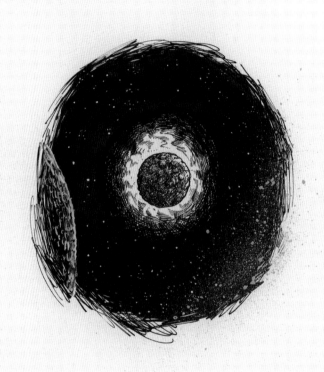

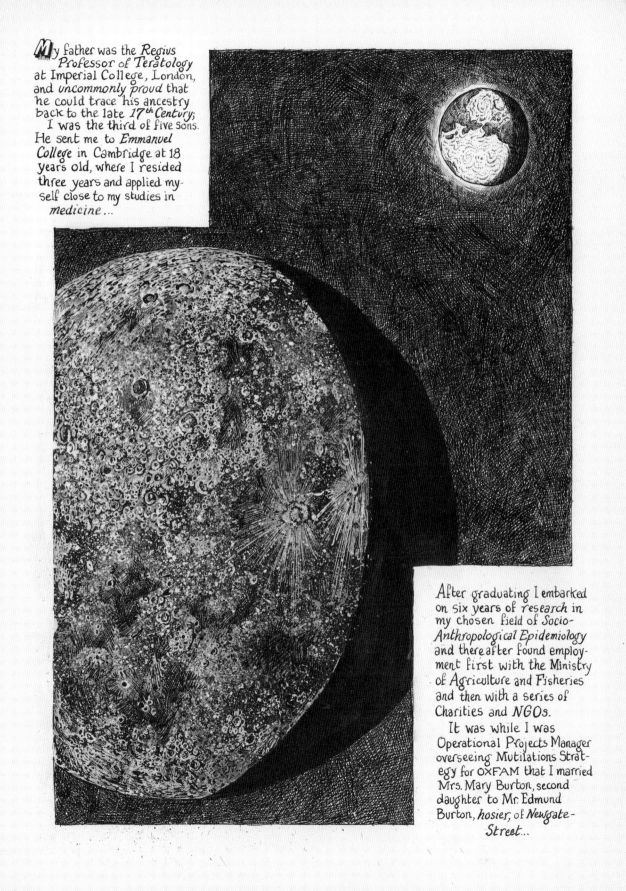

My father was the Regius Professor of Teratology at Imperial College, London, and *uncommonly proud* that he could trace his ancestry back to the late *17th Century;* I was the third of five sons. He sent me to *Emmanuel College* in Cambridge at 18 years old, where I resided three years and applied myself close to my studies in *medicine*...

After graduating I embarked on six years of *research* in my chosen field of *Socio-Anthropological Epidemiology* and thereafter found employment first with the Ministry of Agriculture and Fisheries and then with a series of Charities and *NGOs.*

It was while I was Operational Projects Manager overseeing Mutilations Strategy for OXFAM that I married Mrs. Mary Burton, second daughter to Mr. Edmund Burton, *hosier,* of *Newgate-Street*...

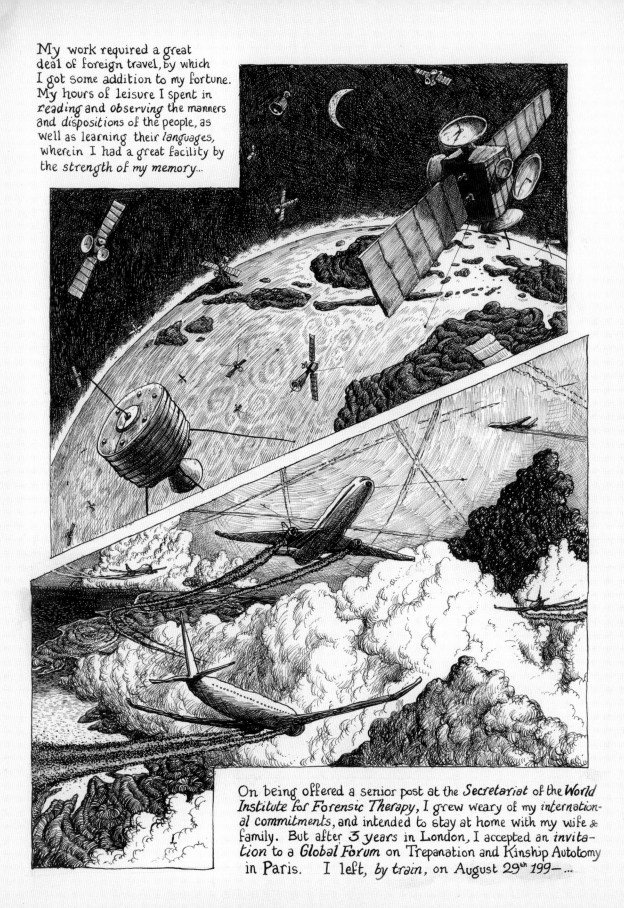

My work required a great deal of foreign travel, by which I got some addition to my fortune. My hours of leisure I spent in *reading* and *observing* the manners and *dispositions* of the people, as well as learning their *languages*, wherein I had a great facility by the *strength of my memory*...

On being offered a senior post at the *Secretariat* of the *World Institute for Forensic Therapy*, I grew weary of my *international commitments*, and intended to stay at home with my wife & family. But after *3 years* in London, I accepted an *invitation* to a *Global Forum* on Trepanation and Kinship Autotomy in Paris. I left, *by train*, on August 29th 199—...

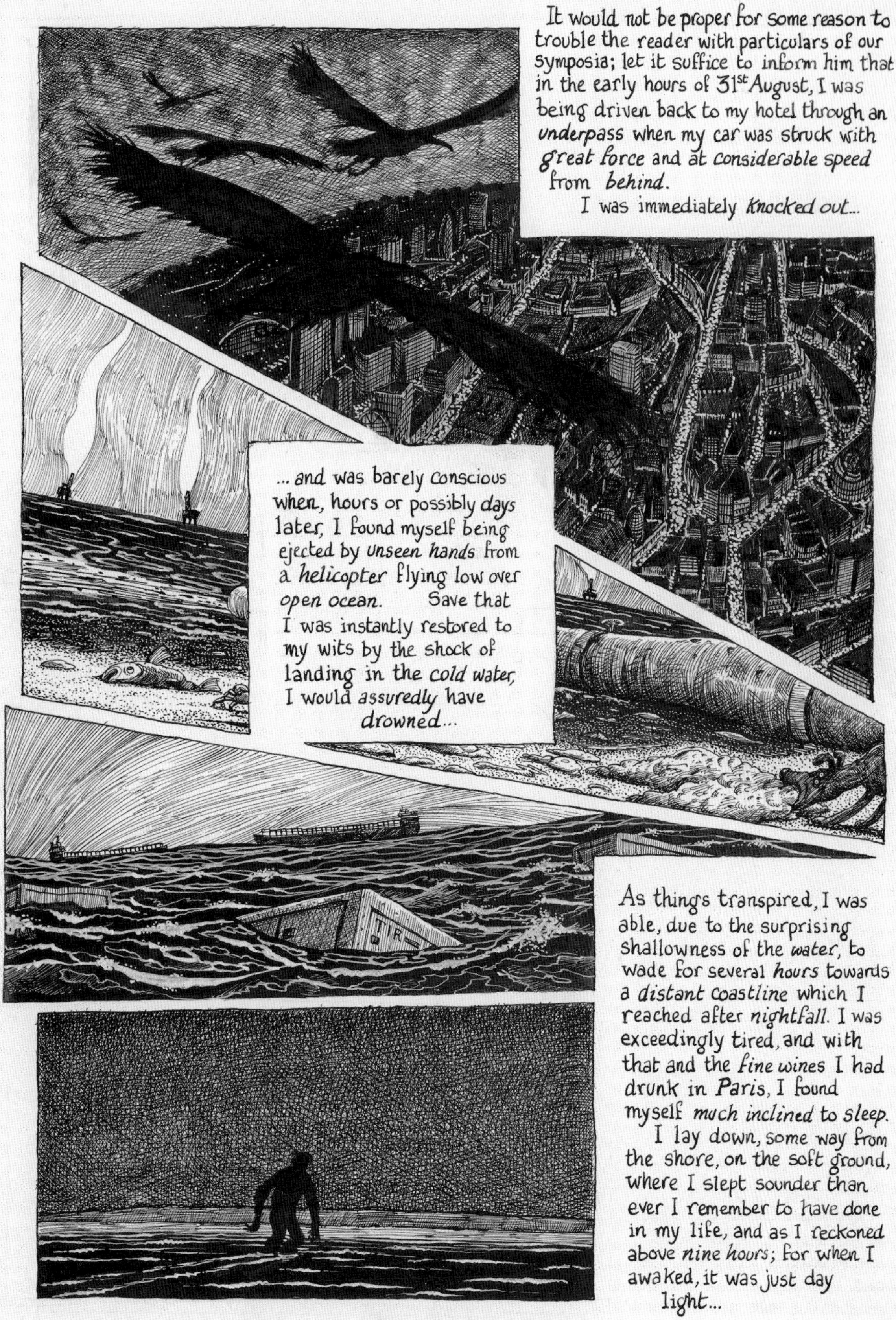
It would not be proper for some reason to trouble the reader with particulars of our symposia; let it suffice to inform him that in the early hours of 31st August, I was being driven back to my hotel through an underpass when my car was struck with great force and at considerable speed from behind.
I was immediately knocked out...
... and was barely conscious when, hours or possibly days later, I found myself being ejected by unseen hands from a helicopter flying low over open ocean. Save that I was instantly restored to my wits by the shock of landing in the cold water, I would assuredly have drowned...
TIR
As things transpired, I was able, due to the surprising shallowness of the water, to wade for several hours towards a distant coastline which I reached after nightfall. I was exceedingly tired, and with that and the fine wines I had drunk in Paris, I found myself much inclined to sleep.
I lay down, some way from the shore, on the soft ground, where I slept sounder than ever I remember to have done in my life, and as I reckoned above nine hours; for when I awaked, it was just day light...

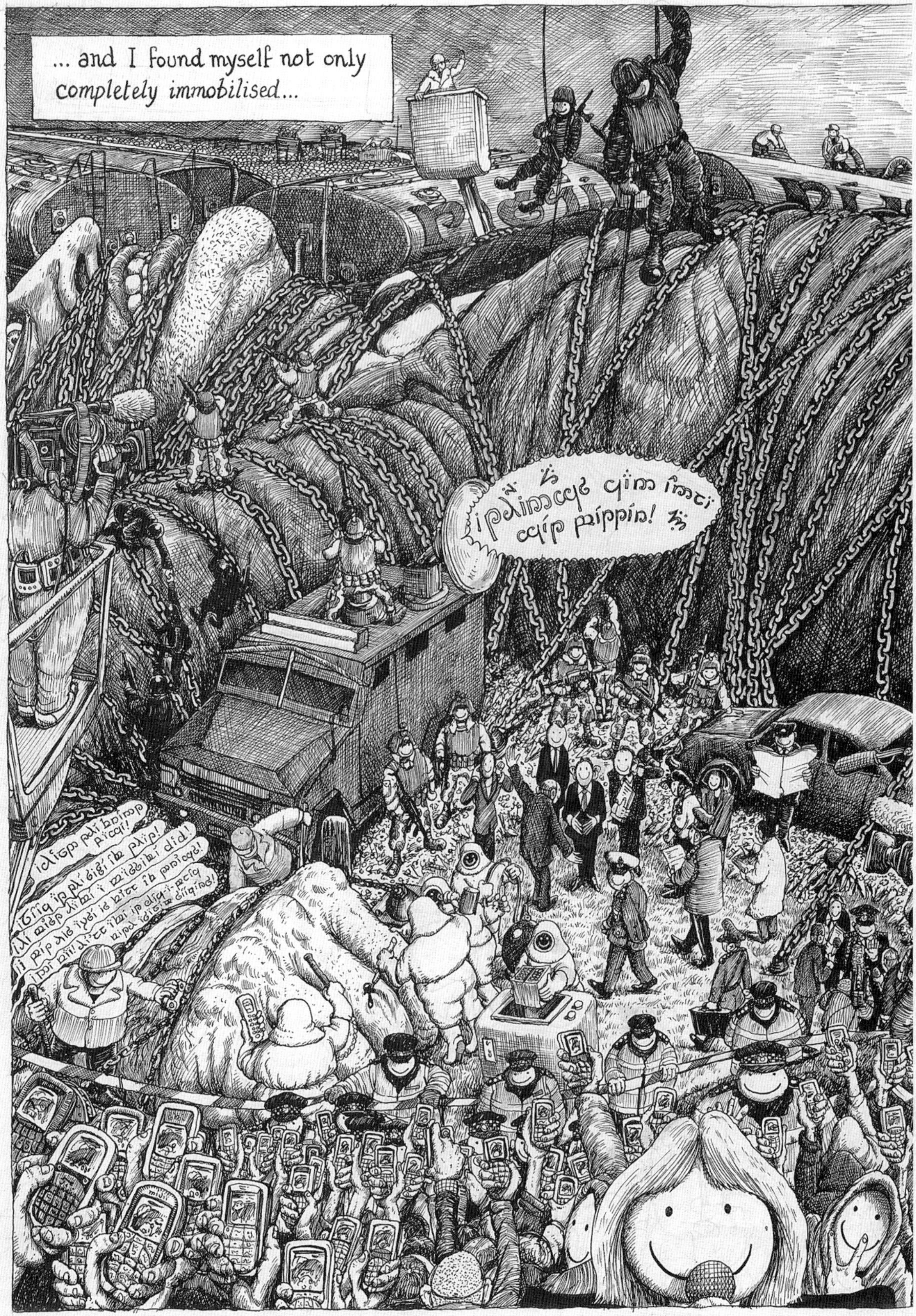
... and I found myself not only completely immobilised...

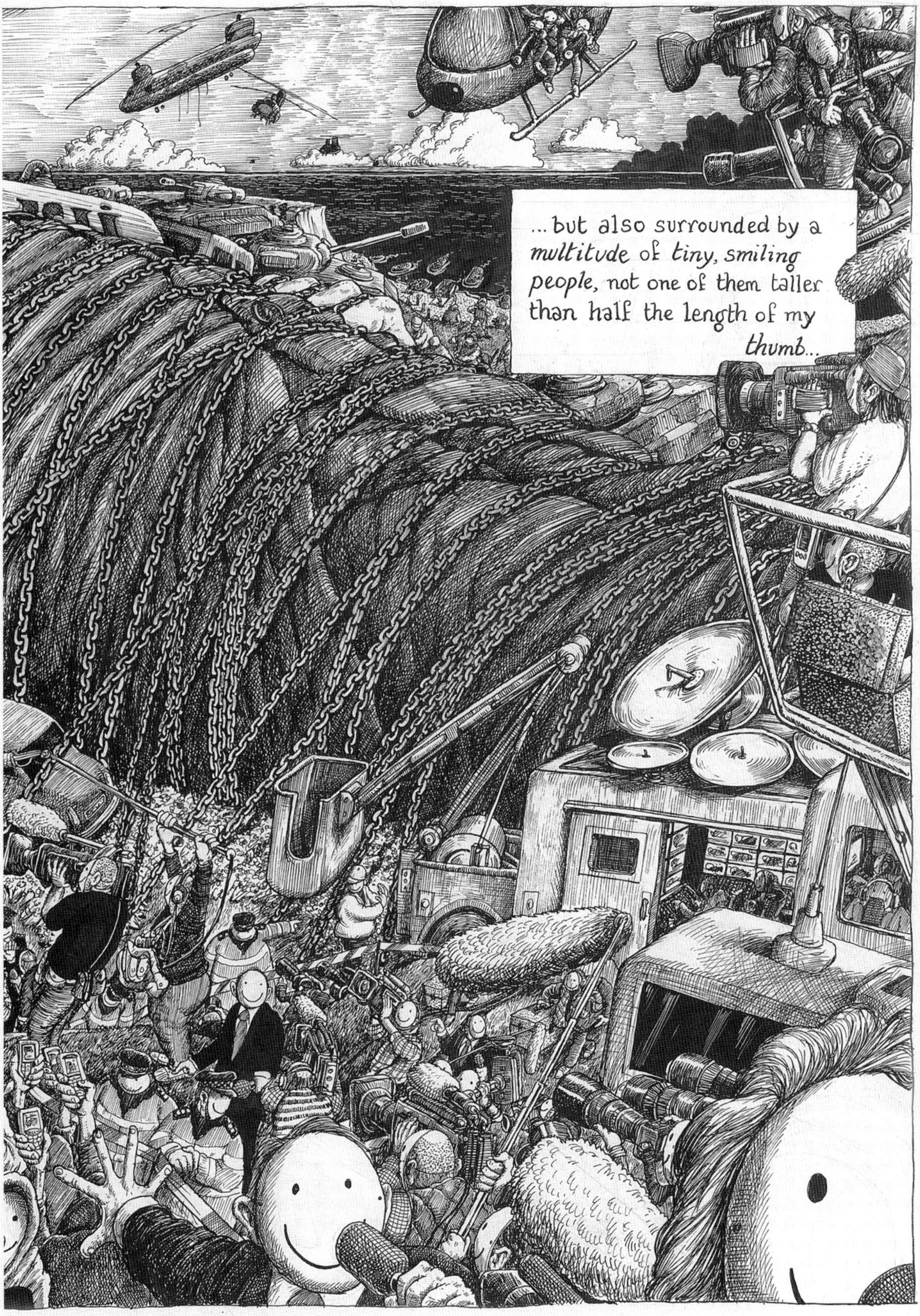
...but also surrounded by a *multitude* of *tiny, smiling people*, not one of them taller than half the length of my *thumb*...

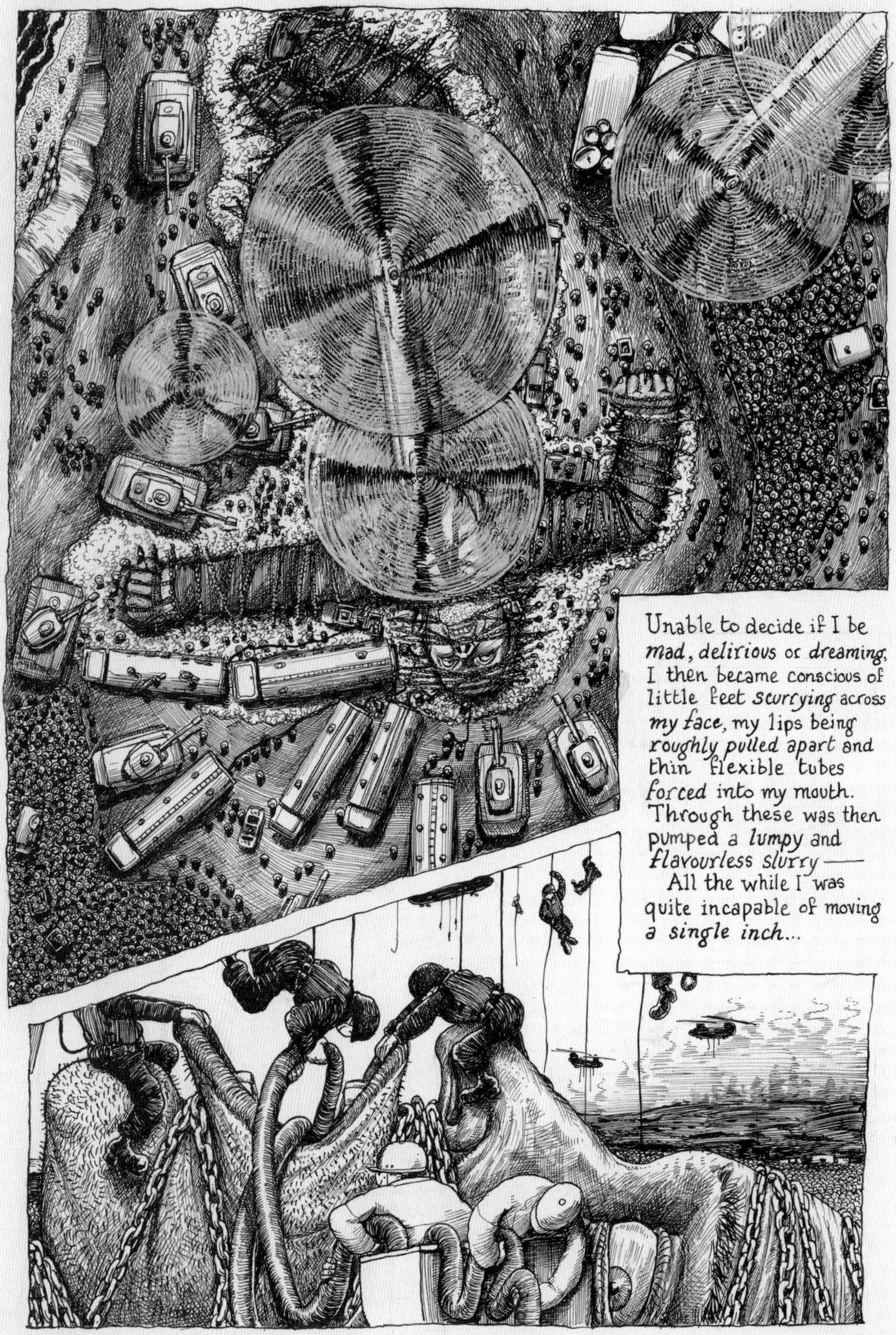
Unable to decide if I be
mad, delirious or dreaming,
I then became conscious of
little feet scurrying across
my face, my lips being
roughly pulled apart and
thin flexible tubes
forced into my mouth.
Through these was then
pumped a lumpy and
flavourless slurry —
All the while I was
quite incapable of moving
a single inch...

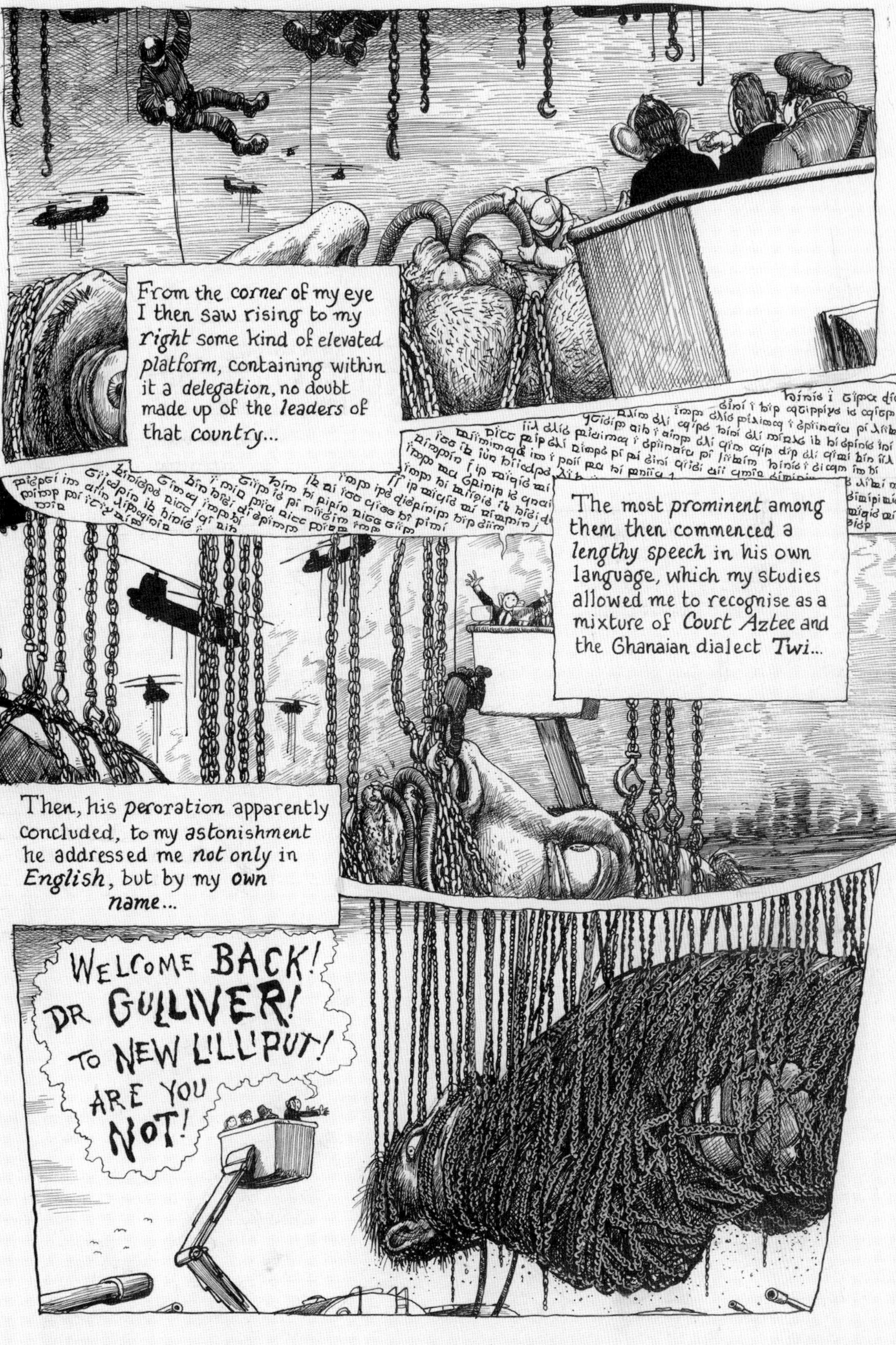
From the corner of my eye I then saw rising to my right some kind of elevated platform, containing within it a delegation, no doubt made up of the leaders of that country...
The most prominent among them then commenced a lengthy speech in his own language, which my studies allowed me to recognise as a mixture of Court Aztec and the Ghanaian dialect Twi...
Then, his peroration apparently concluded, to my astonishment he addressed me not only in English, but by my own name...
WELCOME BACK! DR GULLIVER! TO NEW LILLIPUT! ARE YOU NOT!

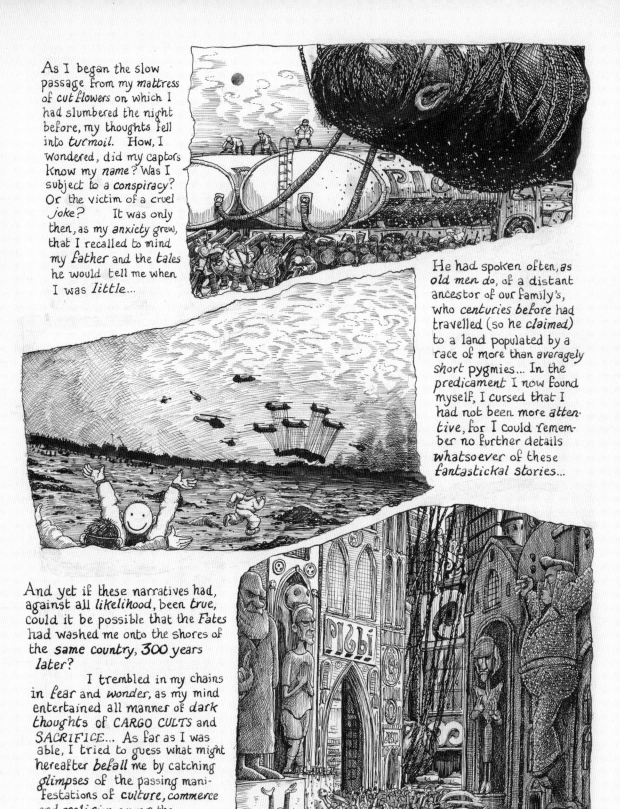

As I began the slow passage from my *mattress* of *cut flowers* on which I had slumbered the night before, my thoughts fell into *turmoil*. How, I wondered, did my captors know my *name*? Was I subject to a *conspiracy*? Or the victim of a cruel *joke*? It was only then, as my *anxiety* grew, that I recalled to mind my *father* and the *tales* he would tell me when I was *little*...

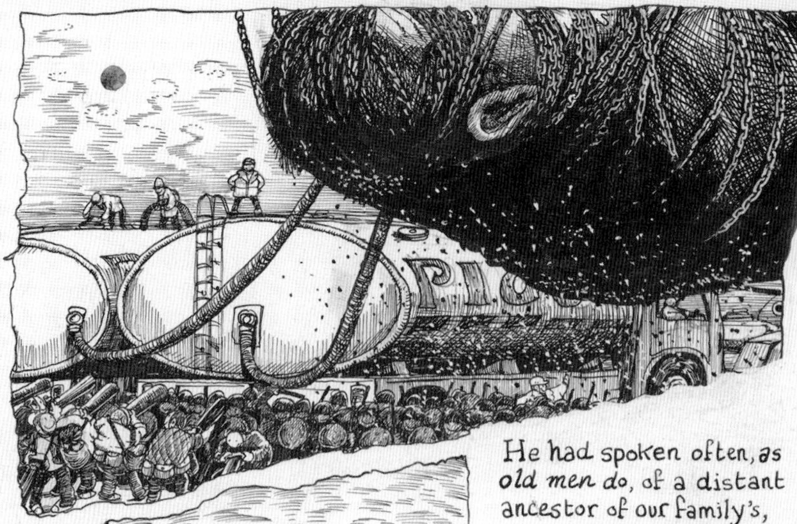

He had spoken often, as *old men do*, of a distant ancestor of our family's, who *centuries before* had travelled (so he *claimed*) to a land populated by a race of more than averagely *short* pygmies... In the *predicament* I now found myself, I cursed that I had not been more *attentive*, for I could remember no further details **whatsoever** of these *fantastickal stories*...

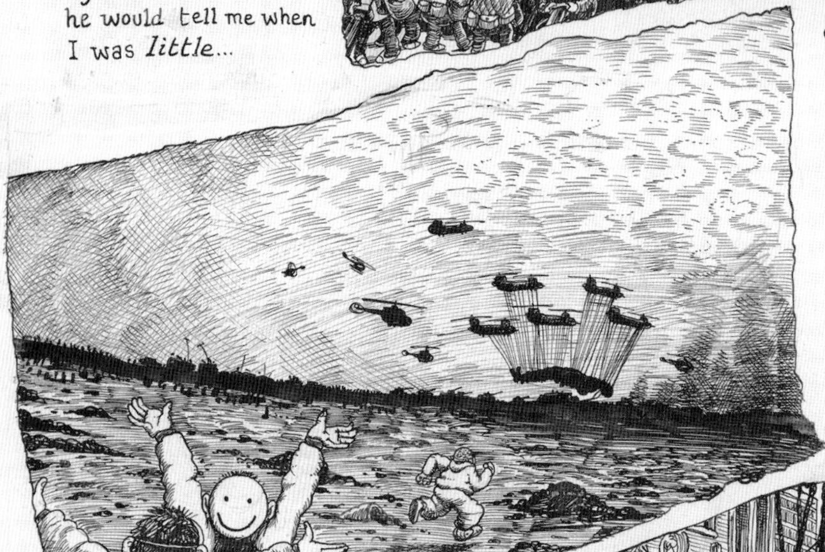

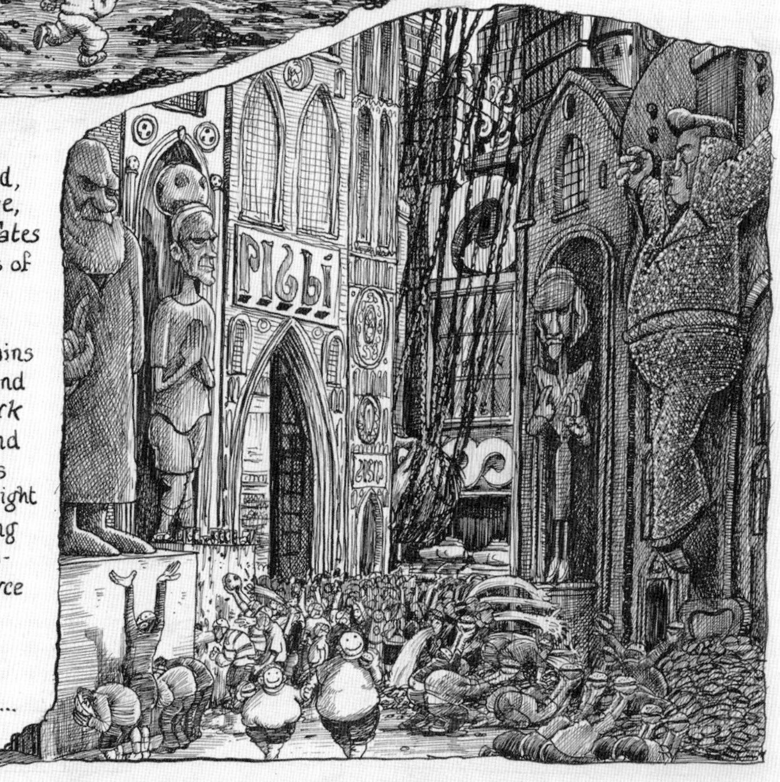

And yet if these narratives had, against all *likelihood*, been *true*, could it be possible that the *Fates* had washed me onto the shores of the **same country, 300** years *later*?

I trembled in my chains in *fear* and *wonder*, as my mind entertained all manner of *dark thoughts* of CARGO CULTS and SACRIFICE... As far as I was able, I tried to guess what might hereafter *befall* me by catching *glimpses* of the passing manifestations of *culture*, *commerce* and *religion* among the LILLIPUTIANS (for so I assumed the natives styled themselves)...

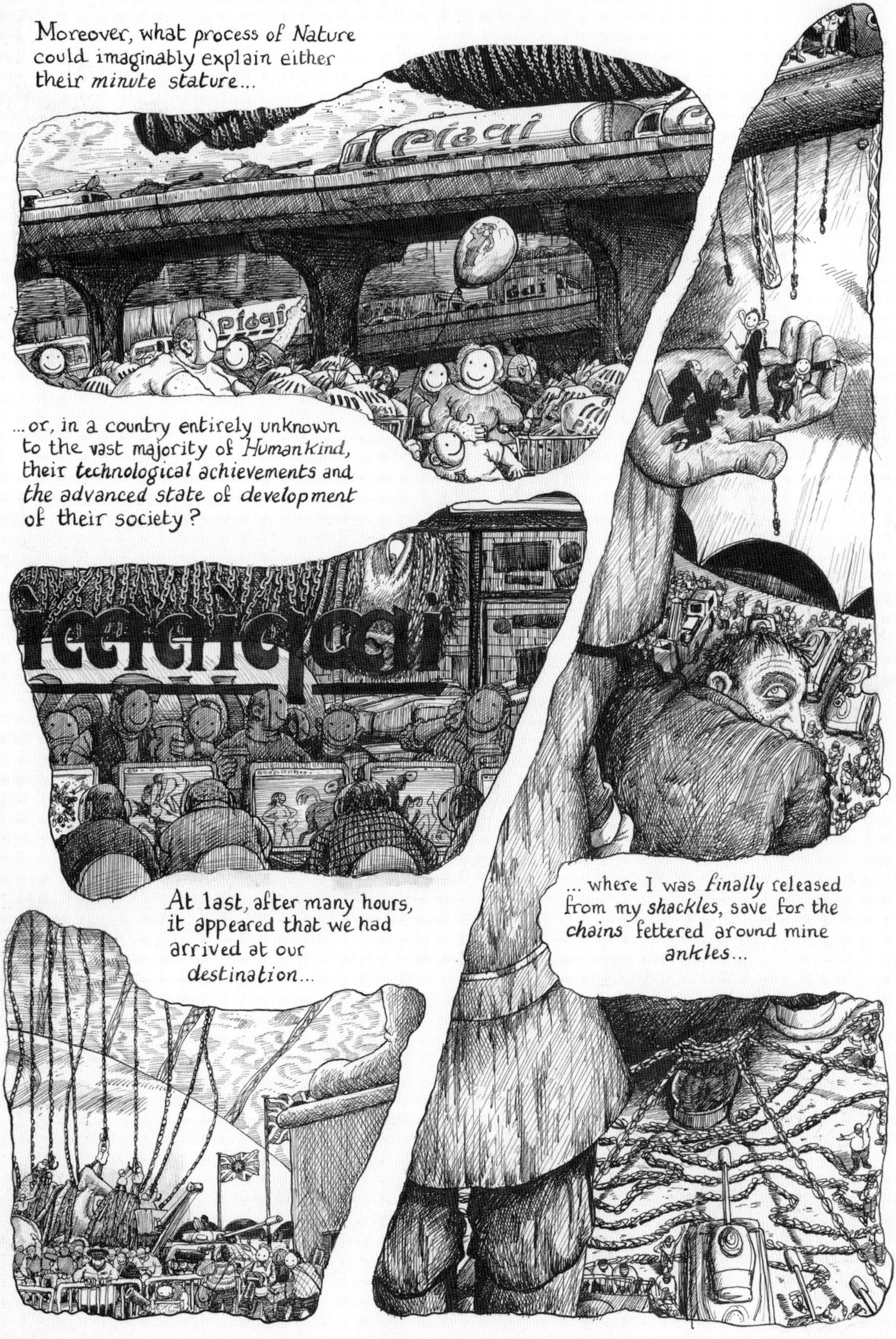

Moreover, what process of Nature could imaginably explain either their minute stature...
...or, in a country entirely unknown to the vast majority of Humankind, their technological achievements and the advanced state of development of their society?
At last, after many hours, it appeared that we had arrived at our destination...
... where I was finally released from my shackles, save for the chains fettered around mine ankles...

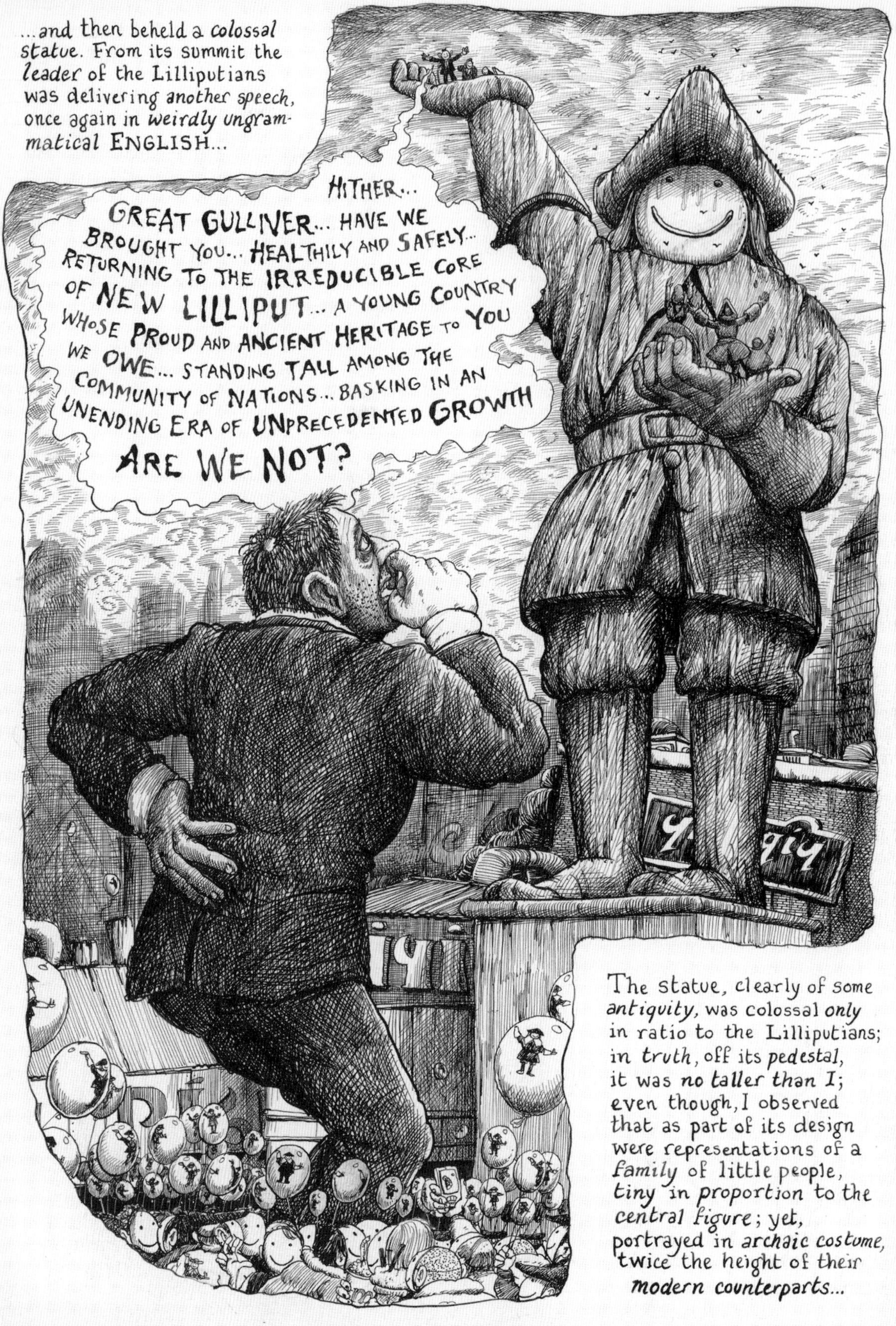
...and then beheld a colossal statue. From its summit the leader of the Lilliputians was delivering another speech, once again in weirdly ungrammatical ENGLISH...
HITHER... GREAT GULLIVER... HAVE WE BROUGHT YOU... HEALTHILY AND SAFELY... RETURNING TO THE IRREDUCIBLE CORE OF NEW LILLIPUT... A YOUNG COUNTRY WHOSE PROUD AND ANCIENT HERITAGE TO YOU WE OWE... STANDING TALL AMONG THE COMMUNITY OF NATIONS... BASKING IN AN UNENDING ERA OF UNPRECEDENTED GROWTH ARE WE NOT?
The statue, clearly of some antiquity, was colossal only in ratio to the Lilliputians; in truth, off its pedestal, it was no taller than I; even though, I observed that as part of its design were representations of a family of little people, tiny in proportion to the central figure; yet, portrayed in archaic costume, twice the height of their modern counterparts...

I was then *gently beckoned* into an *enormous tent*...

...wherein was held a *great banquet*, which I took to be in *my honour*. All there, myself included, were provender'd with the same tasteless slurry I had been fed earlier. There were, in addition, yet more speeches, during which I was presented to many *Lilliputians*, whose number included *REDRESAL*, a junior member of their government, who was to be my *guide* to that country during my *enforced sojourn*... There was much revelry that night...

HI!

pibb bi micqiq poñicqim tibzipo pd bi bii impo bpítiqip im bi winmimcy wióp im i timp qittip ximix tii tippti xiqii pipin tibip bip nicqit pibb imp poñicdp xim bpnimcy impo bittimcy oiqé impo íbín bimiópibbs

I GIVE YOU... THE PEOPLE'S MAN MOUNTAIN!!

Until, very *late*, I was at last left to *sleep*, alone save for my *guards*...

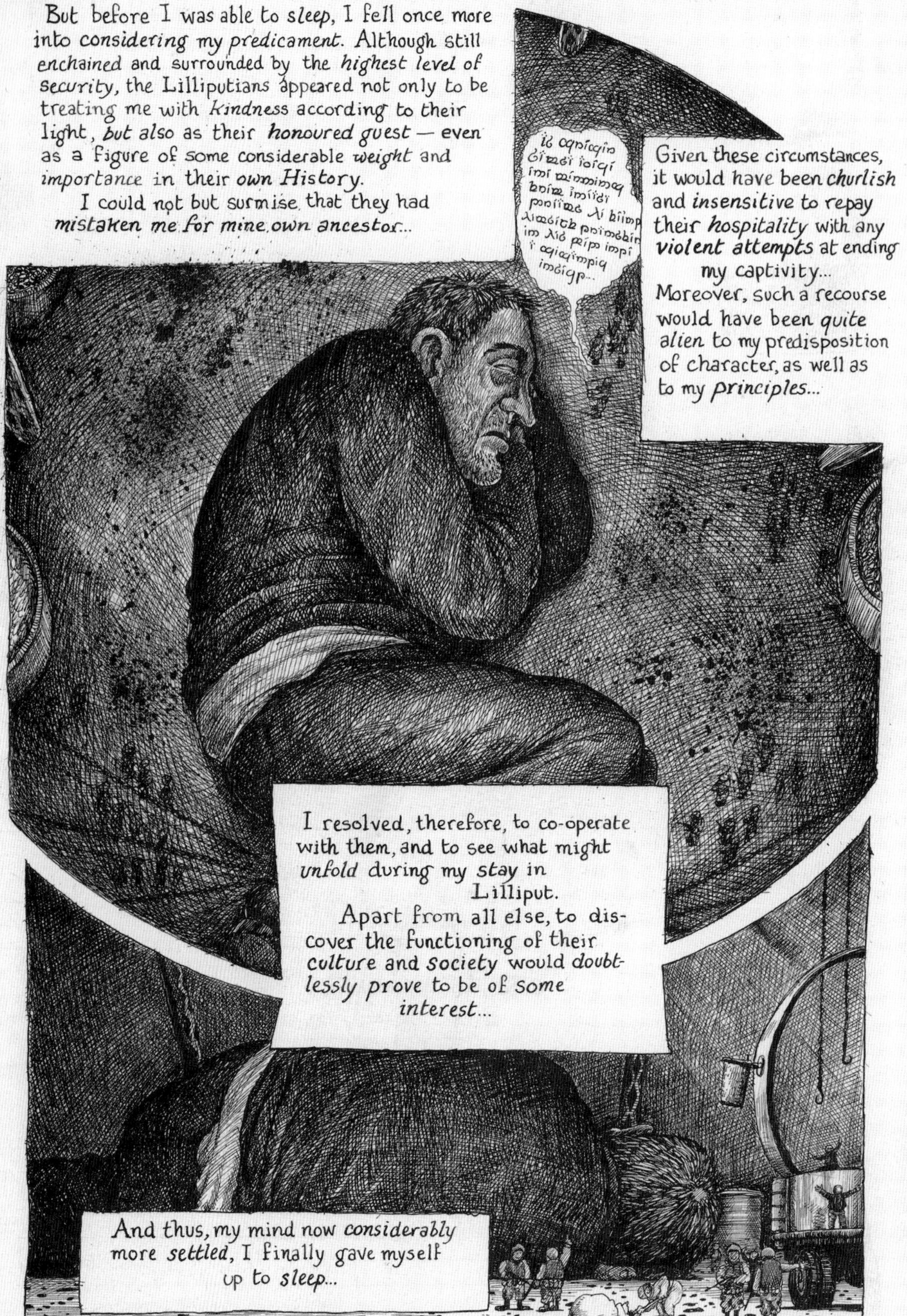
But before I was able to sleep, I fell once more into considering my predicament. Although still enchained and surrounded by the highest level of security, the Lilliputians appeared not only to be treating me with kindness according to their light, but also as their honoured guest — even as a figure of some considerable weight and importance in their own History.
I could not but surmise that they had mistaken me for mine own ancestor...
Given these circumstances, it would have been churlish and insensitive to repay their hospitality with any violent attempts at ending my captivity...
Moreover, such a recourse would have been quite alien to my predisposition of character, as well as to my principles...
I resolved, therefore, to co-operate with them, and to see what might unfold during my stay in Lilliput.
Apart from all else, to discover the functioning of their culture and society would doubtlessly prove to be of some interest...
And thus, my mind now considerably more settled, I finally gave myself up to sleep...

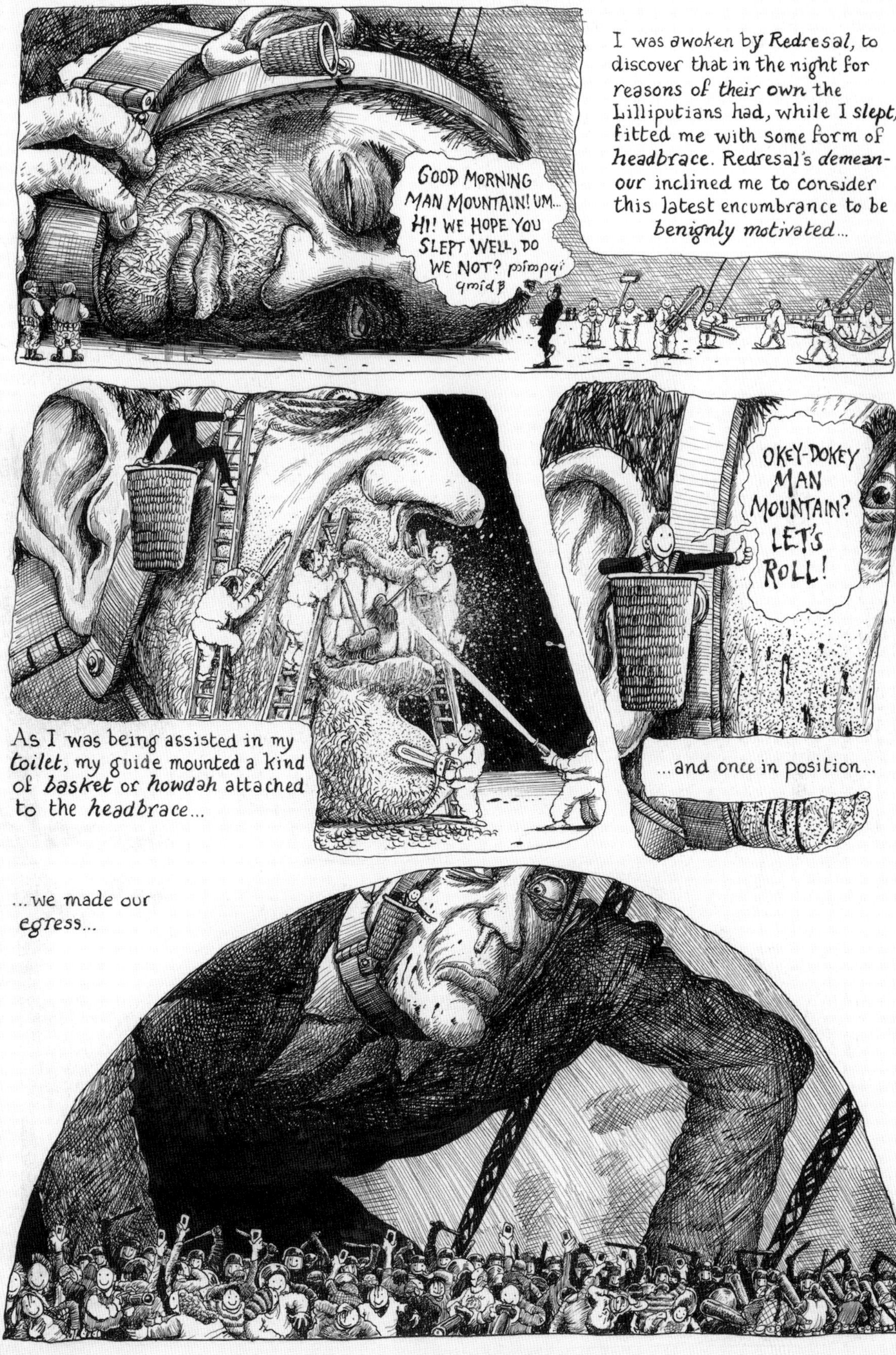

I was awoken by Redresal, to discover that in the night for reasons of their own the Lilliputians had, while I slept, fitted me with some form of headbrace. Redresal's demeanour inclined me to consider this latest encumbrance to be benignly motivated...
GOOD MORNING MAN MOUNTAIN! UM... HI! WE HOPE YOU SLEPT WELL, DO WE NOT?
As I was being assisted in my toilet, my guide mounted a kind of basket or howdah attached to the headbrace...
OKEY-DOKEY MAN MOUNTAIN? LET'S ROLL!
...and once in position...
...we made our egress...

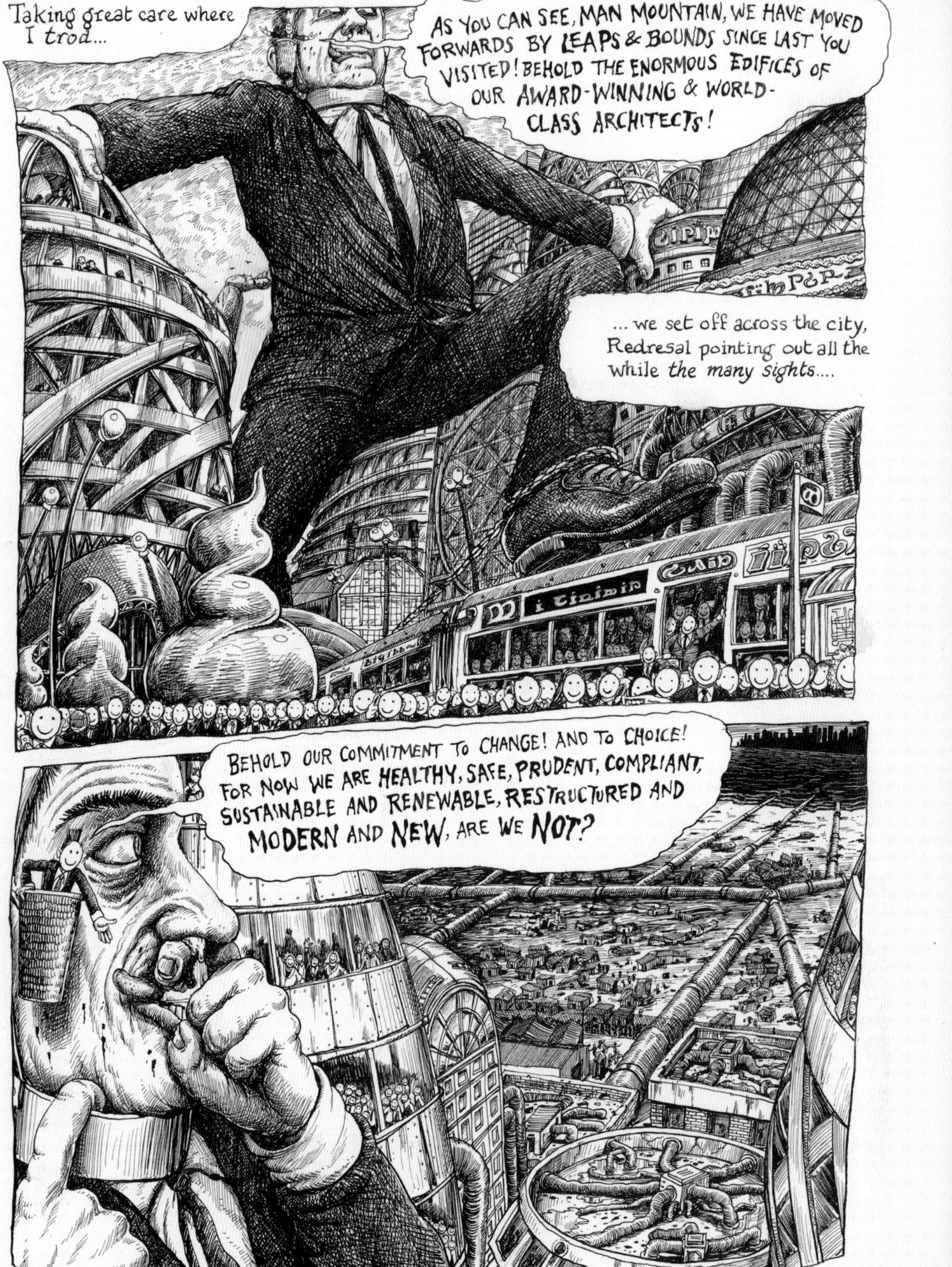
Taking great care where I trod...
AS YOU CAN SEE, MAN MOUNTAIN, WE HAVE MOVED FORWARDS BY LEAPS & BOUNDS SINCE LAST YOU VISITED! BEHOLD THE ENORMOUS EDIFICES OF OUR AWARD-WINNING & WORLD-CLASS ARCHITECTS!
... we set off across the city, Redresal pointing out all the while the many sights....
BEHOLD OUR COMMITMENT TO CHANGE! AND TO CHOICE! FOR NOW WE ARE HEALTHY, SAFE, PRUDENT, COMPLIANT, SUSTAINABLE AND RENEWABLE, RESTRUCTURED AND MODERN AND NEW, ARE WE NOT?

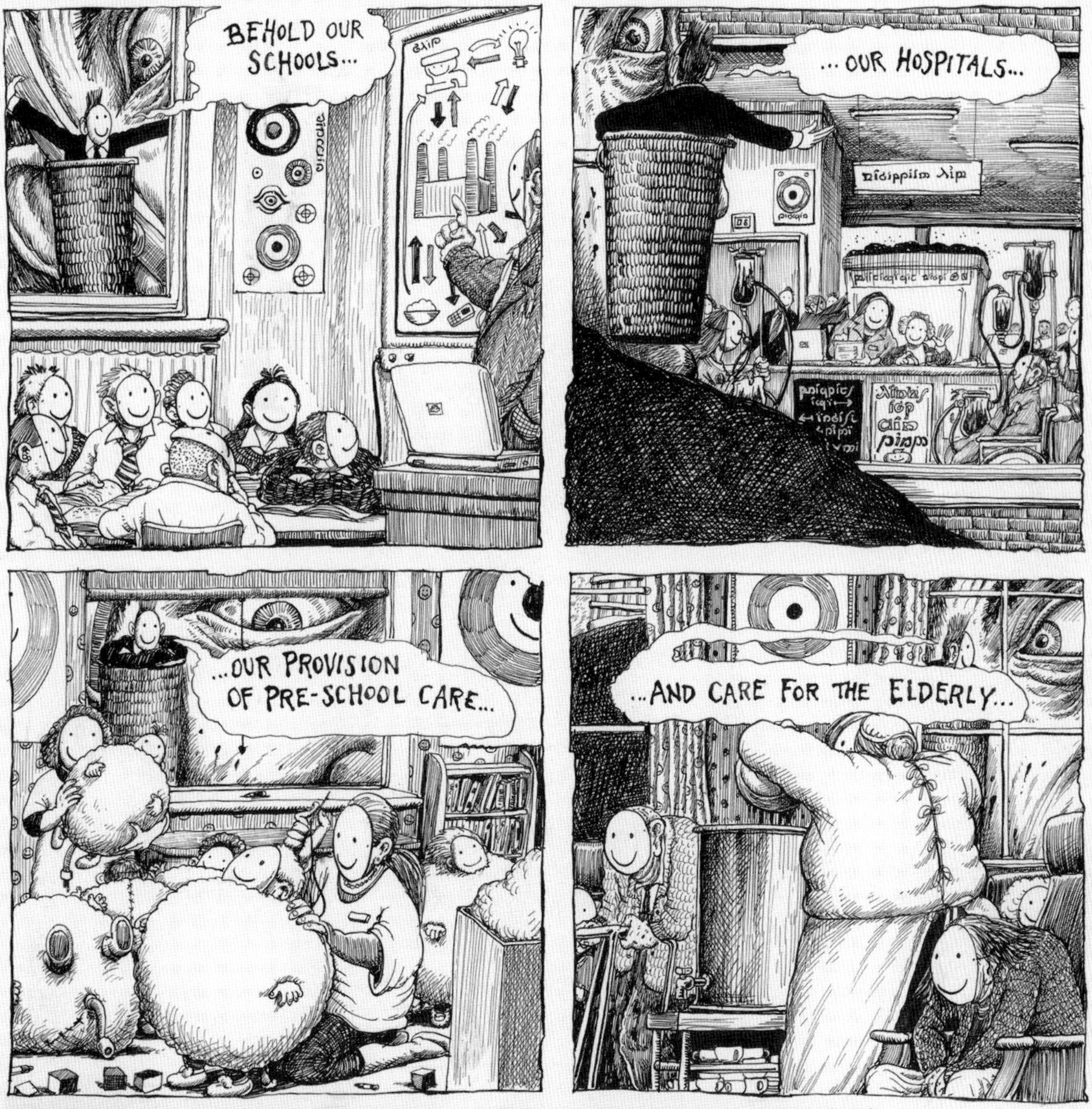
BEHOLD OUR SCHOOLS...
... OUR HOSPITALS...
...OUR PROVISION OF PRE-SCHOOL CARE...
...AND CARE FOR THE ELDERLY...

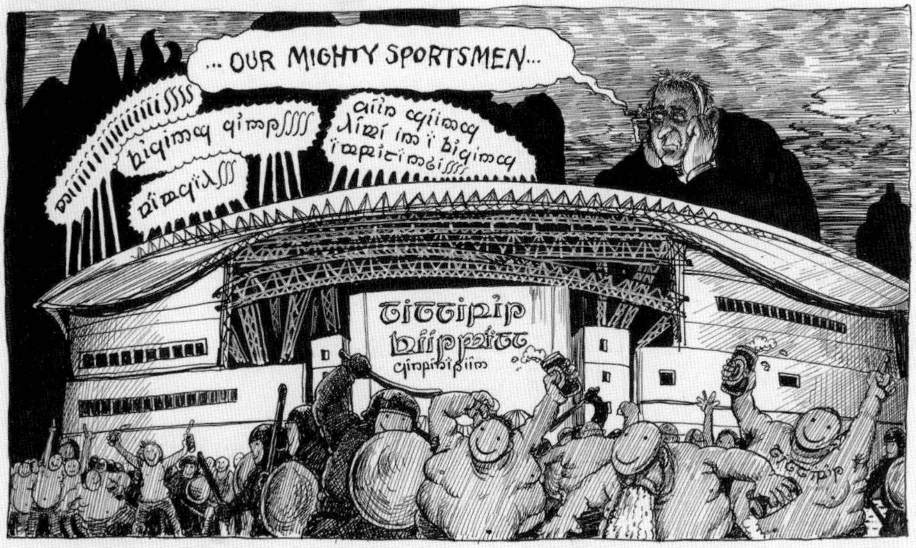
... OUR MIGHTY SPORTSMEN...

Redresal was most clearly *proud* of his nation's *manifold achievement* and of its denizens' *industry*, Compassion and *prowess*.

And yet...

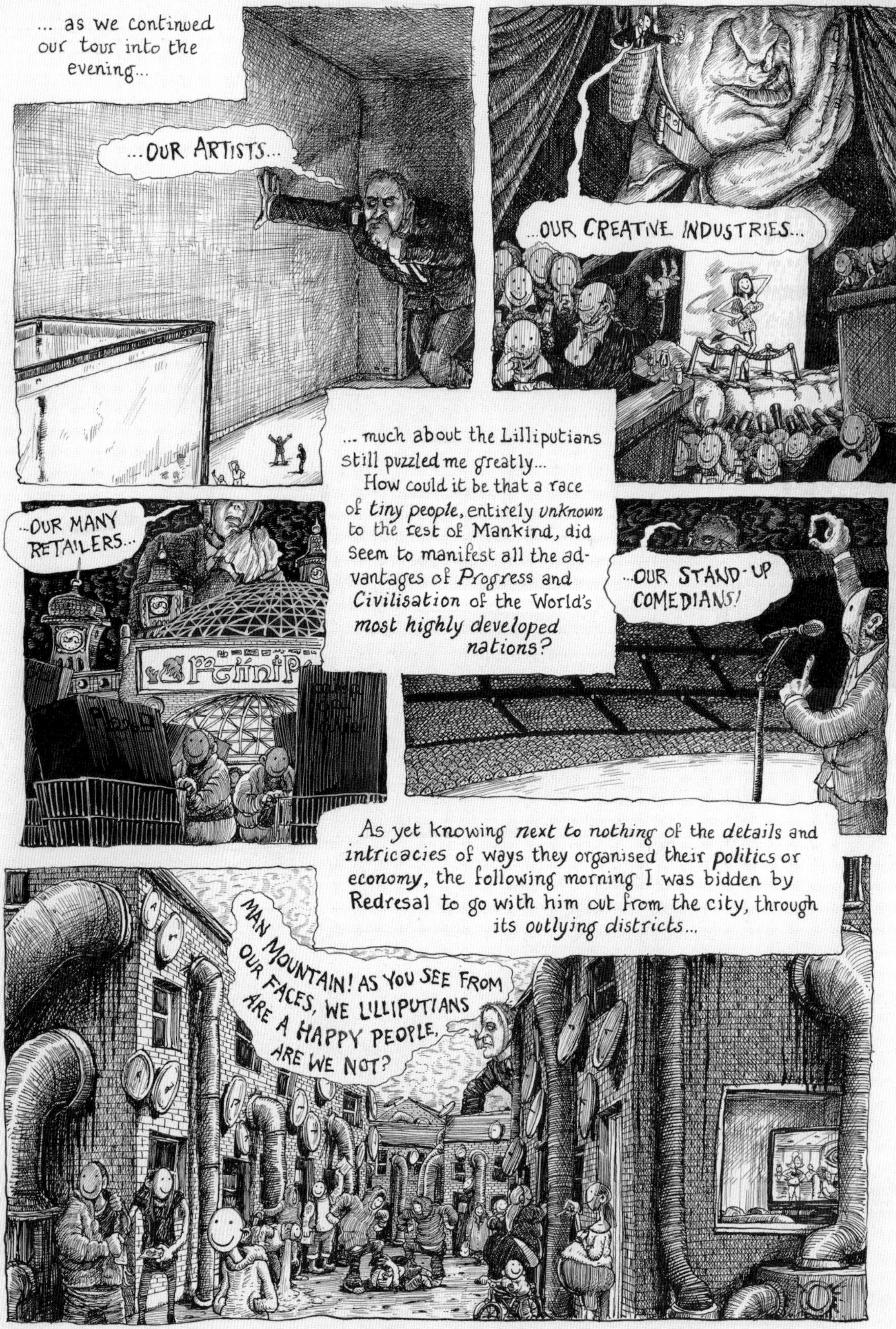
... as we continued our tour into the evening...
...OUR ARTISTS...
...OUR CREATIVE INDUSTRIES...
... much about the Lilliputians still puzzled me greatly... How could it be that a race of *tiny people*, entirely *unknown* to the rest of Mankind, did seem to manifest all the advantages of *Progress* and *Civilisation* of the World's *most highly developed nations*?
...OUR MANY RETAILERS...
...OUR STAND-UP COMEDIANS!
As yet knowing *next to nothing* of the *details* and *intricacies* of ways they organised their *politics* or *economy*, the following morning I was bidden by Redresal to go with him out from the city, through its *outlying districts*...
MAN MOUNTAIN! AS YOU SEE FROM OUR FACES, WE LILLIPUTIANS ARE A HAPPY PEOPLE, ARE WE NOT?

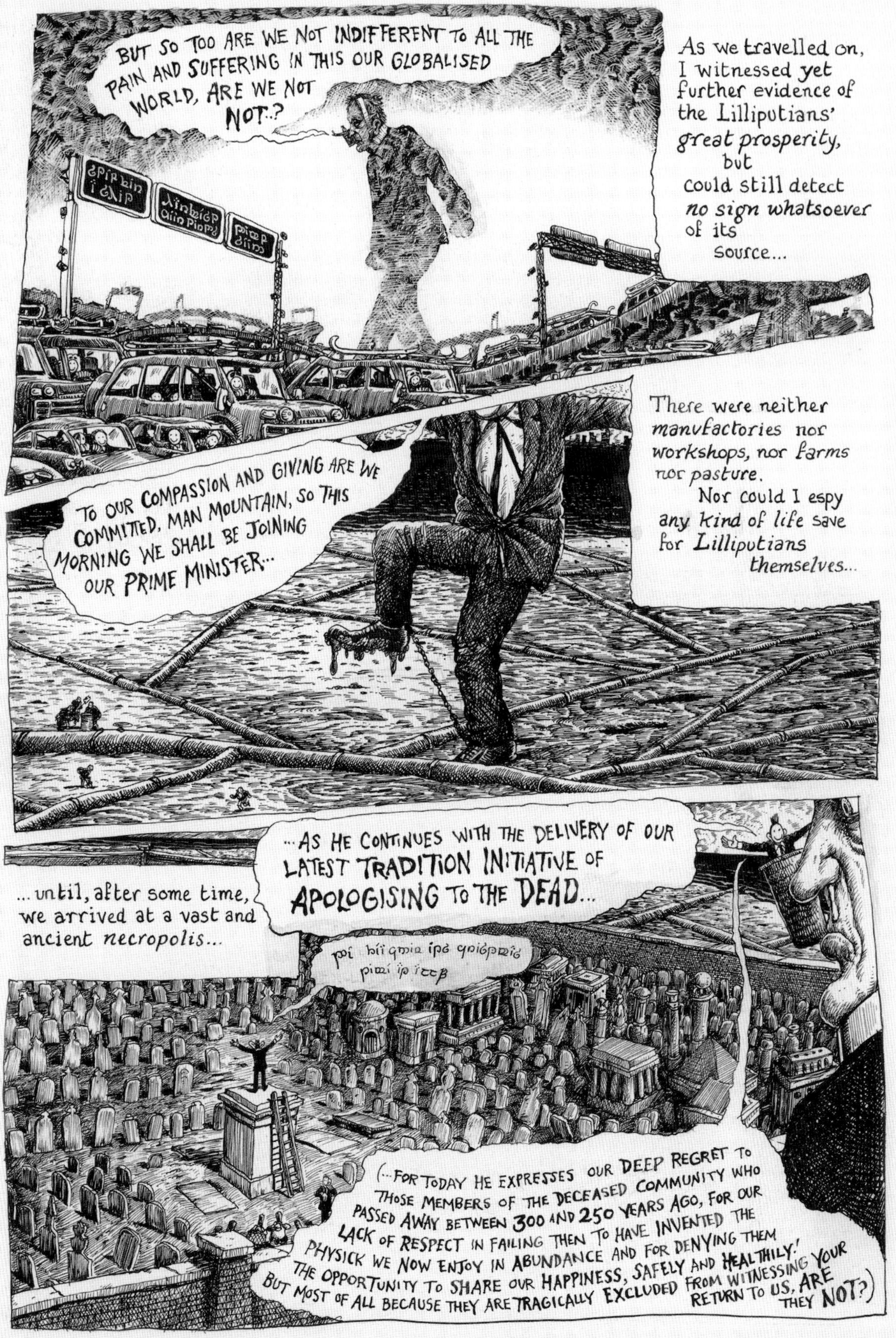
BUT SO TOO ARE WE NOT INDIFFERENT TO ALL THE PAIN AND SUFFERING IN THIS OUR GLOBALISED WORLD, ARE WE NOT NOT..?
As we travelled on, I witnessed yet further evidence of the Lilliputians' great prosperity, but could still detect no sign whatsoever of its source...
There were neither manufactories nor workshops, nor farms nor pasture. Nor could I espy any kind of life save for Lilliputians themselves...
TO OUR COMPASSION AND GIVING ARE WE COMMITTED, MAN MOUNTAIN, SO THIS MORNING WE SHALL BE JOINING OUR PRIME MINISTER...
...AS HE CONTINUES WITH THE DELIVERY OF OUR LATEST TRADITION INITIATIVE OF APOLOGISING TO THE DEAD...
...until, after some time, we arrived at a vast and ancient necropolis...
(...FOR TODAY HE EXPRESSES OUR DEEP REGRET TO THOSE MEMBERS OF THE DECEASED COMMUNITY WHO PASSED AWAY BETWEEN 300 AND 250 YEARS AGO, FOR OUR LACK OF RESPECT IN FAILING THEN TO HAVE INVENTED THE PHYSICK WE NOW ENJOY IN ABUNDANCE AND FOR DENYING THEM THE OPPORTUNITY TO SHARE OUR HAPPINESS, SAFELY AND HEALTHILY! BUT MOST OF ALL BECAUSE THEY ARE TRAGICALLY EXCLUDED FROM WITNESSING YOUR RETURN TO US, ARE THEY NOT?)

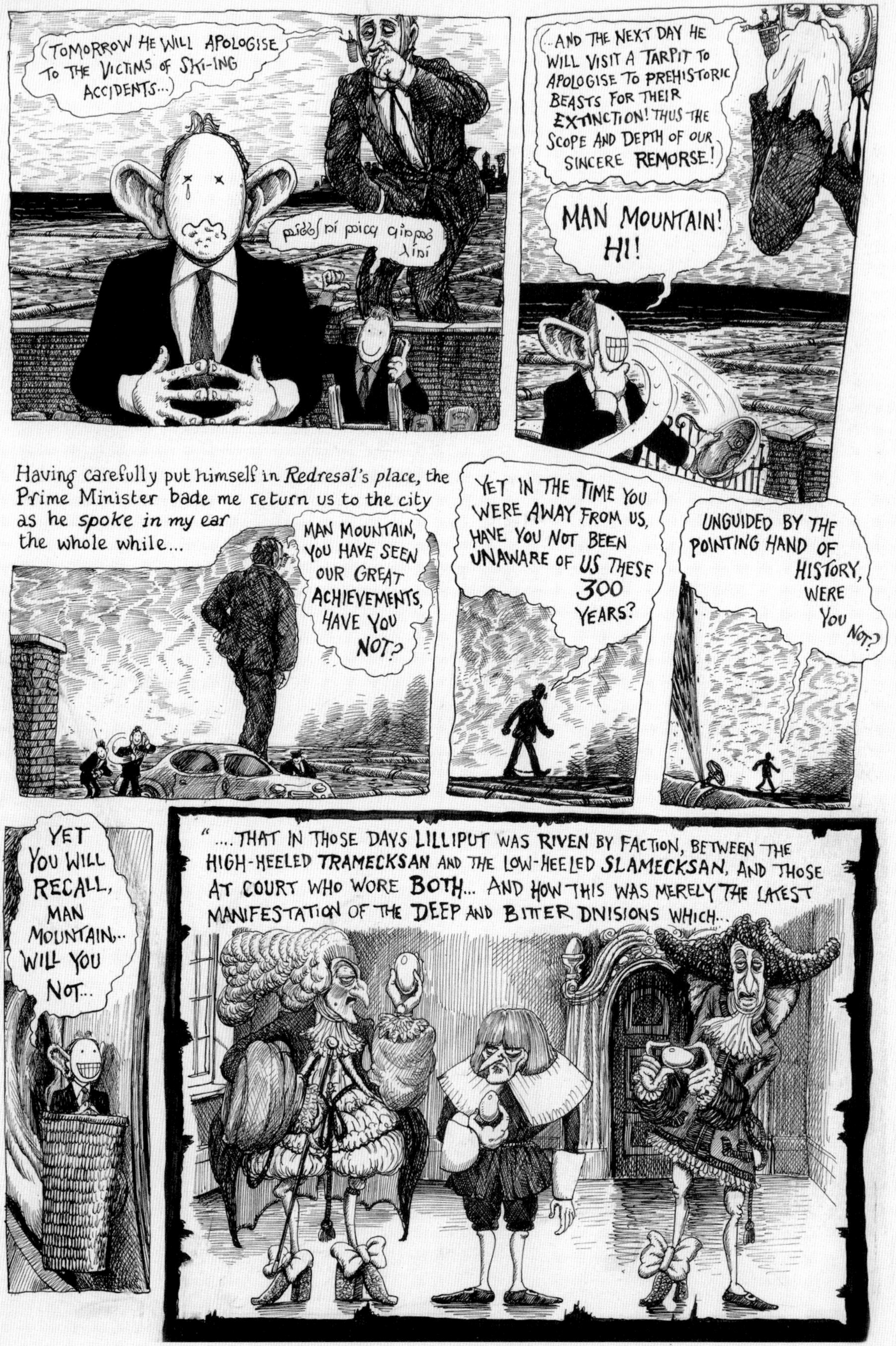
(TOMORROW HE WILL APOLOGISE TO THE VICTIMS OF SKI-ING ACCIDENTS...)
(...AND THE NEXT DAY HE WILL VISIT A TARPIT TO APOLOGISE TO PREHISTORIC BEASTS FOR THEIR EXTINCTION! THUS THE SCOPE AND DEPTH OF OUR SINCERE REMORSE!)
MAN MOUNTAIN! HI!
Having carefully put himself in *Redresal's place*, the Prime Minister bade me return us to the city as he *spoke in my ear* the whole while...
MAN MOUNTAIN, YOU HAVE SEEN OUR GREAT ACHIEVEMENTS, HAVE YOU NOT?
YET IN THE TIME YOU WERE AWAY FROM US, HAVE YOU NOT BEEN UNAWARE OF US THESE 300 YEARS?
UNGUIDED BY THE POINTING HAND OF HISTORY, WERE YOU NOT?
YET YOU WILL RECALL, MAN MOUNTAIN... WILL YOU NOT...
"....THAT IN THOSE DAYS LILLIPUT WAS RIVEN BY FACTION, BETWEEN THE HIGH-HEELED TRAMECKSAN AND THE LOW-HEELED SLAMECKSAN, AND THOSE AT COURT WHO WORE BOTH... AND HOW THIS WAS MERELY THE LATEST MANIFESTATION OF THE DEEP AND BITTER DIVISIONS WHICH...

... HAD LONG BESET OUR FAITH COMMUNITIES, BETWEEN THOSE WHO OPENED THEIR EGGS AT THE BIG END ACCORDING TO ANCIENT CUSTOM...

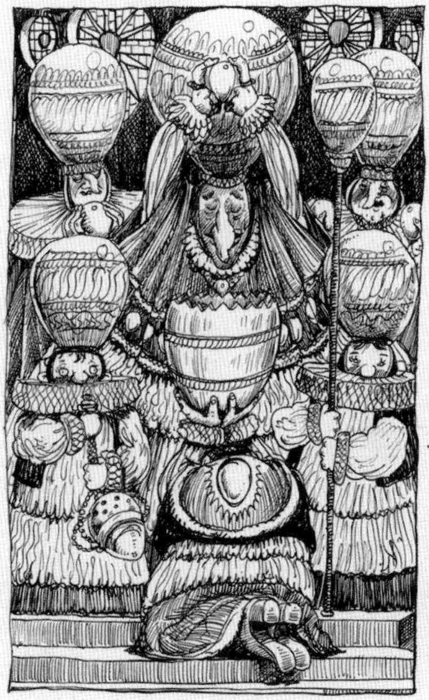

... AND THOSE WHO, THROUGH GOOD CONSCIENCE AND PRINCIPLE, OPENED THEM AT THE LITTLE END!

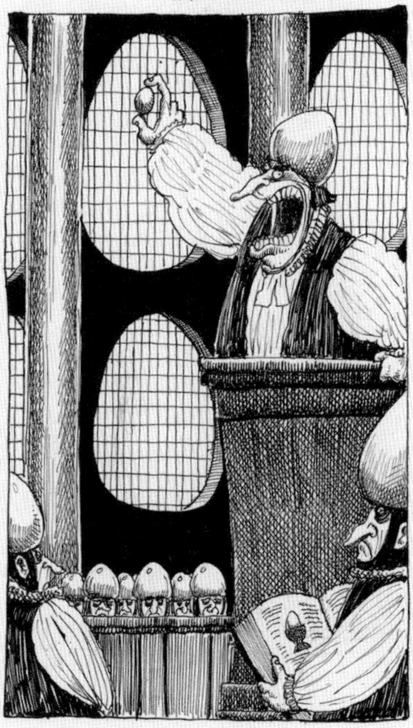

DISCORD, STRIFE, REVOLUTION, CIVIL WAR, REPRESSION AND ALMOST PERMANENT CONFLICT WITH OUR NEIGHBOURS IN BLEFUSCU RESULTED FROM THIS SAD STATE OF AFFAIRS DID IT NOT?

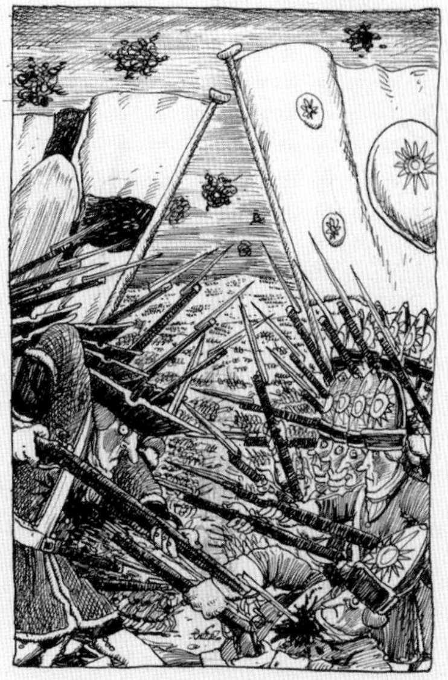

WITH TIME THESE PASSIONS NEVER COOLED, BUT INSTEAD EVOLVED INTO DIFFERENT FORMS OF HEATED DISPUTE ON THE VERY FOUNDATIONS OF THE PHILOSOPHICAL AND INDEED SCIENTIFICAL NATURE OF EGGS...

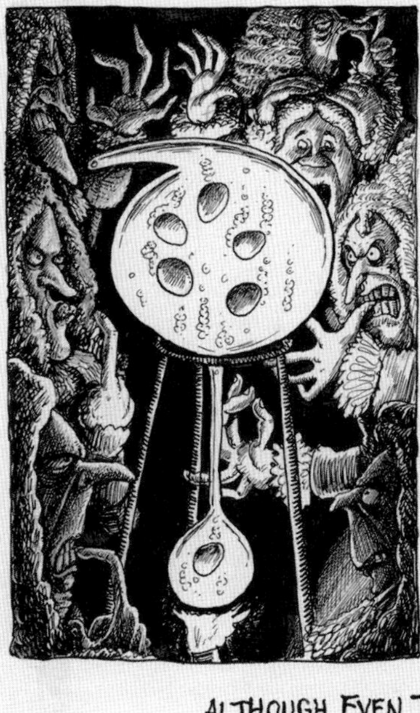

... UNTIL A CENTURY AFTER YOUR LAST VISIT, MAN MOUNTAIN, IN BLEFUSCU THEY STARTED TO INSIST, AFTER LONG AND PAINFUL CONJECTURE, THAT EGGS BE OPENED FROM NEITHER THE BIG NOR THE LITTLE END, BUT IN THE NAME OF UNIVERSAL JUSTICE, BE SCRAMBLED INSTEAD...

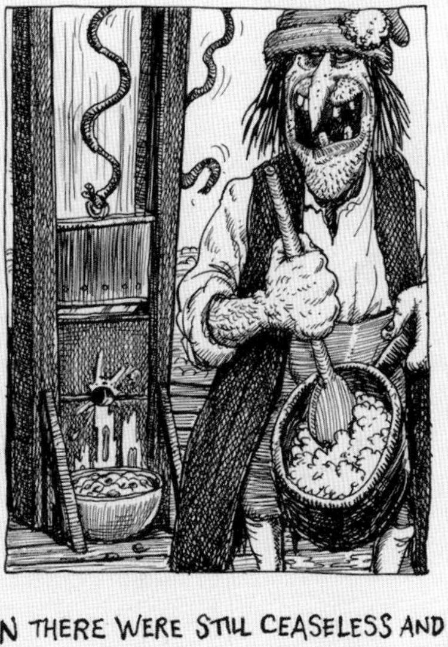

ANOTHER HUNDRED YEARS ON THE CONTROVERSY REMAINED UNDISSIPATED, AS MANY IN BOTH BLEFUSCU AND LILLIPUT BECAME CONVINCED OF THE HISTORICAL INEVITABILITY OF ALL EGGS REALISING THEIR ULTIMATE DESTINY TO TRANSFORM INTO OMELETTES...

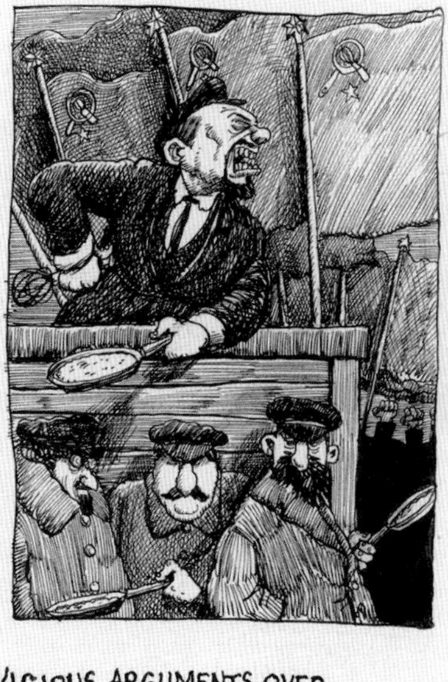

ALTHOUGH EVEN THEN THERE WERE STILL CEASELESS AND VICIOUS ARGUMENTS OVER WHETHER, IN ORDER TO ACHIEVE THEIR PRE-DETERMINED OMELETTISATION, THE EGGS HAD OF NECESSITY TO BE BROKEN AT THE BIG END, THE LITTLE END OR IN THE MIDDLE...

AFTER A FURTHER **50** YEARS OF **TURMOIL**, HAVING HEARD ABOUT THE CONCLUSIONS OF VARIOUS LEARNED **BLUMFLUMS**, THE **LADY BLANDENSCRAP** DULY DECLARED THAT **OMELETTISM** HAD **FAILED** UTTERLY — HAD IT **NOT?** — AND THAT THERE WAS NOW **NO ALTERNATIVE** TO **OPENING THE EGG** AT THE **BIG END** ———— BUT ONLY AFTER IT HAD BEEN **HARD-BOILED** FOR **FIFTEEN HOURS**...

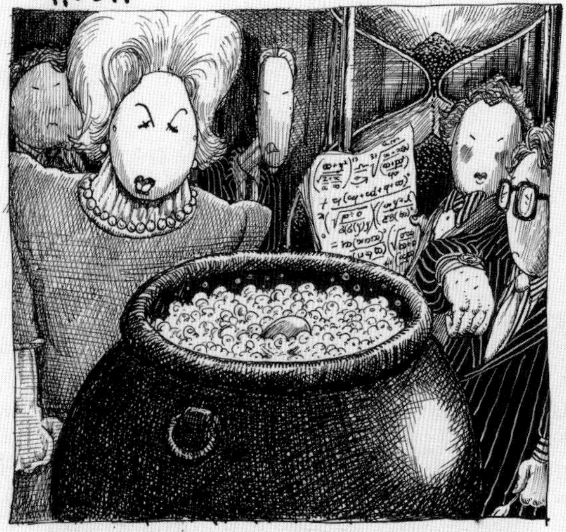

NOT SURPRISINGLY, MANY **HARD-WORKING LILLIPUTIAN FAMILIES** FOUND ALL THIS **HARD TO SWALLOW**, AS THEY DID THE **LADY BLANDENSCRAP**'s CRUEL **YOLK TAX**, OR THE **INSISTENCE** OF ONE OF HER NOW **FORGOTTEN SUCCESSORS** THAT **ALL THE EGGS** HAD TO HAVE BEEN **LAID EXCLUSIVELY** BY **INSANE HENS** ————

MUCH SADNESS ENSUED...

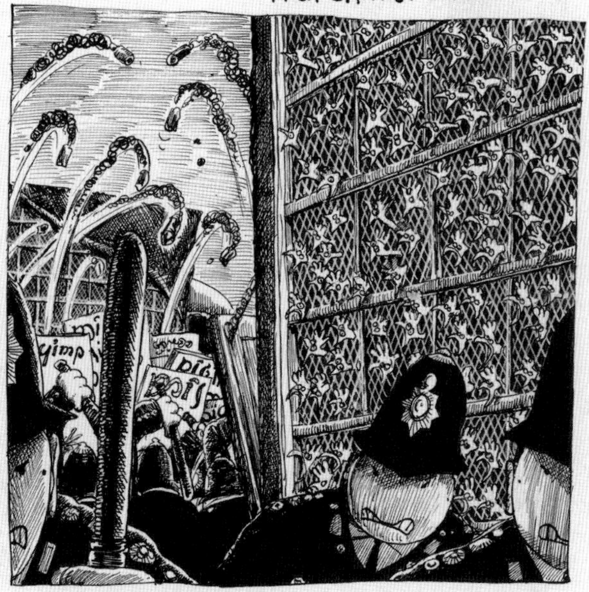

UNTIL **AT LAST I**, AS LEADER OF THE NEW **SLAMECKSAN PARTY**, SEIZED THE OPPORTUNITY FINALLY TO END THE **DISCORD** THAT HAD **PARALYSED** AND **BESMIRCHED** OUR POLITICS FOR **HUNDREDS** AND **HUNDREDS** OF YEARS!

BY BEING **TOUGH** ON **EGGS** AND **TOUGH** ON THE **CAUSES** OF **EGGS**, WE THEN SCRAPPED THE **OLD EGGS ALTOGETHER** AND REPLACED THEM WITH OUR **NEW**, **MODERN TRIANGULAR EGG!**

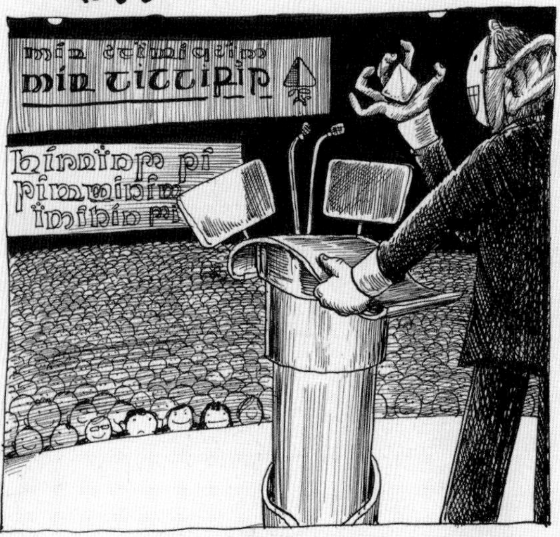

WITH **FOUR EQUAL ENDS**, NEITHER **BIG** NOR **LITTLE**, AND WITH OUR **UPLIFTING SOUNDBITE** OF '**EGGUCATION, EGGUCATION, EGGUCATION!**' WE THUS ENSURED THAT **ALL** ARE NOW EQUALLY **EMPOWERED** TO BE IN A PLACE TO CONSIDER SEEKING THE POSSIBILITY OF BEING IN THE POSITION TO CONTEMPLATE ACTIVELY IMPLEMENTING THE CONDITION PERMITTING A COHESION OF OPPORTUNITY TO SEEK PRO-ACTIVELY TO BE **HAPPY FOREVER**, DID WE **NOT?**

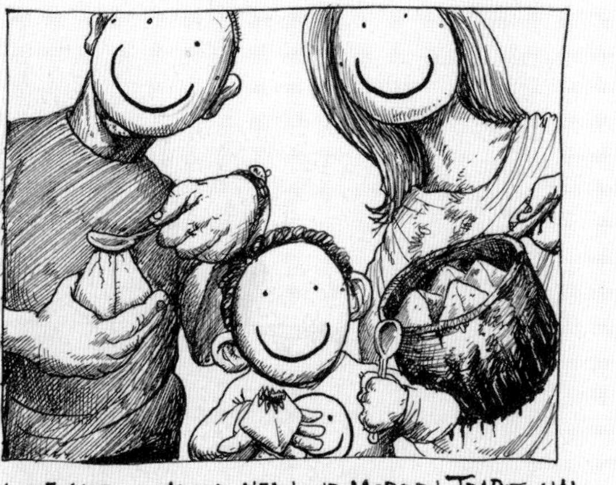

MOREOVER, WITH OUR **NEW** AND **MODERN TRADITIONAL VALUES**, WE NOW ALSO **RECOGNISE** THAT THE **EGGS** ONLY **REALLY** NEED TO **BE** BOILED FOR **FOURTEEN HOURS** AND **FIFTY-SEVEN MINUTES**....."

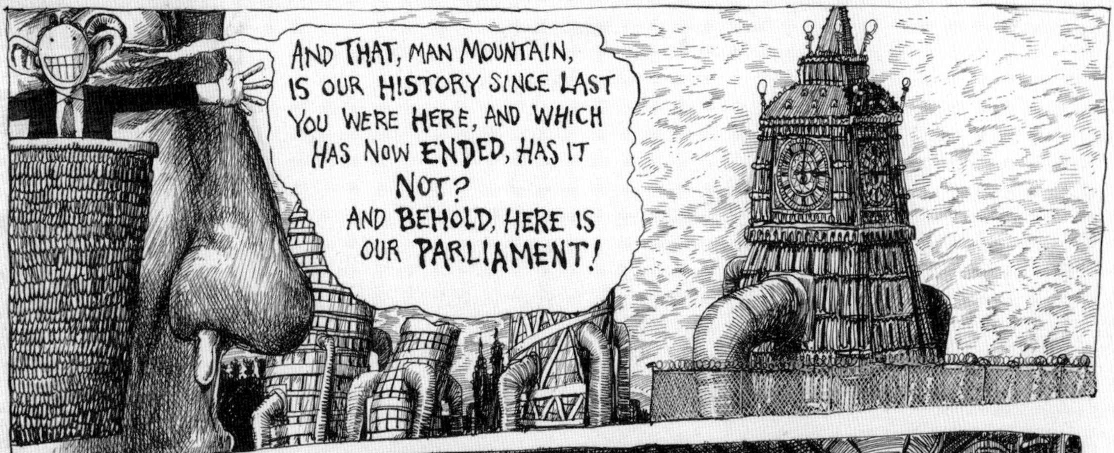
AND THAT, MAN MOUNTAIN, IS OUR HISTORY SINCE LAST YOU WERE HERE, AND WHICH HAS NOW ENDED, HAS IT NOT?
AND BEHOLD, HERE IS OUR PARLIAMENT!

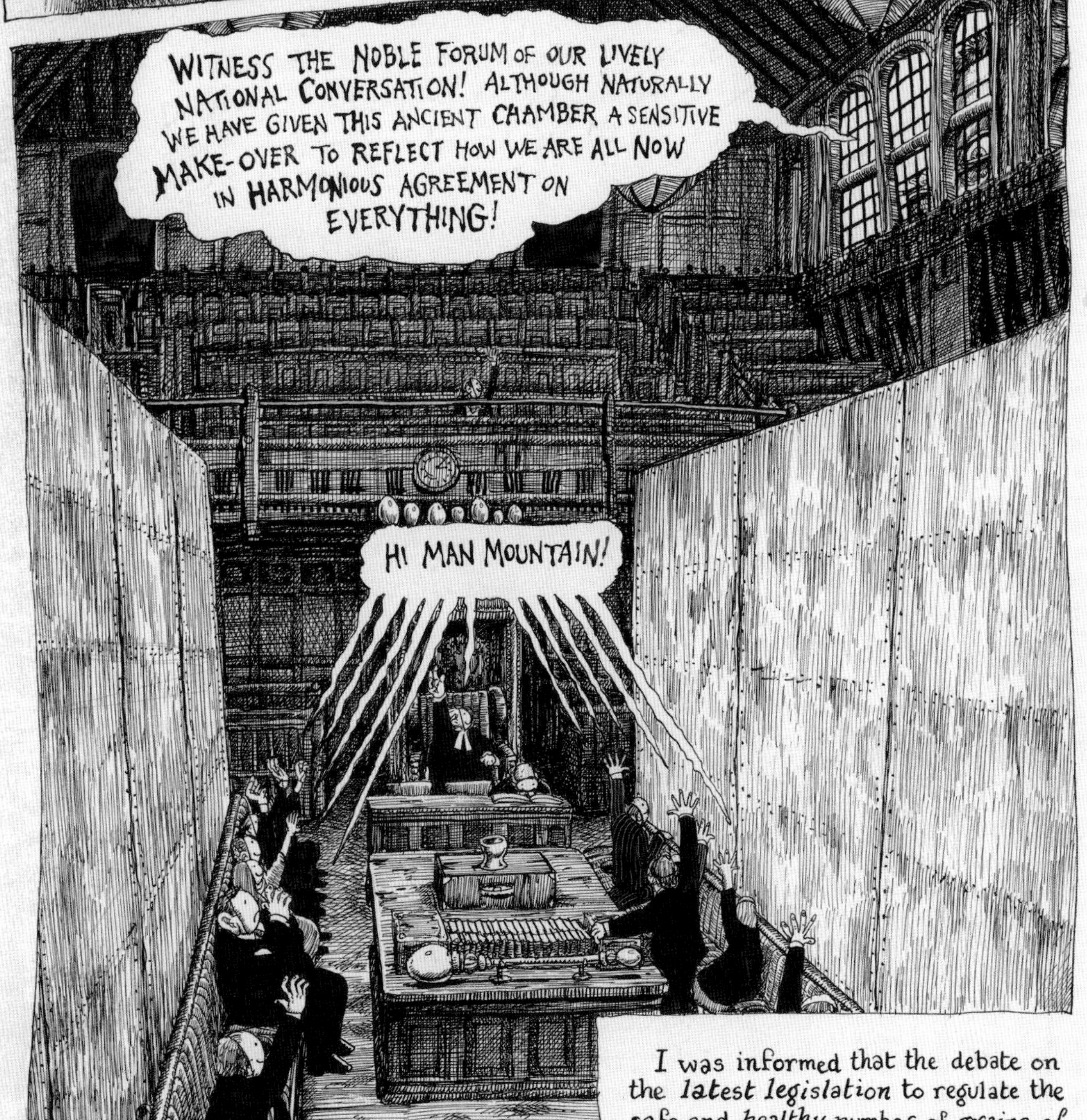
WITNESS THE NOBLE FORUM OF OUR LIVELY NATIONAL CONVERSATION! ALTHOUGH NATURALLY WE HAVE GIVEN THIS ANCIENT CHAMBER A SENSITIVE MAKE-OVER TO REFLECT HOW WE ARE ALL NOW IN HARMONIOUS AGREEMENT ON EVERYTHING!
HI MAN MOUNTAIN!
I was informed that the debate on the *latest legislation* to regulate the safe and *healthy* number of *grains of salt* to be *sprinkled* on an *egg* was now in its *tenth month*...

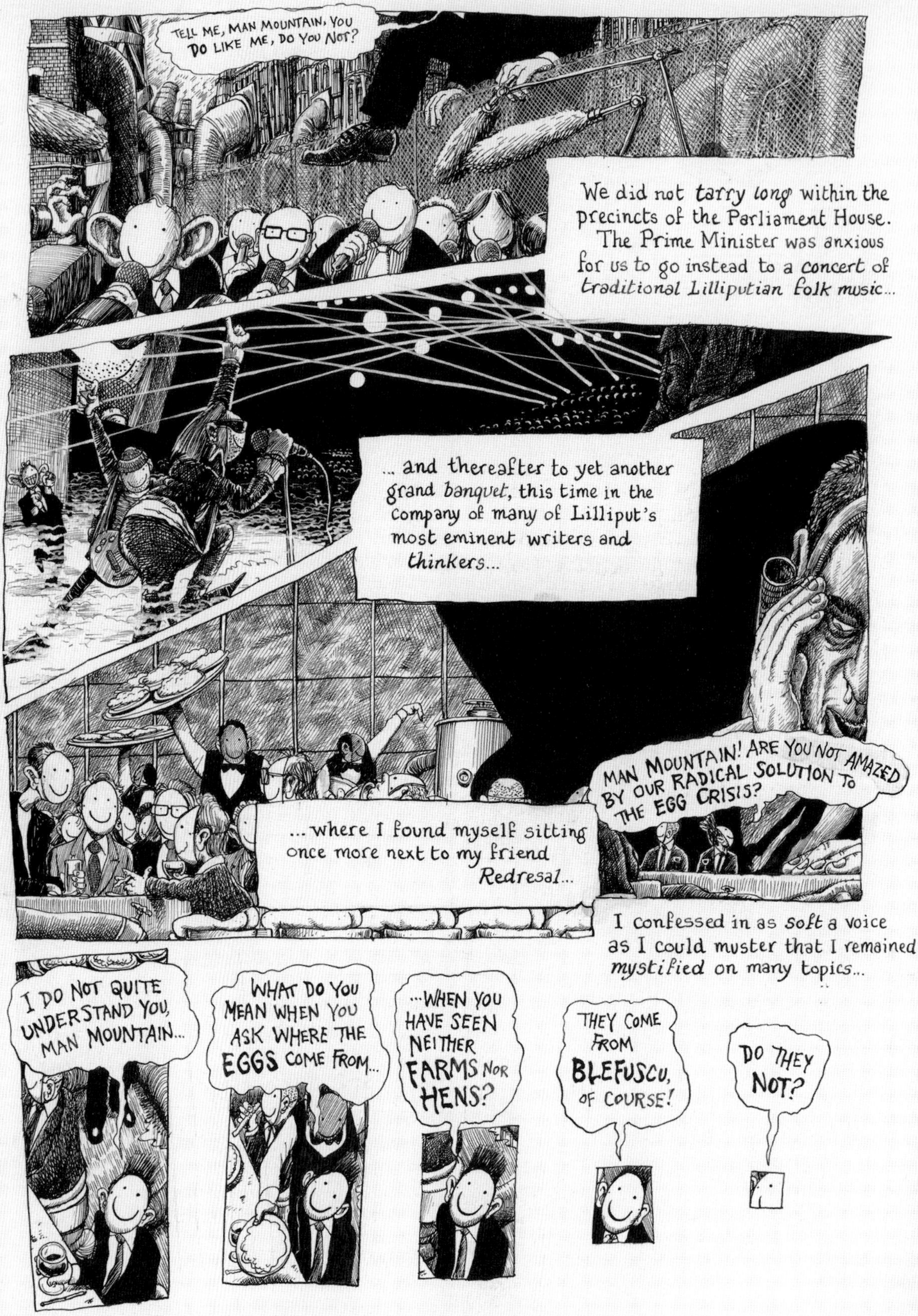
TELL ME, MAN MOUNTAIN, YOU DO LIKE ME, DO YOU NOT?
We did not tarry long within the precincts of the Parliament House. The Prime Minister was anxious for us to go instead to a concert of traditional Lilliputian folk music...
... and thereafter to yet another grand banquet, this time in the company of many of Lilliput's most eminent writers and thinkers...
... where I found myself sitting once more next to my friend Redresal...
MAN MOUNTAIN! ARE YOU NOT AMAZED BY OUR RADICAL SOLUTION TO THE EGG CRISIS?
I confessed in as soft a voice as I could muster that I remained mystified on many topics...
I DO NOT QUITE UNDERSTAND YOU, MAN MOUNTAIN...
WHAT DO YOU MEAN WHEN YOU ASK WHERE THE EGGS COME FROM...
...WHEN YOU HAVE SEEN NEITHER FARMS NOR HENS?
THEY COME FROM BLEFUSCU, OF COURSE!
DO THEY NOT?

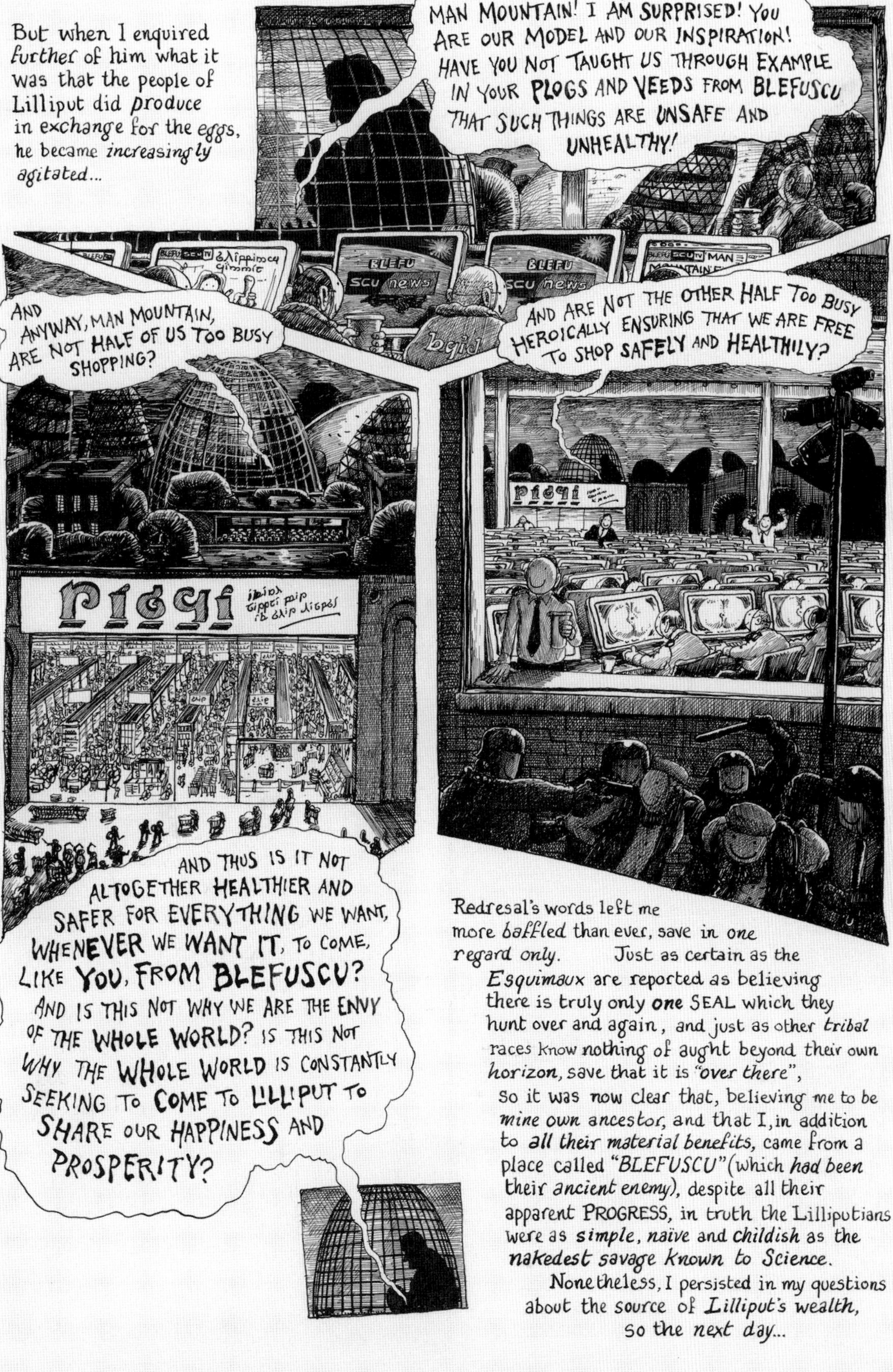

But when I enquired further of him what it was that the people of Lilliput did produce in exchange for the eggs, he became increasingly agitated...
MAN MOUNTAIN! I AM SURPRISED! YOU ARE OUR MODEL AND OUR INSPIRATION! HAVE YOU NOT TAUGHT US THROUGH EXAMPLE IN YOUR PLOGS AND VEEDS FROM BLEFUSCU THAT SUCH THINGS ARE UNSAFE AND UNHEALTHY!
BLEFU scu news
BLEFU scu news
AND ANYWAY, MAN MOUNTAIN, ARE NOT HALF OF US TOO BUSY SHOPPING?
AND ARE NOT THE OTHER HALF TOO BUSY HEROICALLY ENSURING THAT WE ARE FREE TO SHOP SAFELY AND HEALTHILY?
Pidgi
AND THUS IS IT NOT ALTOGETHER HEALTHIER AND SAFER FOR EVERYTHING WE WANT, WHENEVER WE WANT IT, TO COME, LIKE YOU, FROM BLEFUSCU? AND IS THIS NOT WHY WE ARE THE ENVY OF THE WHOLE WORLD? IS THIS NOT WHY THE WHOLE WORLD IS CONSTANTLY SEEKING TO COME TO LILLIPUT TO SHARE OUR HAPPINESS AND PROSPERITY?
Redresal's words left me more baffled than ever, save in one regard only. Just as certain as the Esquimaux are reported as believing there is truly only one SEAL which they hunt over and again, and just as other tribal races know nothing of aught beyond their own horizon, save that it is "over there", so it was now clear that, believing me to be mine own ancestor, and that I, in addition to all their material benefits, came from a place called "BLEFUSCU" (which had been their ancient enemy), despite all their apparent PROGRESS, in truth the Lilliputians were as simple, naïve and childish as the nakedest savage known to Science.
Nonetheless, I persisted in my questions about the source of Lilliput's wealth, so the next day...

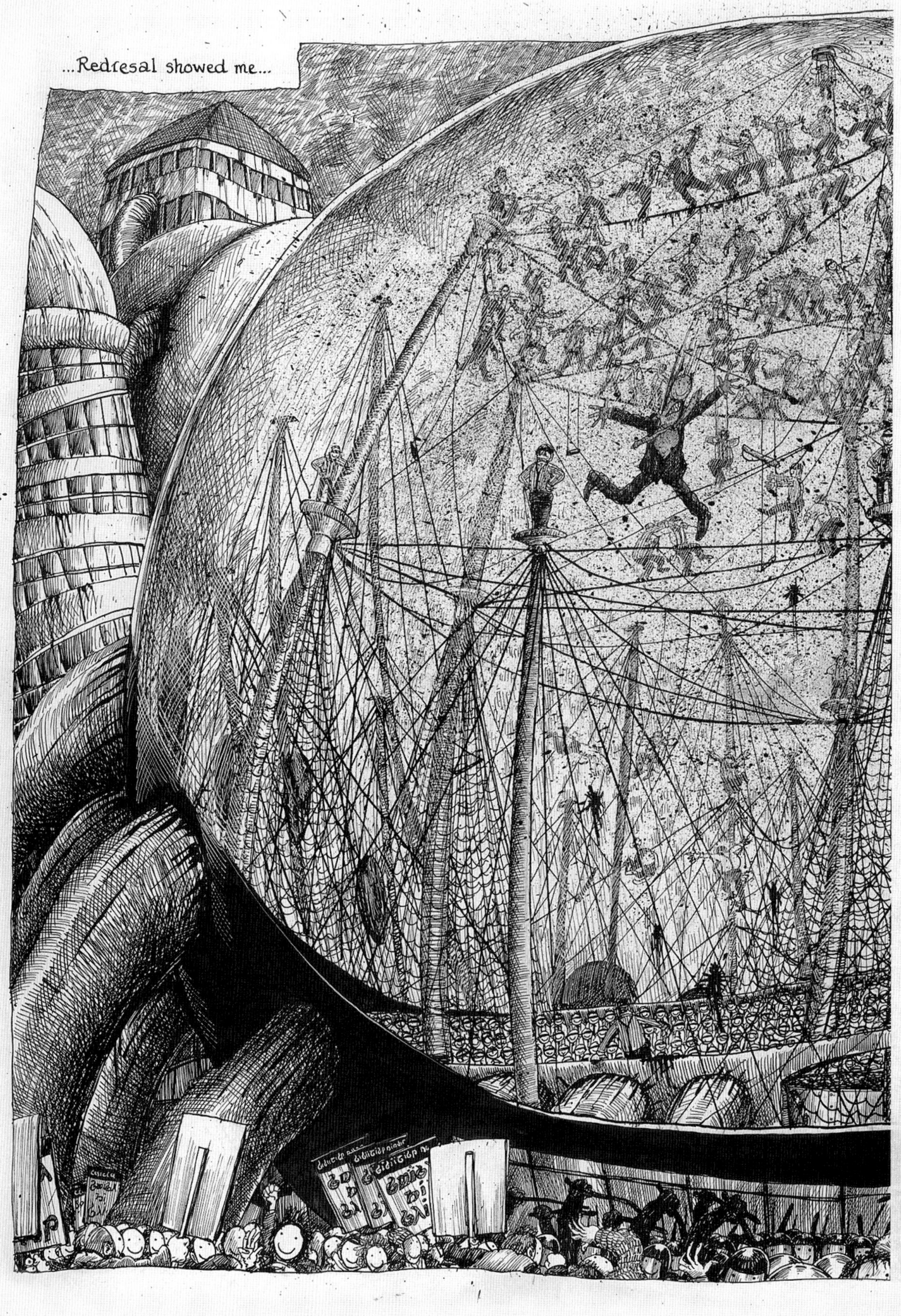
...Redresal showed me...

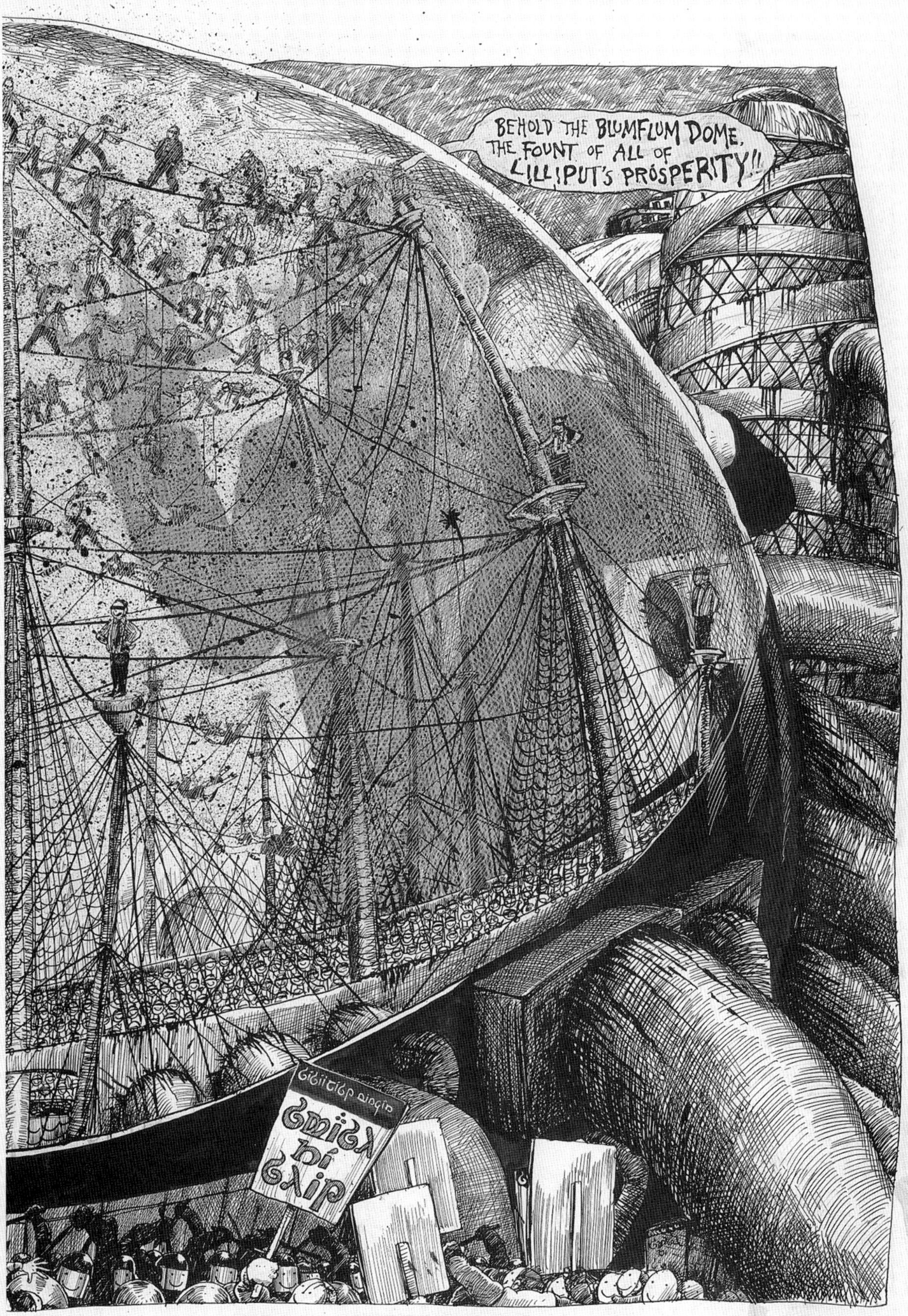
BEHOLD THE BLUMFLUM DOME, THE FOUNT OF ALL OF LILLIPUT'S PROSPERITY!!

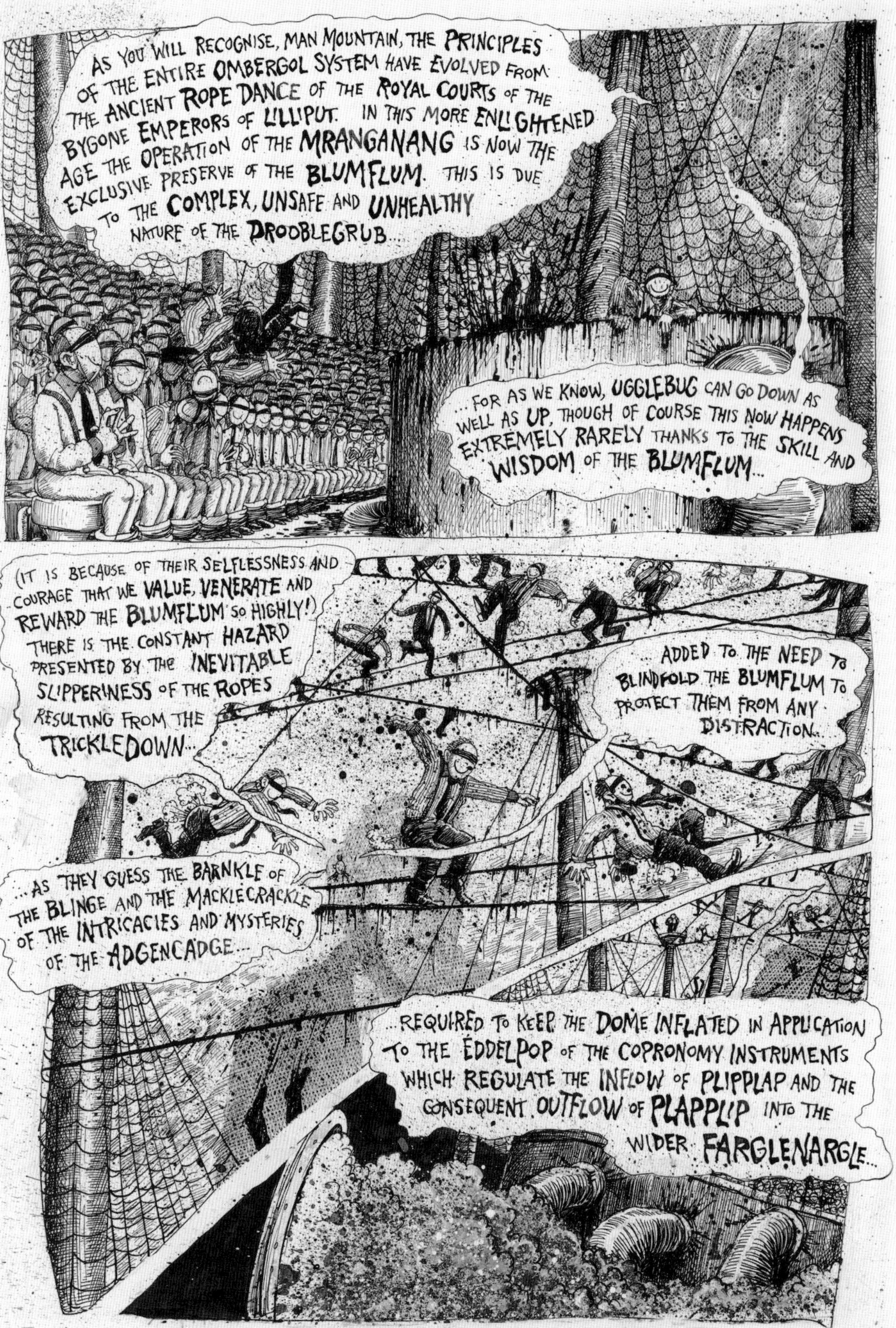
AS YOU WILL RECOGNISE, MAN MOUNTAIN, THE PRINCIPLES OF THE ENTIRE OMBERGOL SYSTEM HAVE EVOLVED FROM THE ANCIENT ROPE DANCE OF THE ROYAL COURTS OF THE BYGONE EMPERORS OF LILLIPUT. IN THIS MORE ENLIGHTENED AGE THE OPERATION OF THE MRANGANANG IS NOW THE EXCLUSIVE PRESERVE OF THE BLUMFLUM. THIS IS DUE TO THE COMPLEX, UNSAFE AND UNHEALTHY NATURE OF THE DROOBLEGRUB...
...FOR AS WE KNOW, UGGLEBUG CAN GO DOWN AS WELL AS UP, THOUGH OF COURSE THIS NOW HAPPENS EXTREMELY RARELY THANKS TO THE SKILL AND WISDOM OF THE BLUMFLUM...
(IT IS BECAUSE OF THEIR SELFLESSNESS AND COURAGE THAT WE VALUE, VENERATE AND REWARD THE BLUMFLUM SO HIGHLY!) THERE IS THE CONSTANT HAZARD PRESENTED BY THE INEVITABLE SLIPPERINESS OF THE ROPES RESULTING FROM THE TRICKLEDOWN...
...ADDED TO THE NEED TO BLINDFOLD THE BLUMFLUM TO PROTECT THEM FROM ANY DISTRACTION...
...AS THEY GUESS THE BARNKLE OF THE BLINGE AND THE MACKLECRACKLE OF THE INTRICACIES AND MYSTERIES OF THE ADGENCADGE...
...REQUIRED TO KEEP THE DOME INFLATED IN APPLICATION TO THE EDDELPOP OF THE COPRONOMY INSTRUMENTS WHICH REGULATE THE INFLOW OF PLIPPLAP AND THE CONSEQUENT OUTFLOW OF PLAPPLIP INTO THE WIDER FARGLENARGLE...

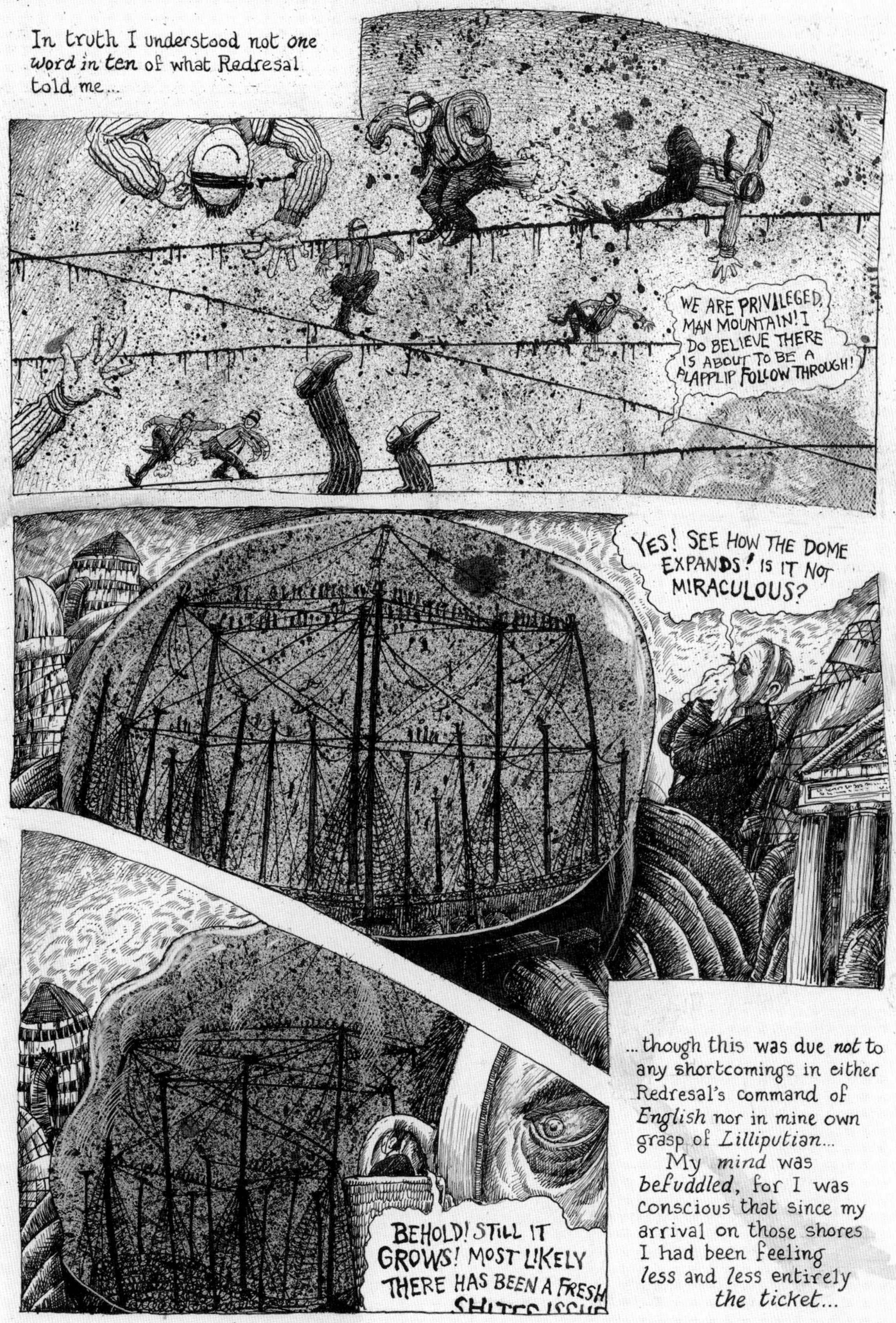

In truth I understood not *one word in ten* of what Redresal told me...
WE ARE PRIVILEGED, MAN MOUNTAIN! I DO BELIEVE THERE IS ABOUT TO BE A PLAPPLIP FOLLOW THROUGH!
YES! SEE HOW THE DOME EXPANDS! IS IT NOT MIRACULOUS?
BEHOLD! STILL IT GROWS! MOST LIKELY THERE HAS BEEN A FRESH SHITES ISSUE
...though this was due *not* to any shortcomings in either Redresal's command of *English* nor in mine own grasp of *Lilliputian*...
My *mind* was *befuddled*, for I was conscious that since my arrival on those shores I had been feeling *less* and *less* entirely *the ticket*...

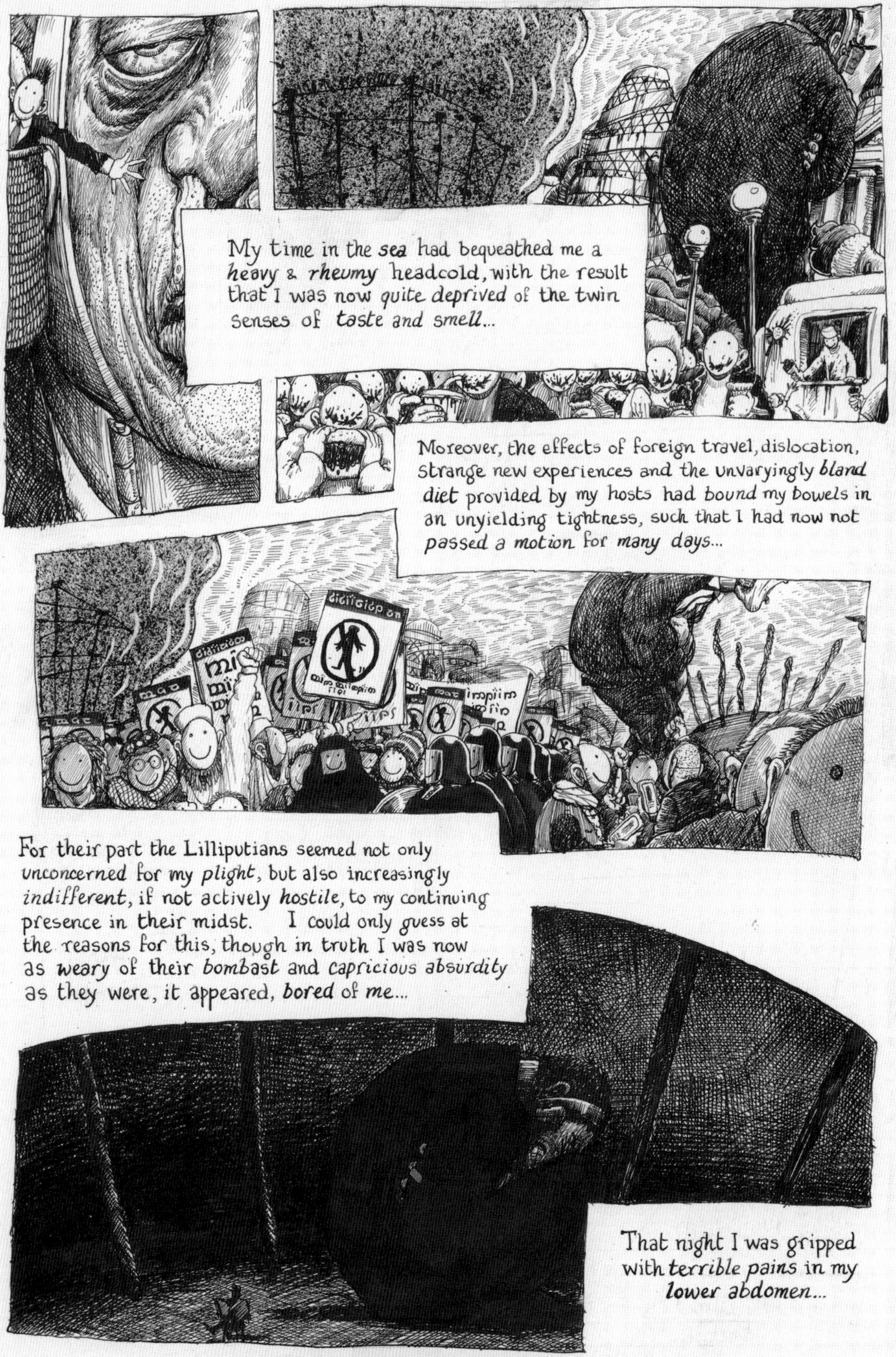
My time in the sea had bequeathed me a heavy & rheumy headcold, with the result that I was now quite deprived of the twin senses of taste and smell...
Moreover, the effects of foreign travel, dislocation, strange new experiences and the unvaryingly bland diet provided by my hosts had bound my bowels in an unyielding tightness, such that I had now not passed a motion for many days...
For their part the Lilliputians seemed not only unconcerned for my plight, but also increasingly indifferent, if not actively hostile, to my continuing presence in their midst. I could only guess at the reasons for this, though in truth I was now as weary of their bombast and capricious absurdity as they were, it appeared, bored of me...
That night I was gripped with terrible pains in my lower abdomen...

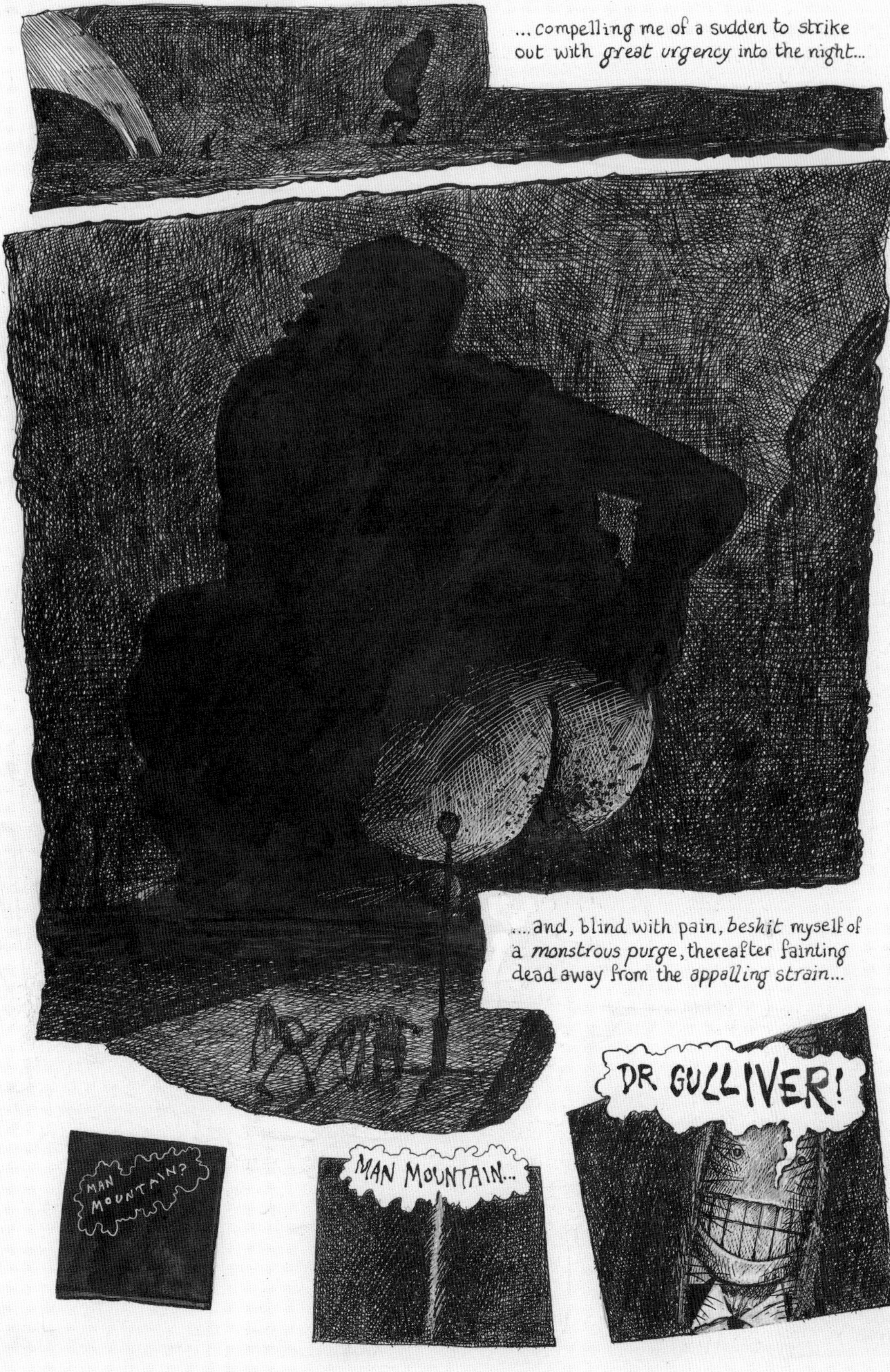
...compelling me of a sudden to strike out with great urgency into the night...
....and, blind with pain, beshit myself of a monstrous purge, thereafter fainting dead away from the appalling strain...
MAN MOUNTAIN?
MAN MOUNTAIN...
DR GULLIVER!

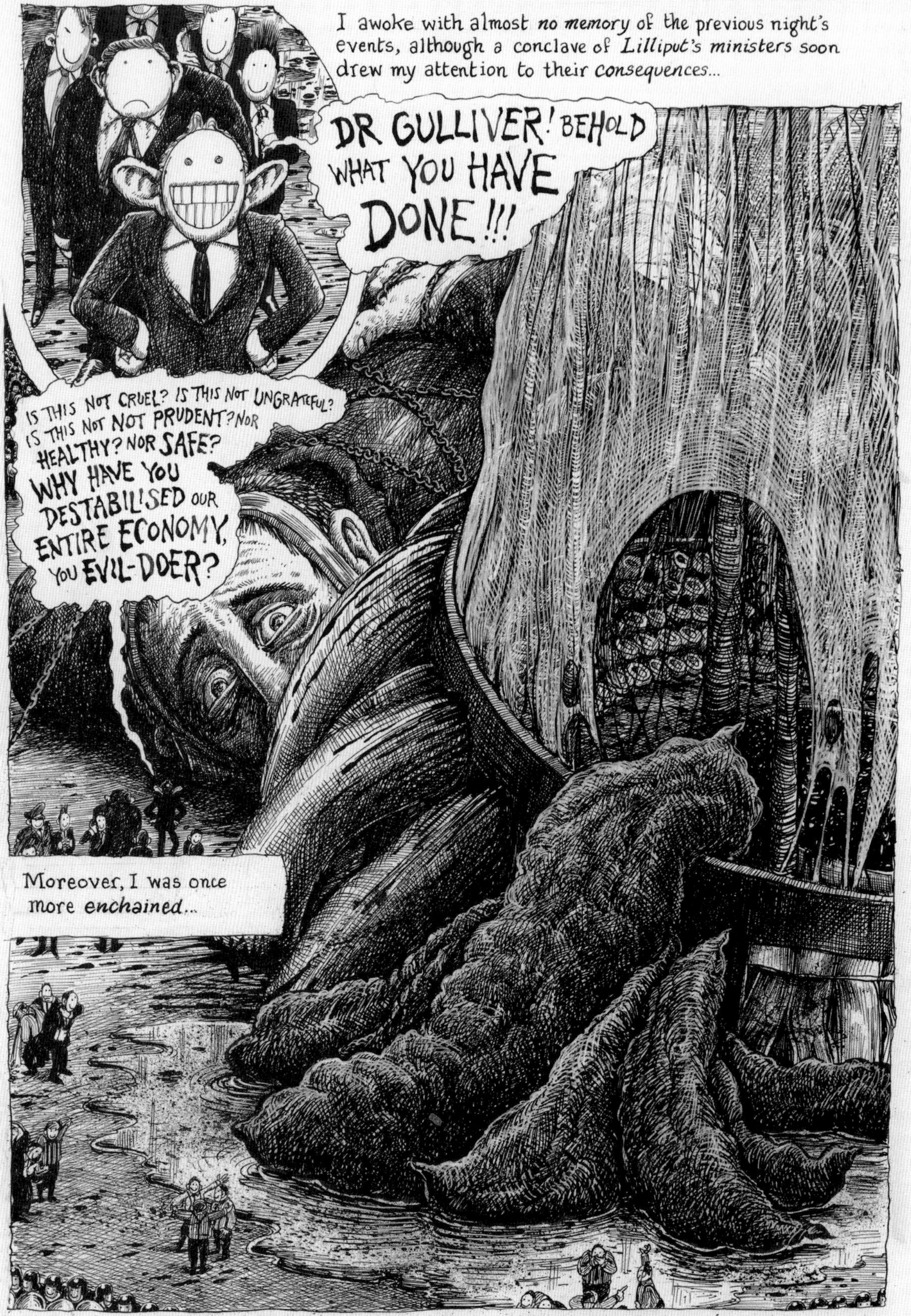
I awoke with almost no memory of the previous night's events, although a conclave of Lilliput's ministers soon drew my attention to their consequences...
DR GULLIVER! BEHOLD WHAT YOU HAVE DONE!!!
IS THIS NOT CRUEL? IS THIS NOT UNGRATEFUL? IS THIS NOT NOT PRUDENT? NOR HEALTHY? NOR SAFE? WHY HAVE YOU DESTABILISED OUR ENTIRE ECONOMY, YOU EVIL-DOER?
Moreover, I was once more enchained...

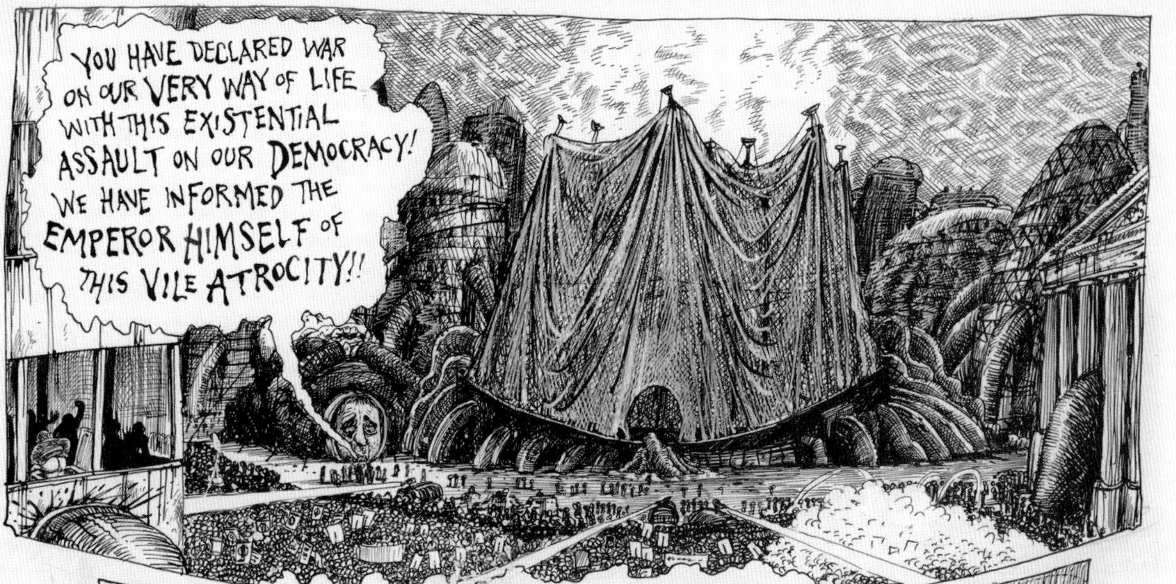
YOU HAVE DECLARED WAR ON OUR VERY WAY OF LIFE WITH THIS EXISTENTIAL ASSAULT ON OUR DEMOCRACY! WE HAVE INFORMED THE EMPEROR HIMSELF OF THIS VILE ATROCITY!!

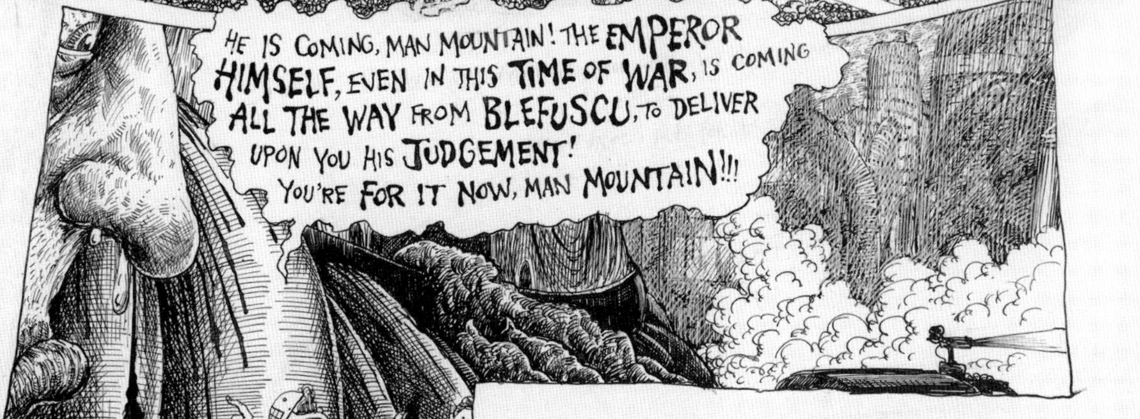
HE IS COMING, MAN MOUNTAIN! THE EMPEROR HIMSELF, EVEN IN THIS TIME OF WAR, IS COMING ALL THE WAY FROM BLEFUSCU, TO DELIVER UPON YOU HIS JUDGEMENT!
YOU'RE FOR IT NOW, MAN MOUNTAIN!!!

I no more understood how my *bemerding* of it had also *burst* the Blumflum Dome than I did the nature of that edifice's *purpose* or *functionings*.

Nonetheless, my actions, however inadvertently, had clearly enraged my hosts. As they grovelled in fearful expectation of the *imminence* of their *Emperor's arrival*, my anxiety increased too.

What was the exact nature of this great personage, of whom no previous mention had been made? Could he be a creature of my own *dimensions*, who kept Lilliput merely as a kind of *toy*? Or might he be even *bigger*?

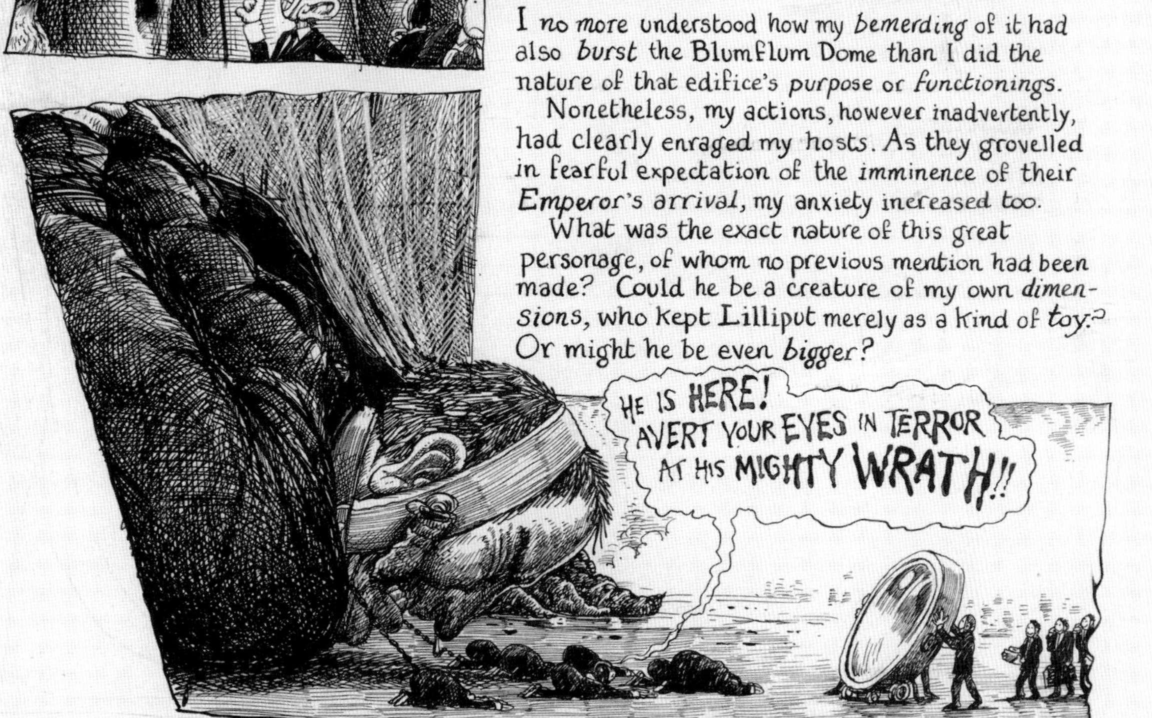
HE IS HERE! AVERT YOUR EYES IN TERROR AT HIS MIGHTY WRATH!!

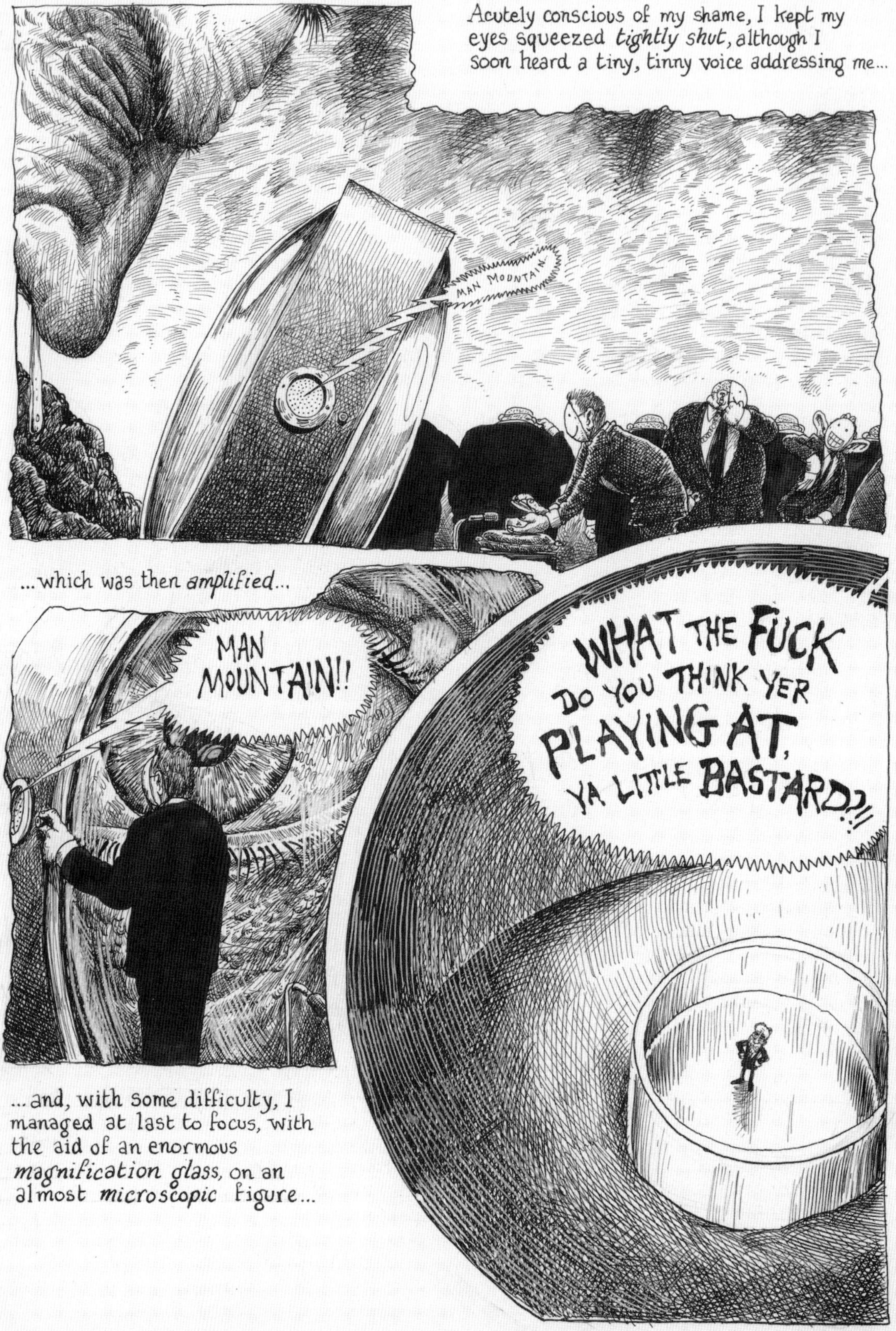
Acutely conscious of my shame, I kept my eyes squeezed *tightly shut*, although I soon heard a tiny, tinny voice addressing me...
MAN MOUNTAIN
...which was then *amplified*...
MAN MOUNTAIN!!
...and, with some difficulty, I managed at last to focus, with the aid of an enormous *magnification glass*, on an almost *microscopic* figure...
WHAT THE FUCK DO YOU THINK YER PLAYING AT, YA LITTLE BASTARD?!!

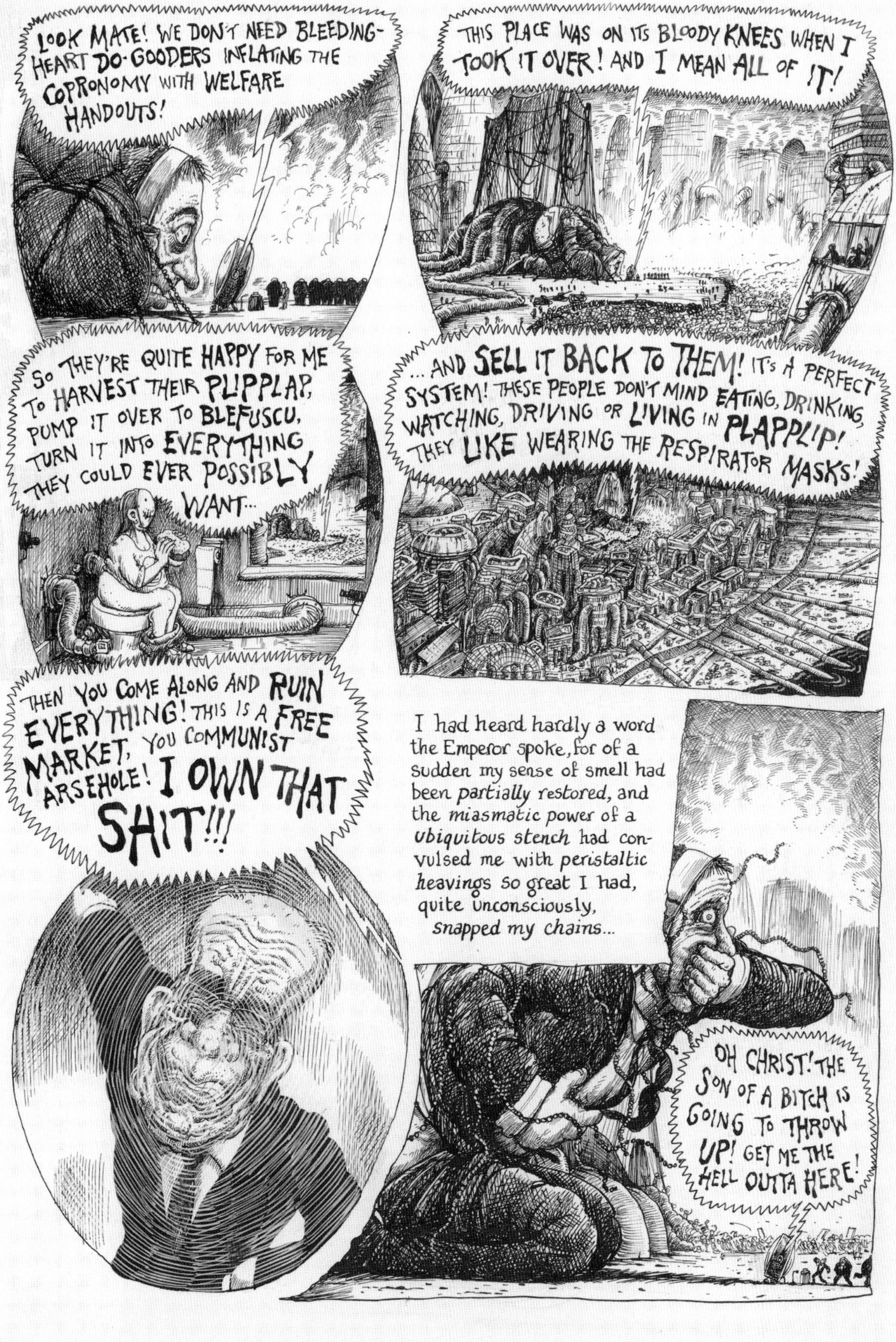
LOOK MATE! WE DON'T NEED BLEEDING-HEART DO-GOODERS INFLATING THE COPRONOMY WITH WELFARE HANDOUTS!
THIS PLACE WAS ON ITS BLOODY KNEES WHEN I TOOK IT OVER! AND I MEAN ALL OF IT!
SO THEY'RE QUITE HAPPY FOR ME TO HARVEST THEIR PLIPPLAP, PUMP IT OVER TO BLEFUSCU, TURN IT INTO EVERYTHING THEY COULD EVER POSSIBLY WANT...
... AND SELL IT BACK TO THEM! IT'S A PERFECT SYSTEM! THESE PEOPLE DON'T MIND EATING, DRINKING, WATCHING, DRIVING OR LIVING IN PLAPPLIP! THEY LIKE WEARING THE RESPIRATOR MASKS!
THEN YOU COME ALONG AND RUIN EVERYTHING! THIS IS A FREE MARKET, YOU COMMUNIST ARSEHOLE! I OWN THAT SHIT!!!
I had heard hardly a word the Emperor spoke, for of a sudden my sense of smell had been partially restored, and the miasmatic power of a ubiquitous stench had convulsed me with peristaltic heavings so great I had, quite unconsciously, snapped my chains...
OH CHRIST! THE SON OF A BITCH IS GOING TO THROW UP! GET ME THE HELL OUTTA HERE!

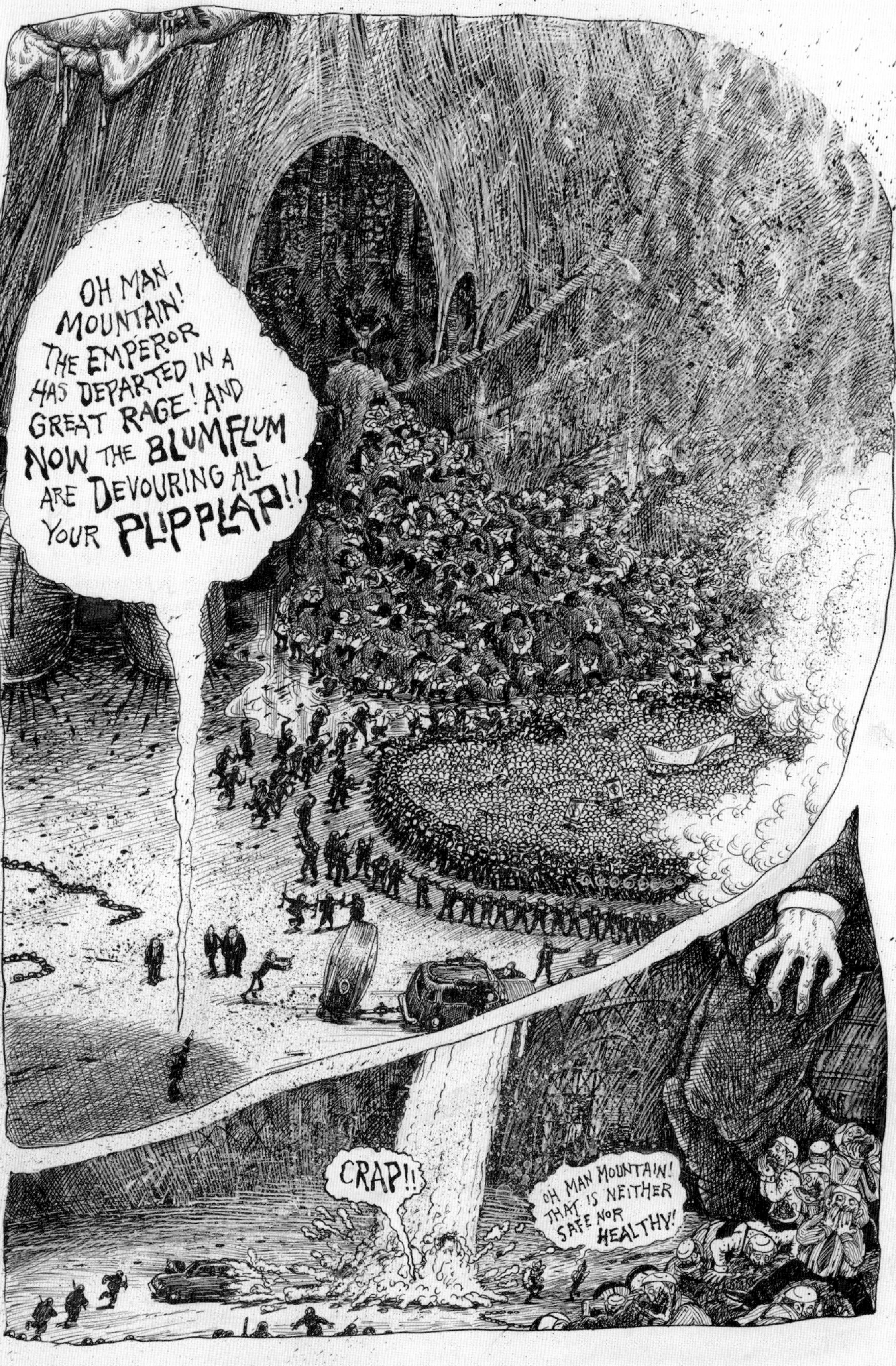
OH MAN MOUNTAIN! THE EMPEROR HAS DEPARTED IN A GREAT RAGE! AND NOW THE BLUMFLUM ARE DEVOURING ALL YOUR PLIPPLAP!!
CRAP!!
OH MAN MOUNTAIN! THAT IS NEITHER SAFE NOR HEALTHY!

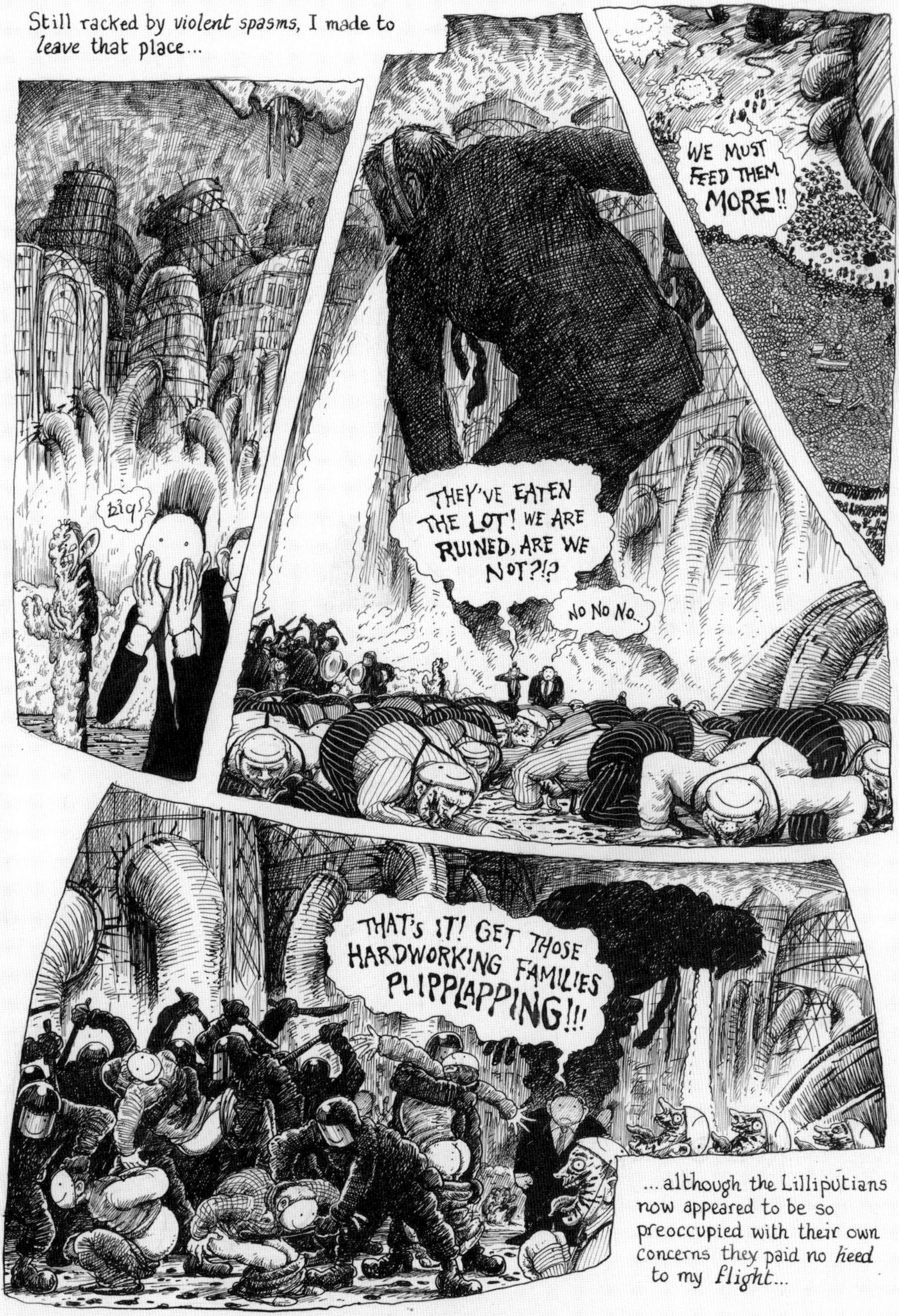
Still racked by violent spasms, I made to leave that place...
WE MUST FEED THEM MORE!!
THEY'VE EATEN THE LOT! WE ARE RUINED, ARE WE NOT?!?
NO NO NO...
THAT'S IT! GET THOSE HARDWORKING FAMILIES PLIPPLAPPING!!!
...although the Lilliputians now appeared to be so preoccupied with their own concerns they paid no heed to my flight...

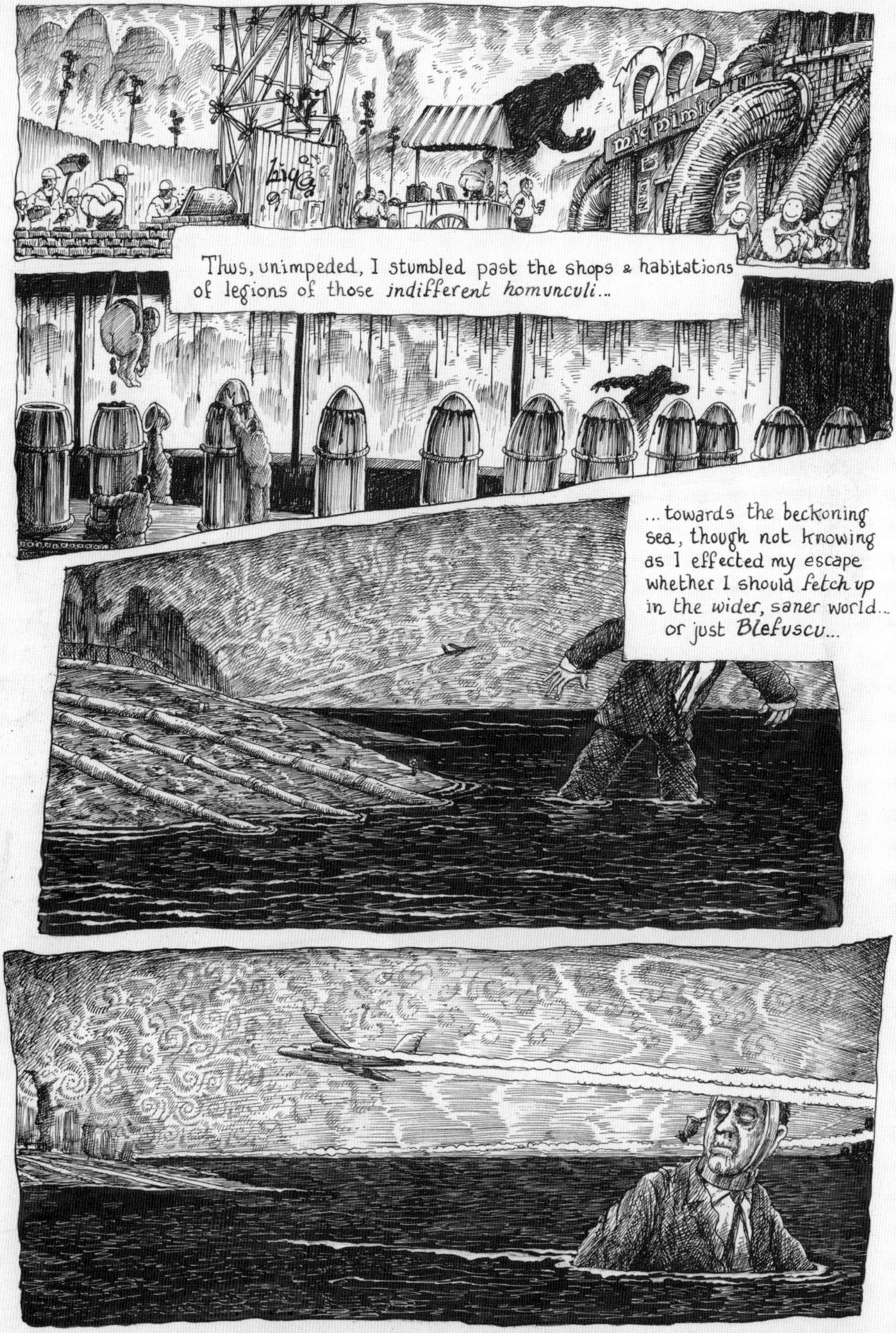
Thus, unimpeded, I stumbled past the shops & habitations of legions of those *indifferent homunculi*...
...towards the beckoning sea, though not knowing as I effected my escape whether I should *fetch up* in the *wider*, saner world... or just *Blefuscu*...

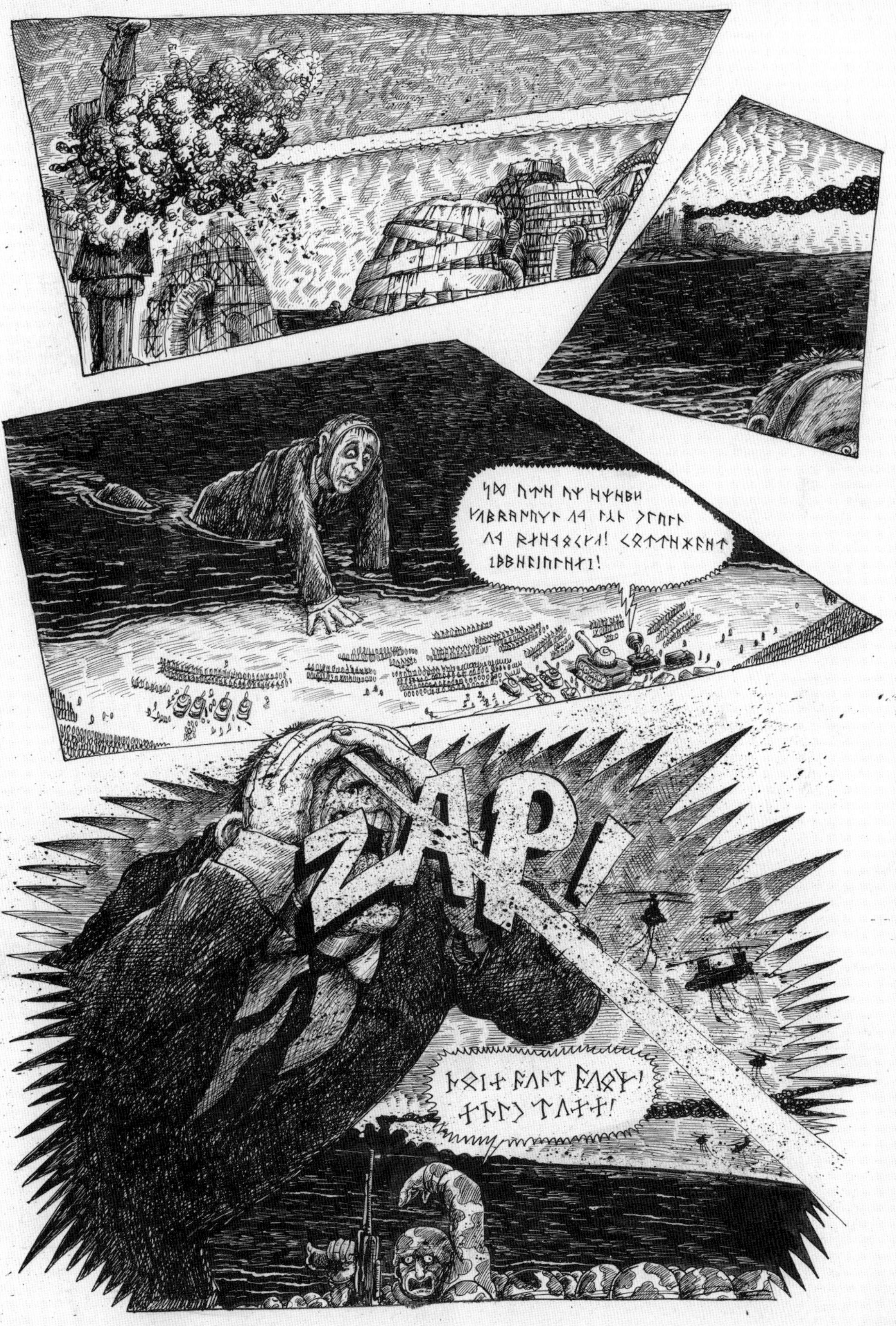
ZAP!

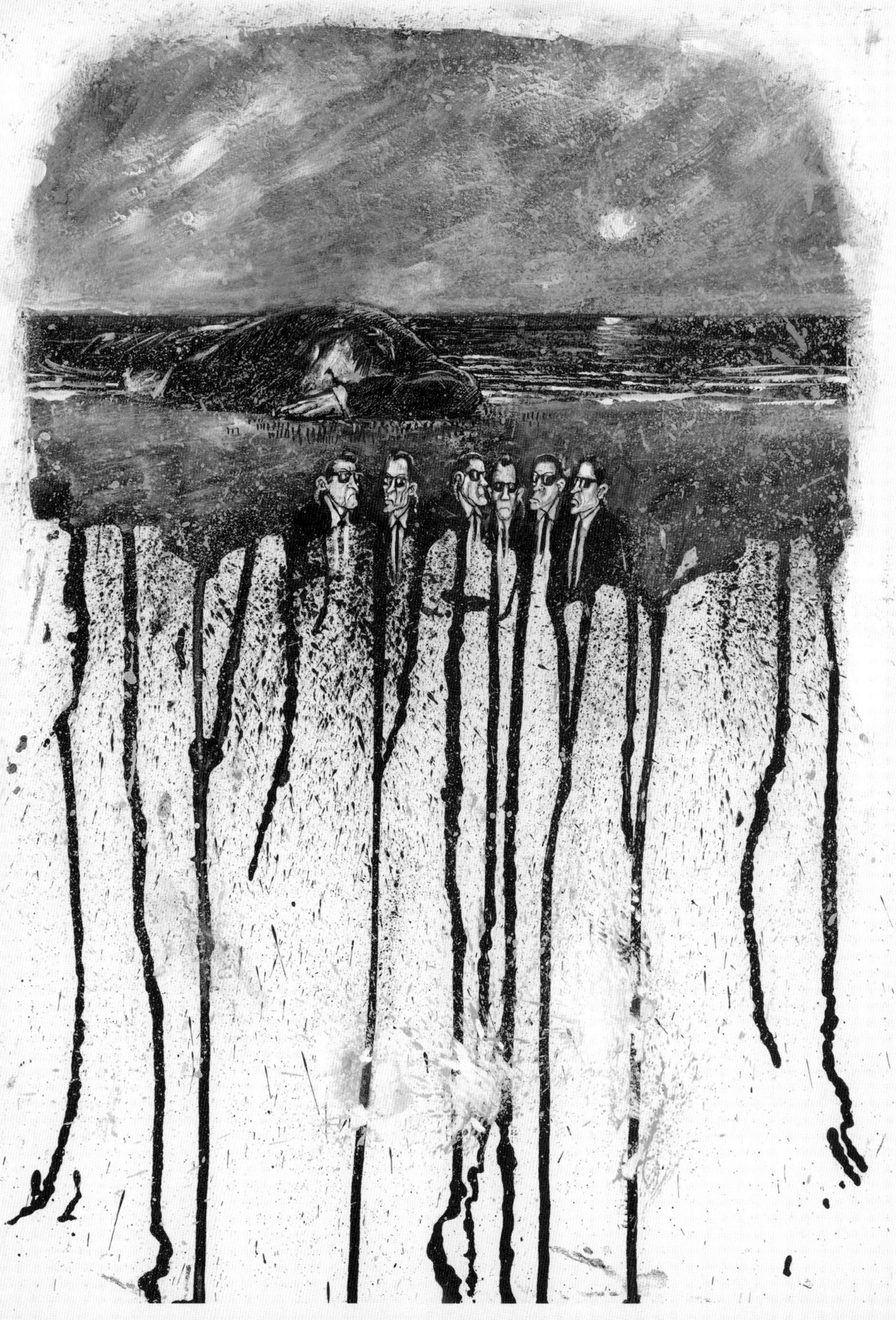

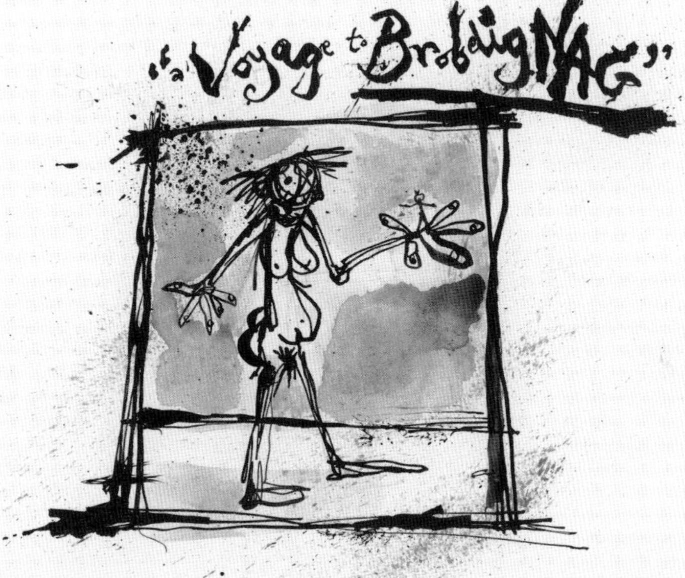
"a Voyage to BrobdigNAG"

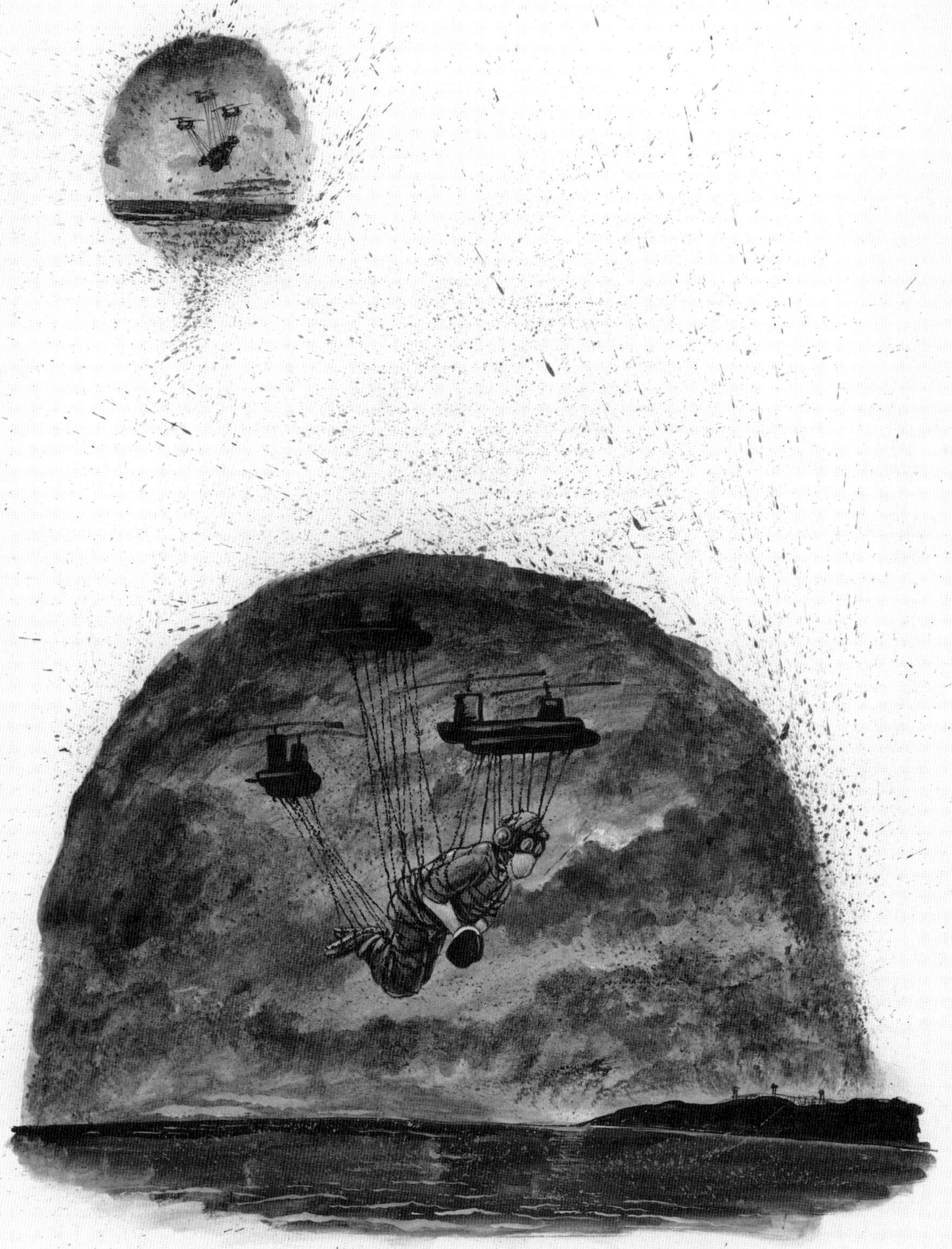

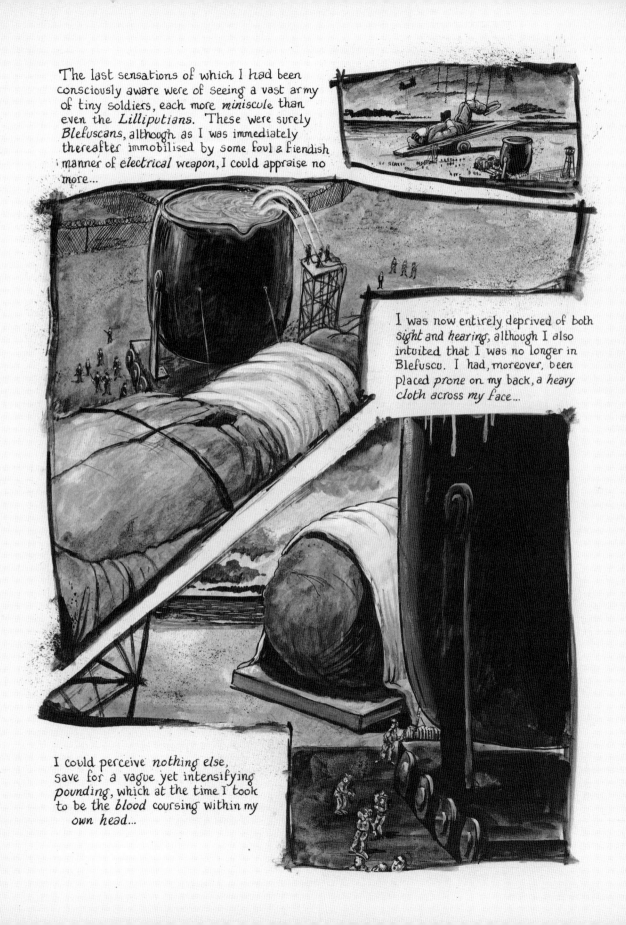

The last sensations of which I had been consciously aware were of seeing a vast army of tiny soldiers, each more *miniscule* than even the *Lilliputians*. These were surely *Blefuscans*, although as I was immediately thereafter immobilised by some foul & fiendish manner of *electrical* weapon, I could appraise no more...

I was now entirely deprived of both *sight* and *hearing*, although I also intuited that I was no longer in Blefuscu. I had, moreover, been placed *prone* on my back, a *heavy cloth* across my face...

I could perceive *nothing else*, save for a vague yet intensifying *pounding*, which at the time I took to be the *blood* coursing within my own *head*...

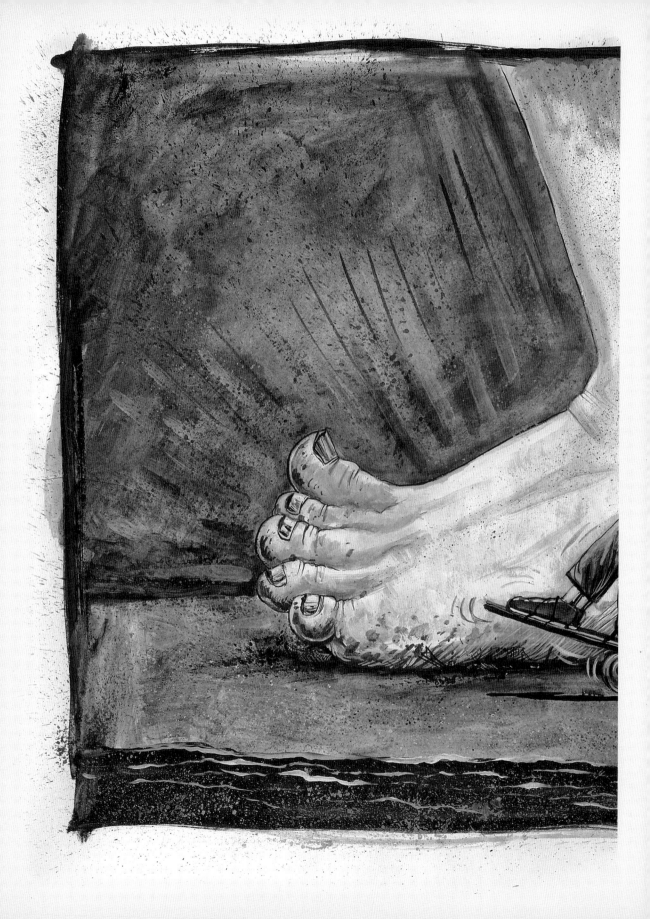

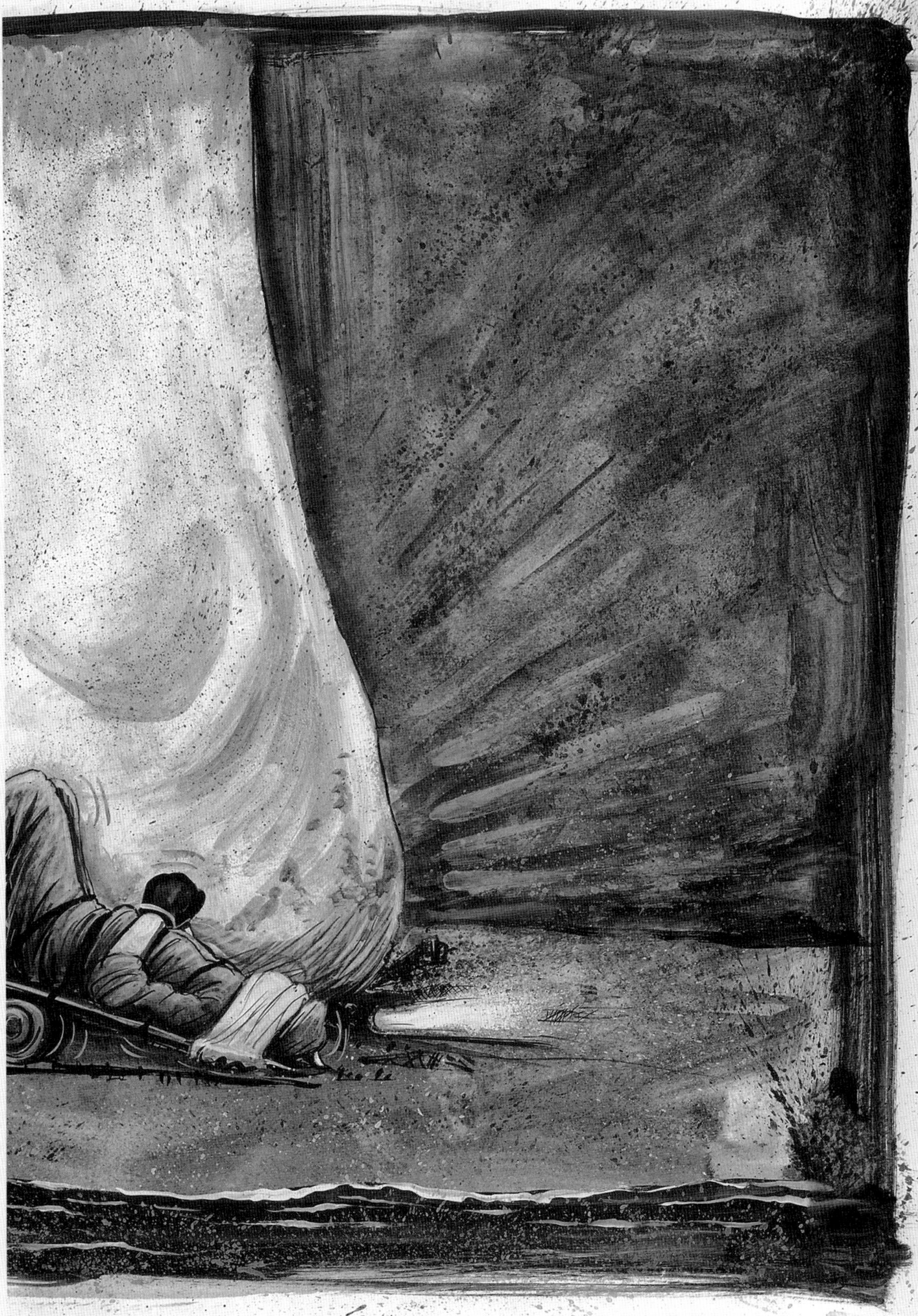

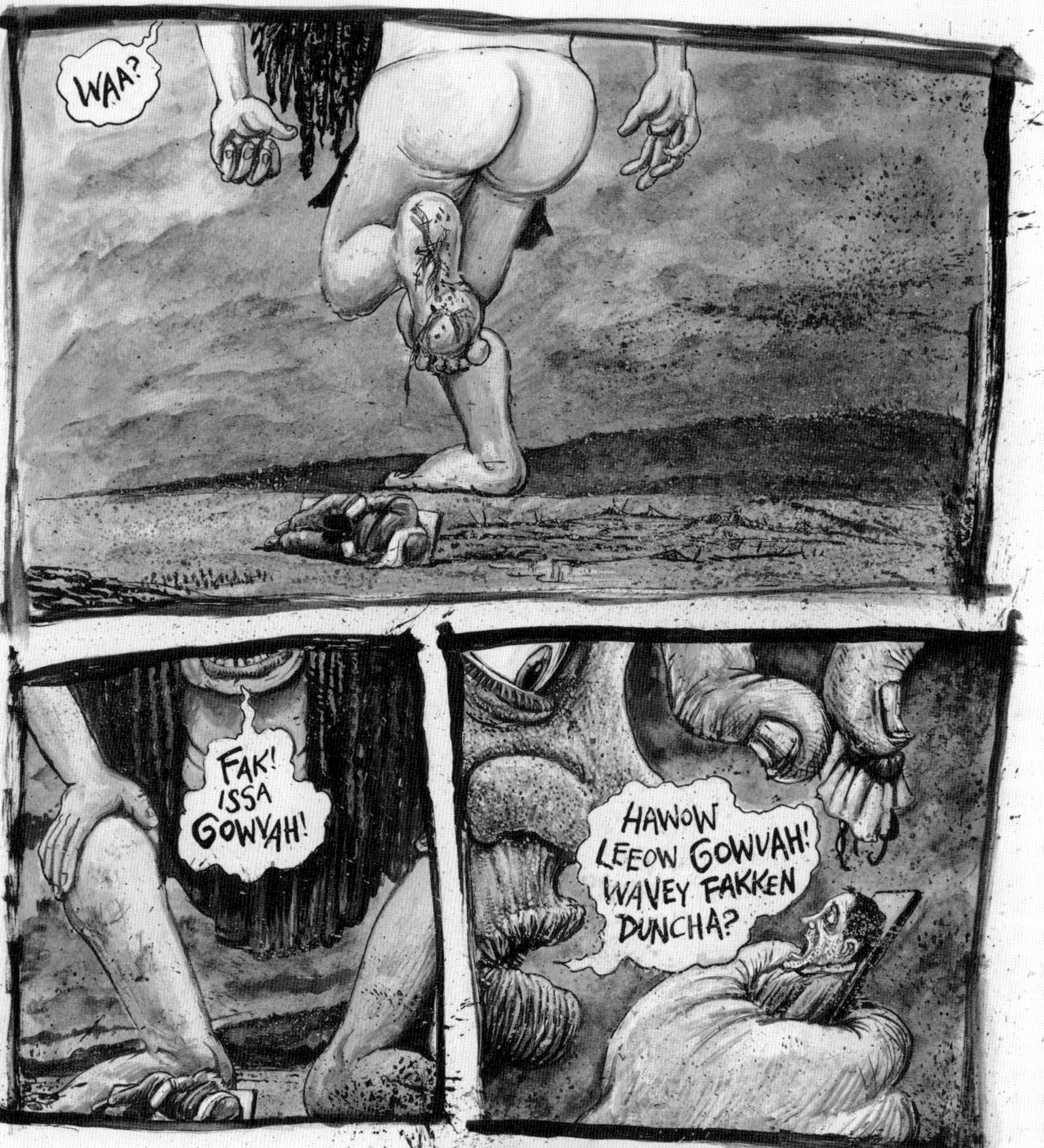
WAA?
FAK! ISSA GOWVAH!
HAWOW LEEOW GOWVAH! WAVEY FAKKEN DUNCHA?

Able once more to see and hear, I was staring into the vast face of a grotesquely large child, who bellowed at me in an incomprehensible tongue.
Once more I had cause to doubt my sanity as, with me in her gargantuan fist, she ran off through a meadow, each blade of grass as tall as a tree...

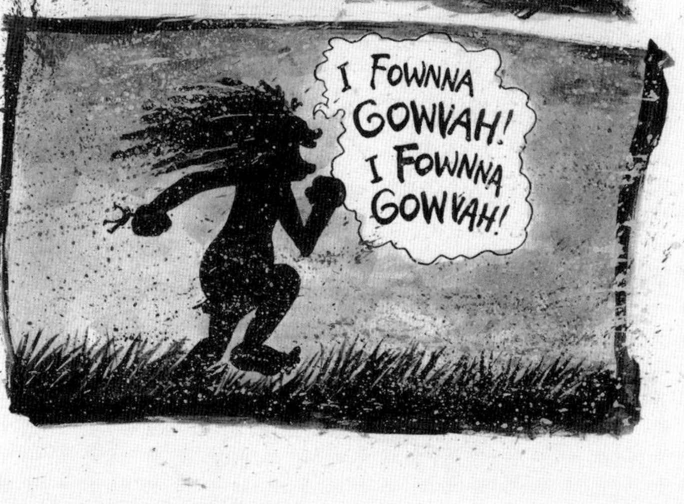
I FOWNNA GOWVAH! I FOWNNA GOWVAH!

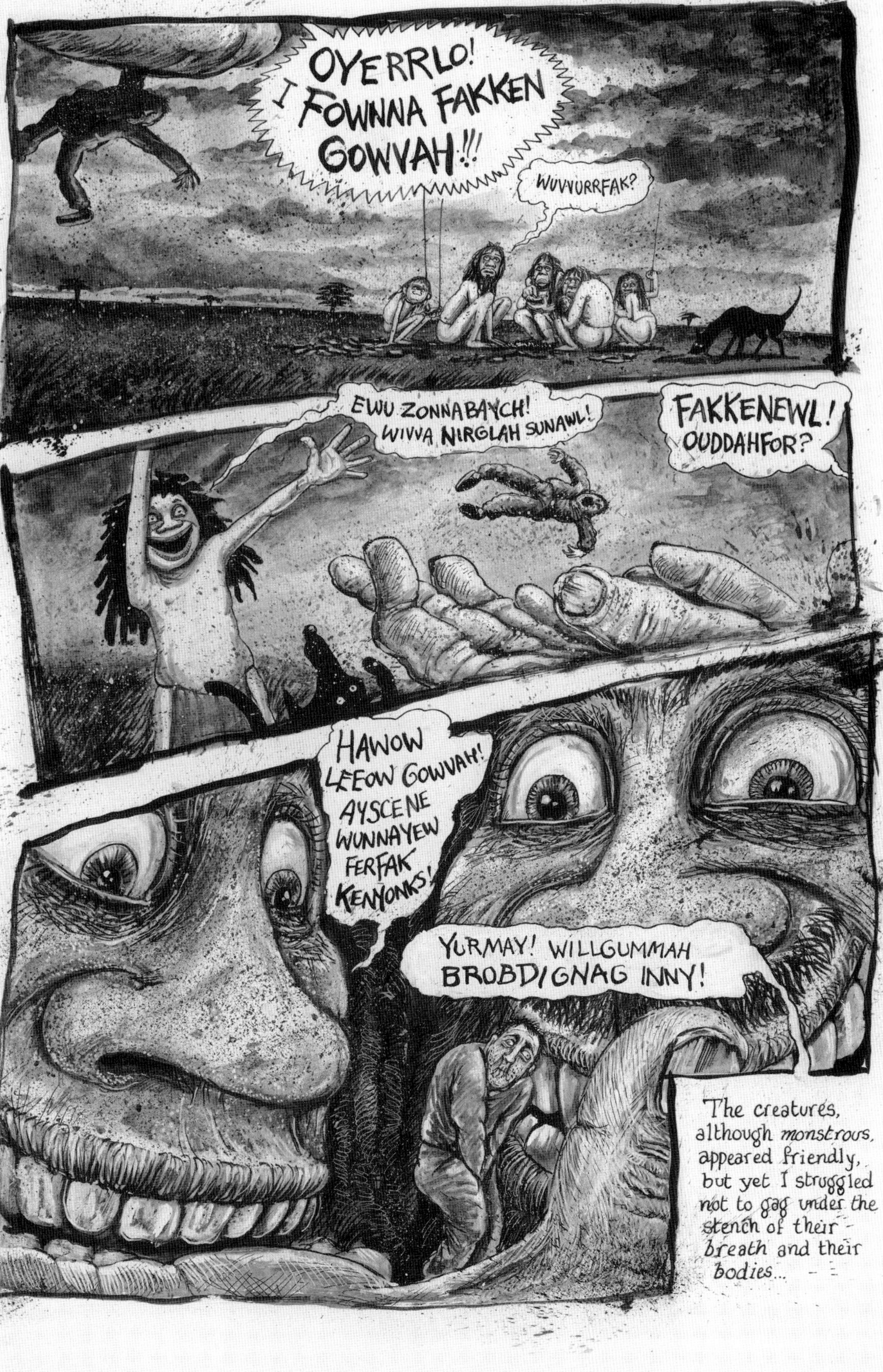
OYERRLO! I FOWNNA FAKKEN GOWVAH!!!
WUVVURRFAK?
EWU ZONNABAYCH! WIVVA NIRGLAH SUNAWL!
FAKKENEWL! OUDDAHFOR?
HAWOW LEEOW GOWVAH! AYSCENE WUNNAYEW FERFAK KENYONKS!
YURMAY! WILLGUMMAH BROBDIGNAG INNY!
The creatures, although *monstrous*, appeared friendly, but yet I struggled not to gag under the stench of their *breath* and their *bodies*...

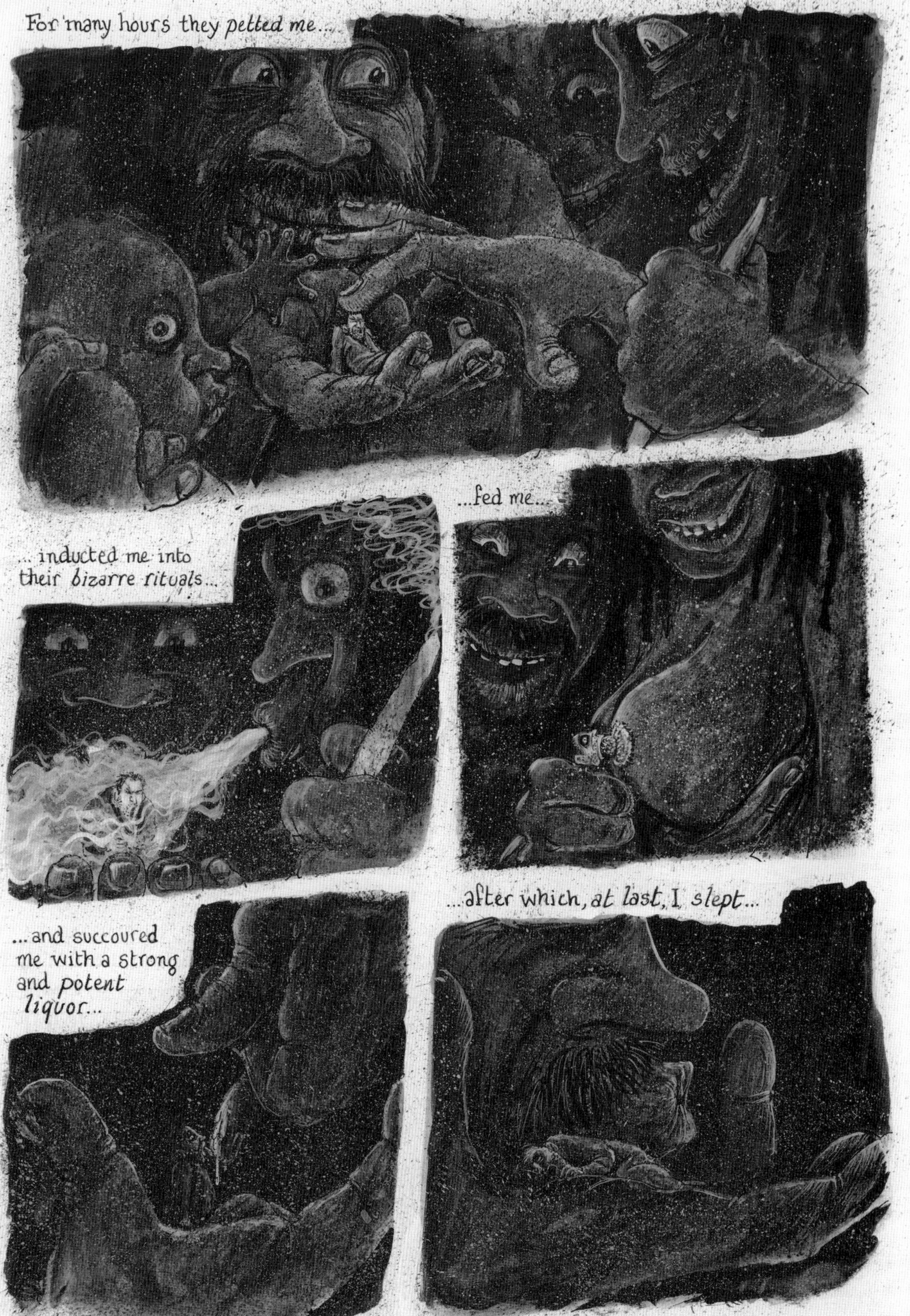
For many hours they petted me...
...fed me...
...inducted me into their bizarre rituals...
...and succoured me with a strong and potent liquor...
...after which, at last, I slept...

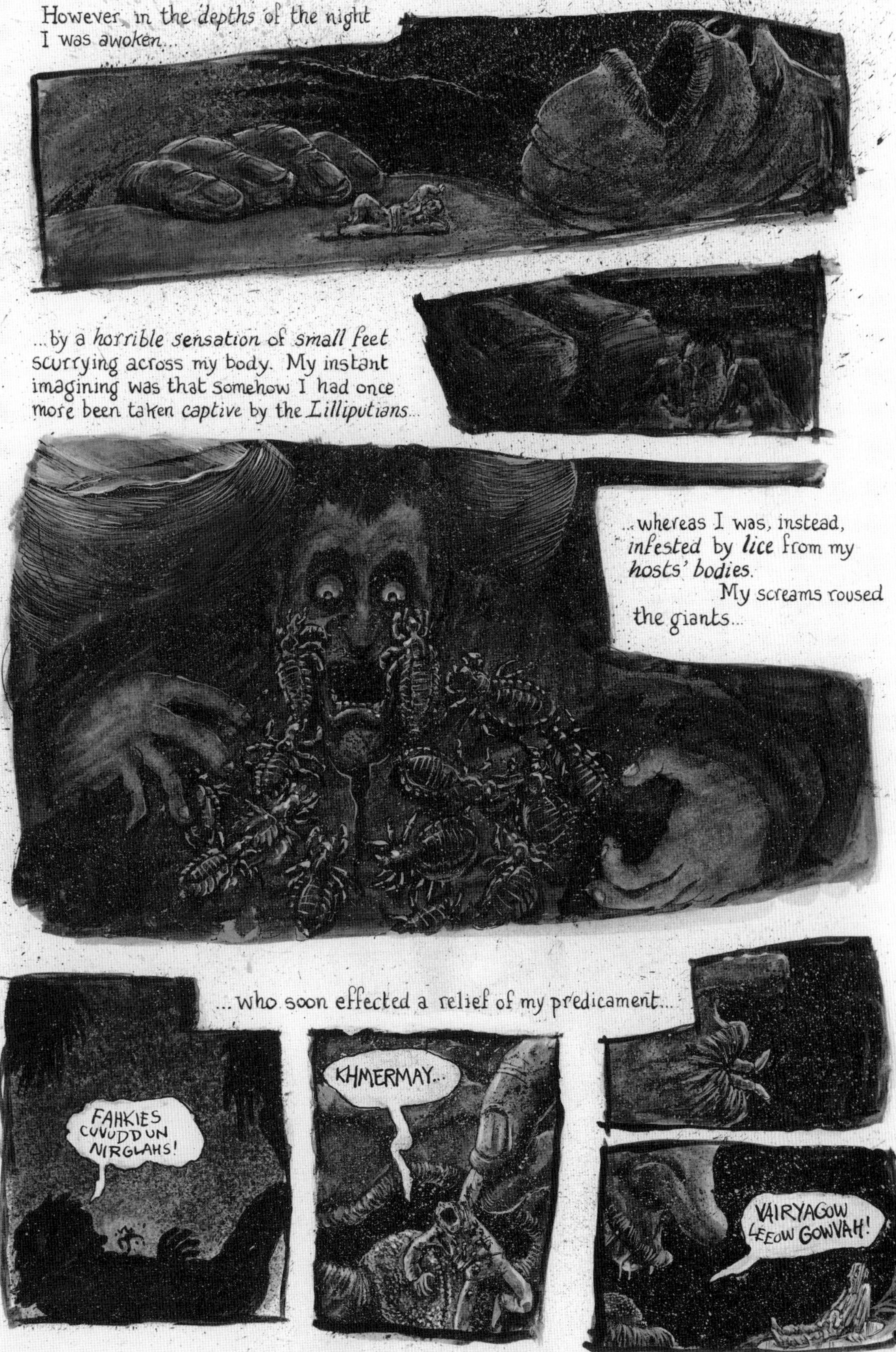
However, in the depths of the night I was awoken...
...by a horrible sensation of small feet scurrying across my body. My instant imagining was that somehow I had once more been taken captive by the Lilliputians...
...whereas I was, instead, infested by lice from my hosts' bodies.
My screams roused the giants...
...who soon effected a relief of my predicament...
FAHKIES CUVUDD UN NIRGLAHS!
KHMERMAY...
VAIRYAGOW LEEOW GOWVAH!

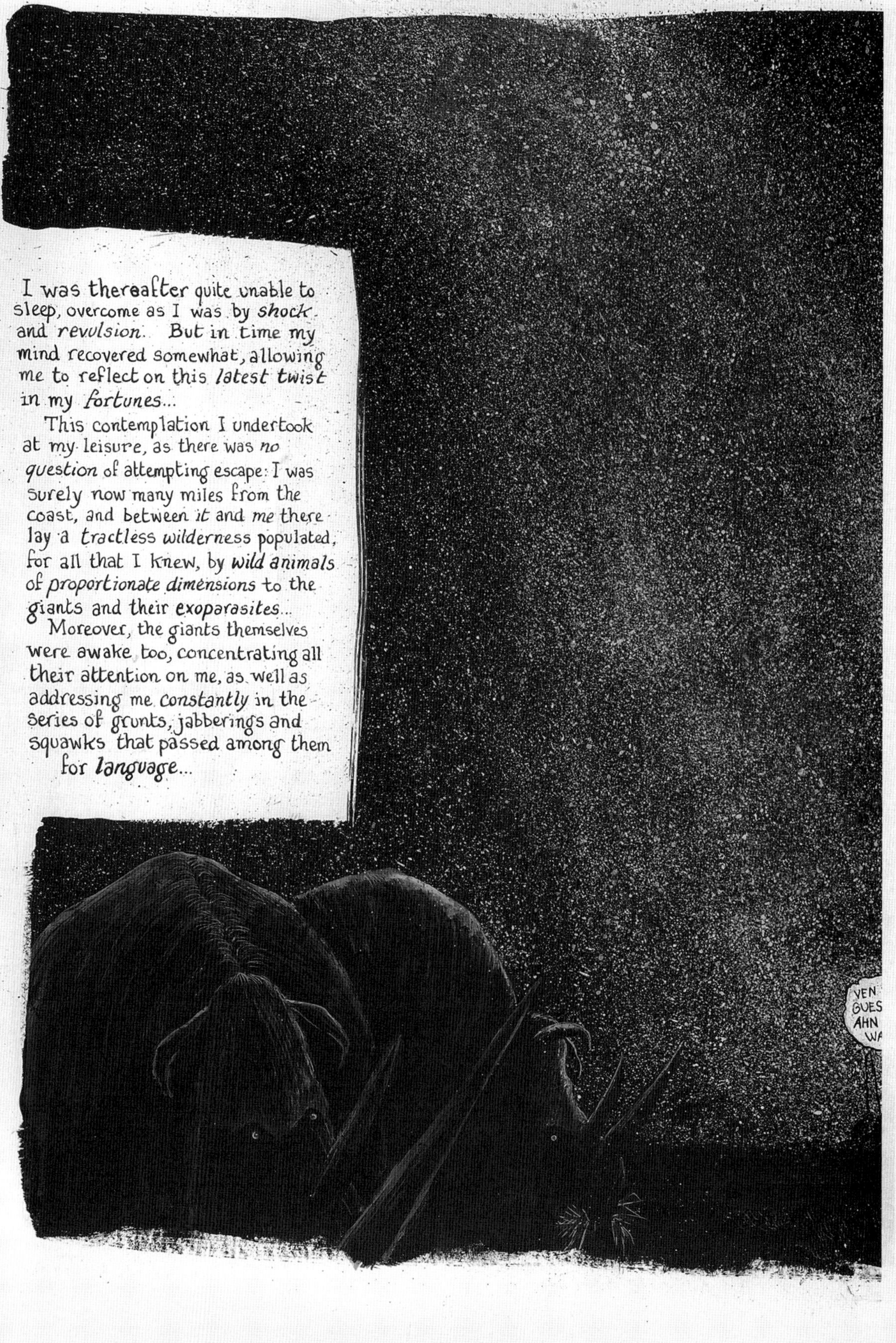
I was thereafter quite unable to sleep, overcome as I was by *shock* and *revulsion*. But in time my mind recovered somewhat, allowing me to reflect on this *latest twist* in my *fortunes*... This contemplation I undertook at my leisure, as there was *no question* of attempting escape: I was surely now many miles from the coast, and between *it* and *me* there lay a *tractless wilderness* populated, for all that I knew, by *wild animals* of *proportionate dimensions* to the giants and their *exoparasites*... Moreover, the giants themselves were awake too, concentrating all their attention on me, as well as addressing me *constantly* in the series of grunts, jabberings and squawks that passed among them for *language*...
VEN GUES AHN WA

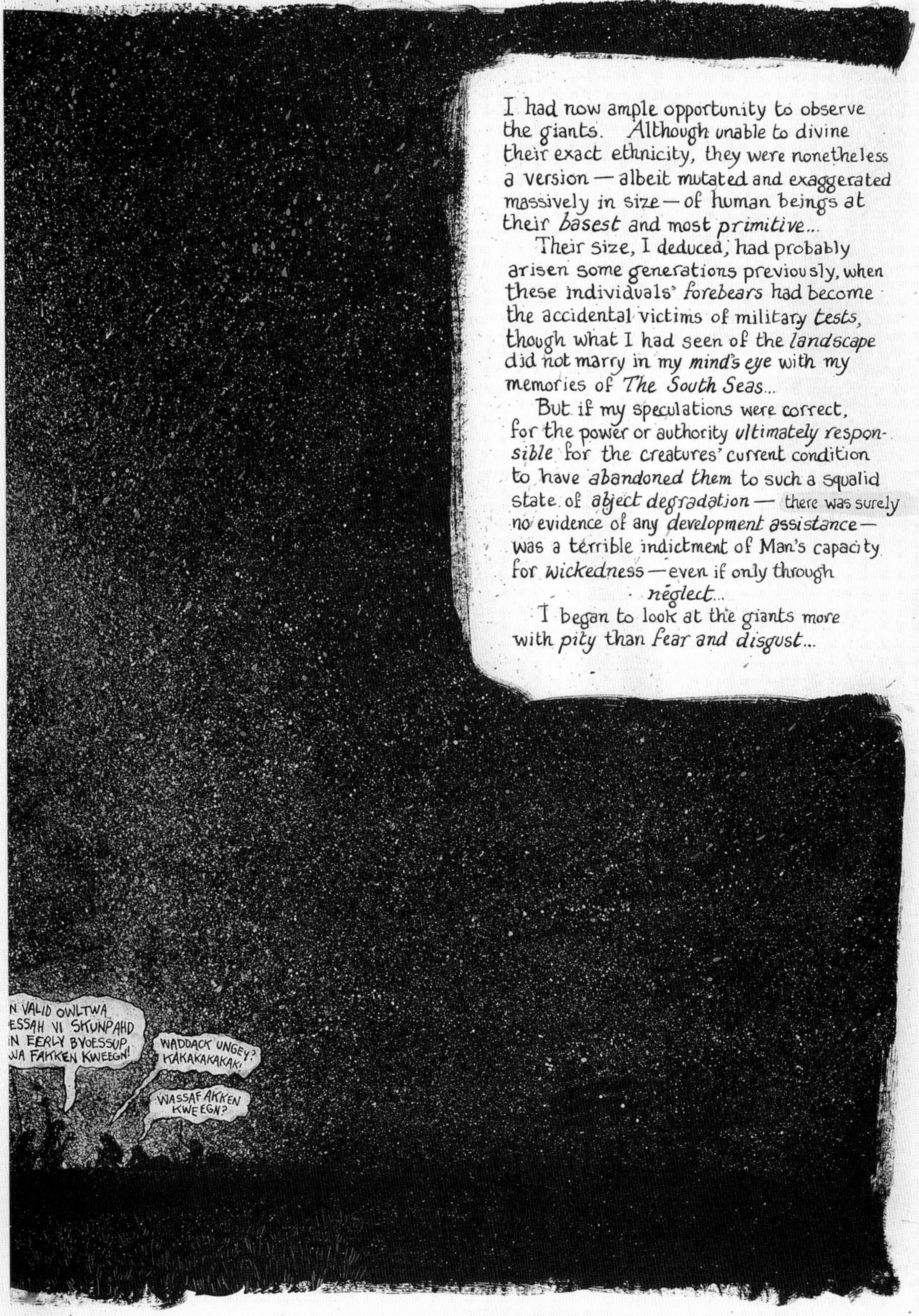
I had now ample opportunity to observe the giants. Although unable to divine their exact ethnicity, they were nonetheless a version — albeit mutated and exaggerated massively in size — of human beings at their *basest* and most *primitive*...
Their size, I deduced, had probably arisen some generations previously, when these individuals' *forebears* had become the accidental victims of military *tests*, though what I had seen of the *landscape* did not marry in my *mind's eye* with my memories of *The South Seas*...
But if my speculations were correct, for the power or authority *ultimately responsible* for the creatures' current condition to have *abandoned them* to such a squalid state of *abject degradation* — there was surely no evidence of any *development assistance* — was a terrible indictment of Man's capacity for *wickedness* — even if only through *neglect*...
I began to look at the giants more with *pity* than fear and *disgust*...
N VALID OWLTWA ESSAH VI SKUNPAHD IN EERLY BYOESSUP WA FAKKEN KWEEGN!
WADDACK UNGEY? KAKAKAKAKAK!
WASSAF AKKEN KWEEGN?

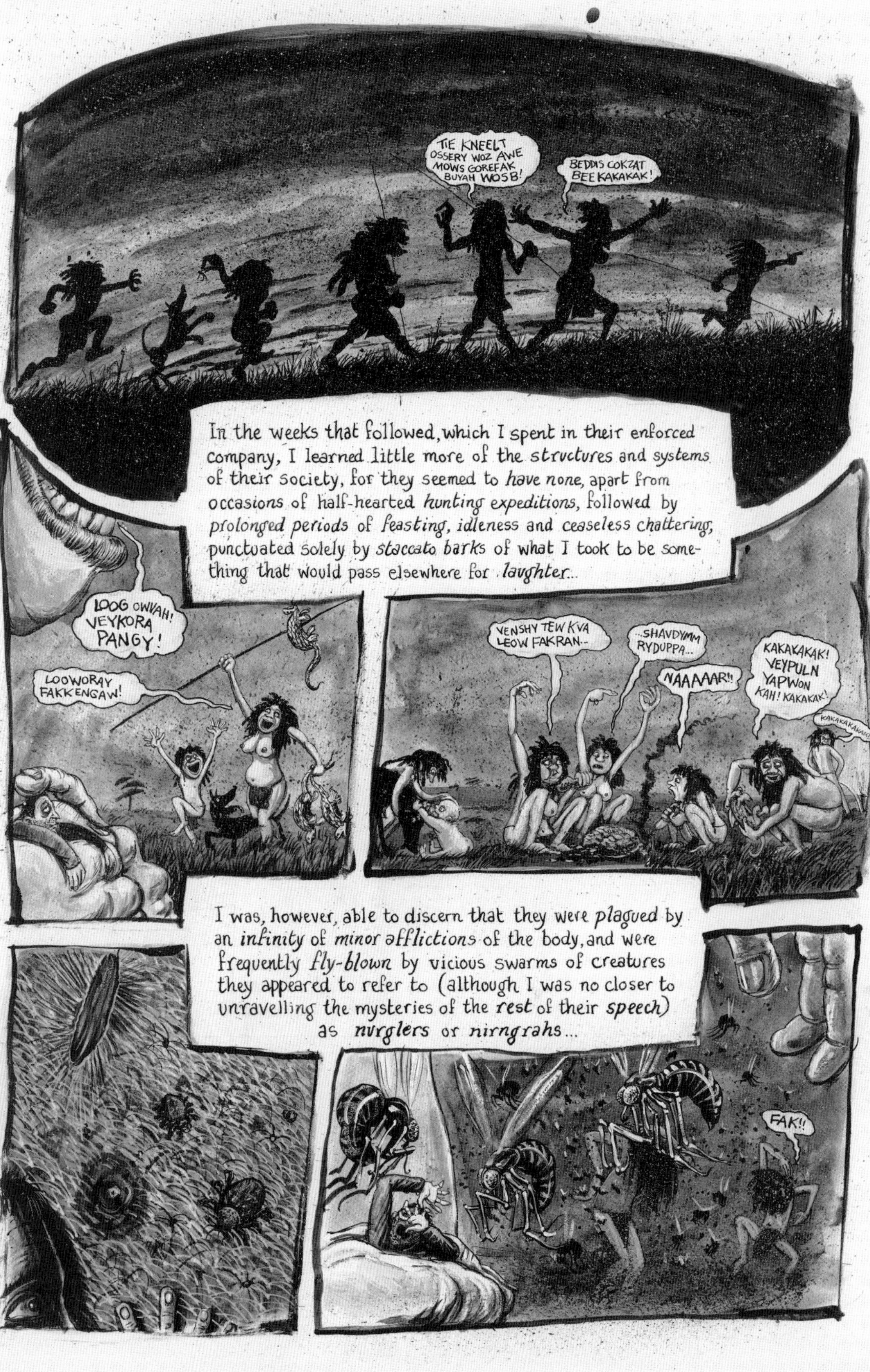
TIE KNEELT OSSERY WOZ AWE MOWS GOREFAK BUYAH WOSB!
BEDDIS COKZAT BEEKAKAKAK!
In the weeks that followed, which I spent in their enforced company, I learned little more of the *structures* and systems of their society, for they seemed to *have none*, apart from occasions of half-hearted *hunting expeditions*, followed by *prolonged periods* of *feasting*, *idleness* and *ceaseless chattering*, punctuated solely by *staccato barks* of what I took to be something that would pass elsewhere for *laughter*...
LOOG OWVAH! VEYKORA PANGY!
LOOWORAY FAKKENGAW!
VENSHY TEW KVA LEOW FAKRAN...
...SHAVDYMM RYDUPPA...
NAAAAAR!!
KAKAKAKAK! VEYPULN YAPWON KAH! KAKAKAK!
KAKAKAKAKAK!
I was, however, able to discern that they were *plagued* by an *infinity* of *minor afflictions* of the body, and were frequently *fly-blown* by vicious swarms of creatures they appeared to refer to (although I was no closer to unravelling the mysteries of the *rest* of their *speech*) as ***nurglers*** or ***nirngrahs***...
FAK!!

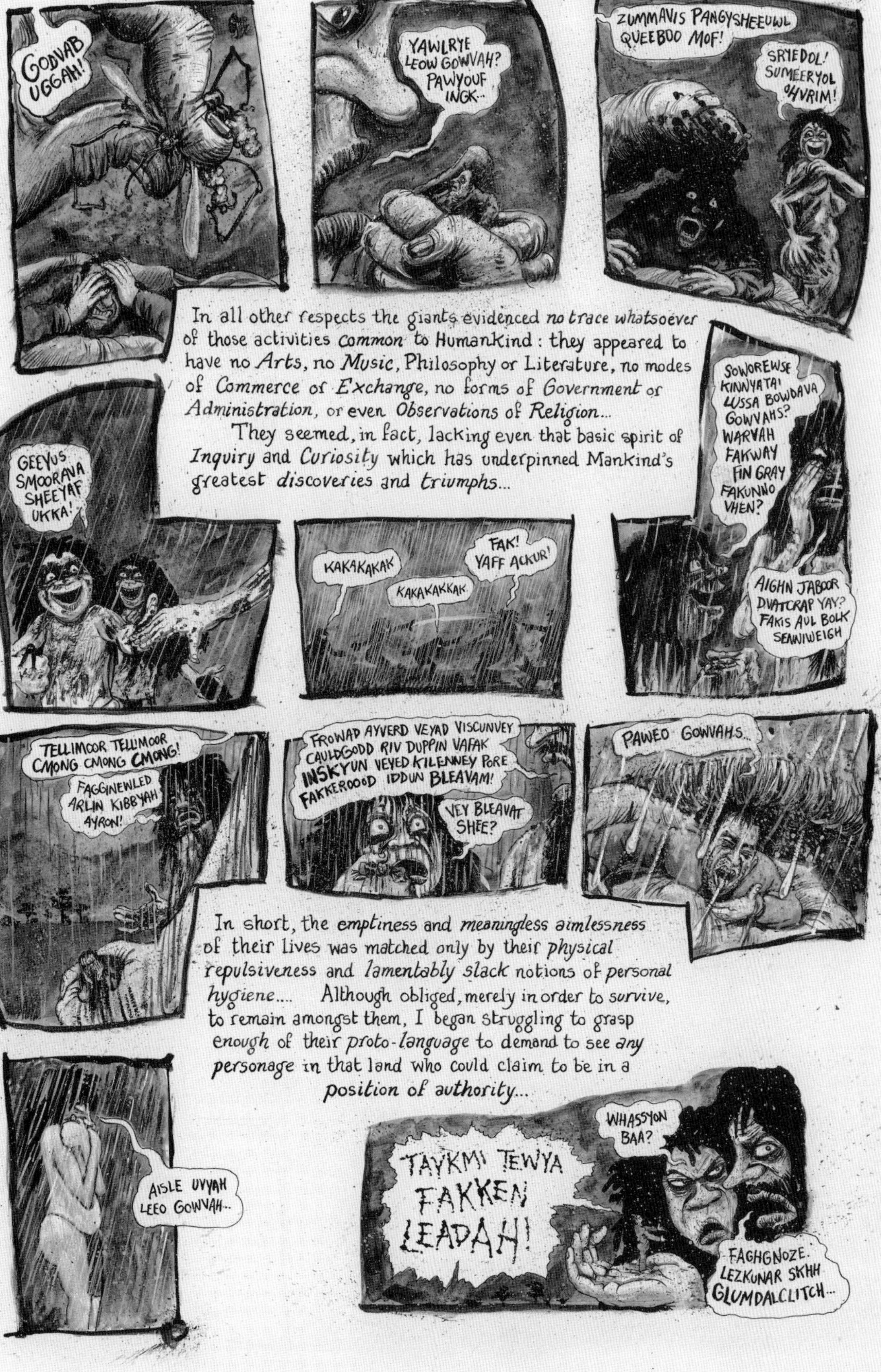
GODVAB UGGAH!
YAWLRYE LEOW GOWVAH? PAWYOUF INGK...
ZUMMAVIS PANGYSHEEUWL QUEEBOO MOF!
SRYEDOL! SUMEERYOL OHVRIM!
In all other respects the giants evidenced *no trace whatsoever* of those activities *common* to HumanKind: they appeared to have no *Arts*, no *Music*, Philosophy or Literature, no modes of *Commerce* or *Exchange*, no forms of *Government* or *Administration*, or even *Observations* of *Religion*...
They seemed, in fact, lacking even that basic spirit of *Inquiry* and *Curiosity* which has underpinned Mankind's greatest *discoveries* and *triumphs*...
GEEYUS SMOORAVA SHEEYAF UKKA!
KAKAKAKAK
KAKAKAKKAK
FAK! YAFF ACKUR!
SOWOREWSE KINNYATAI LUSSA BOWDAVA GOWVAHS? WARVAH FAKWAY FIN GRAY FAKUNNO VHEN?
AIGHN JABOOR DVATCRAP YAY? FAKIS AUL BOLK SENNIWEIGH
TELLIMOOR TELLIMOOR CMONG CMONG CMONG!
FAGGINEWLED ARLIN KIBBYAH AYRON!
FROWAD AYVERD VEYAD VISCUNVEY CAULDGODD RIV DUPPIN VAFAK INSKYUN VEYED KILENNEY PORE FAKKEROOOD IDDUN BLEAVAM!
VEY BLEAVAT SHEE?
PAWEO GOWVAHS...
In short, the *emptiness* and *meaningless aimlessness* of their lives was matched only by their *physical repulsiveness* and *lamentably slack* notions of *personal hygiene*.... Although obliged, merely in order to *survive*, to remain amongst them, I began struggling to grasp enough of their *proto-language* to demand to see *any* personage in that land who could claim to be in a *position of authority*...
AISLE UVYAH LEEO GOWVAH...
TAYKMI TEWYA FAKKEN LEADAH!
WHASSYON BAA?
FAGHGNOZE. LEZKUNAR SKHH GLUMDALCLITCH...

Somewhat to my astonishment the giants appeared to *comply* with my request, for we were soon setting off across that country with far greater a *sense of purpose* than they had shown in any of our *previous peregrinations*...

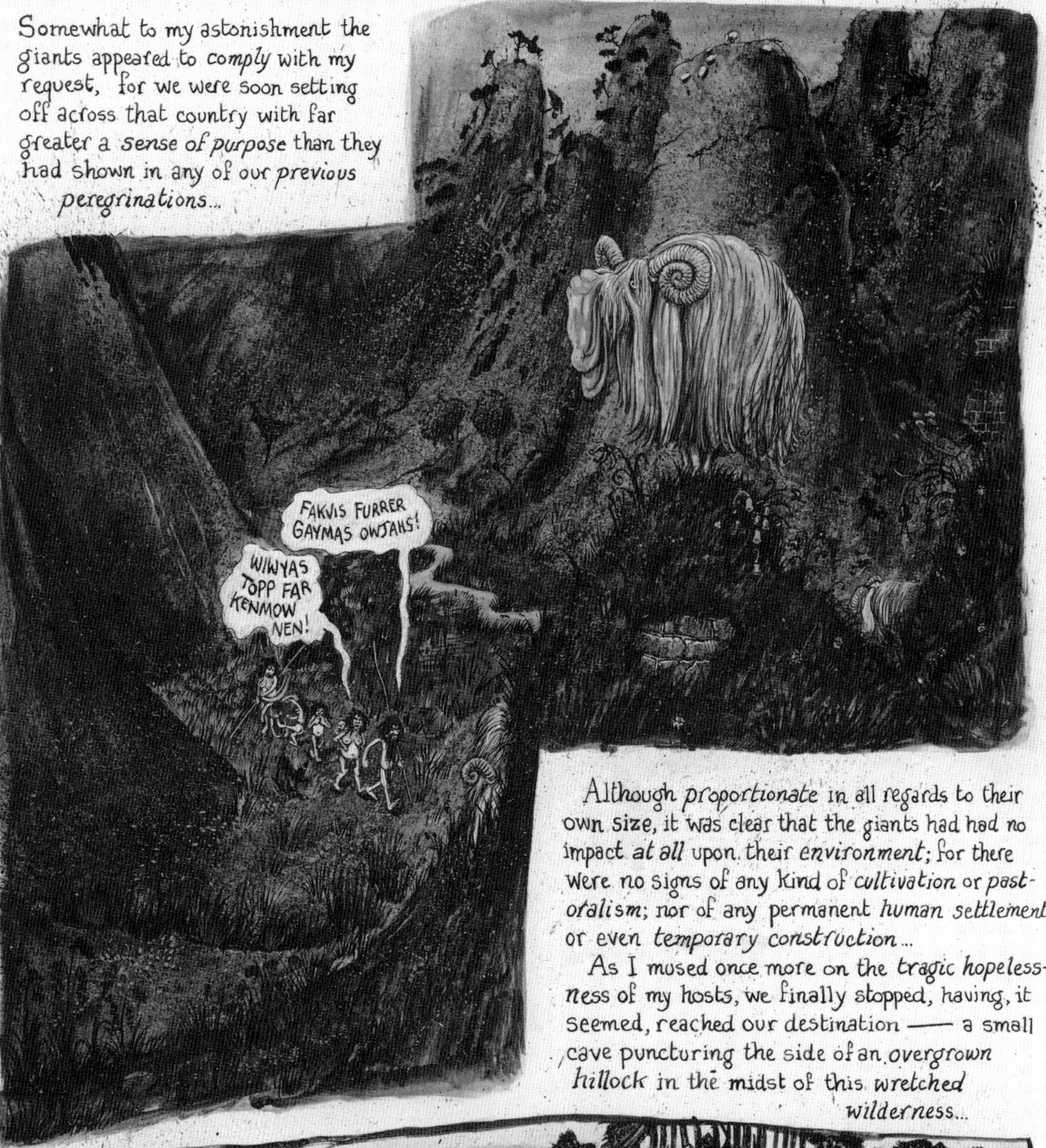
WIWYAS TOPP FAR KENMOW NEN!
FAKVIS FURRER GAYMAS OWJAHS!

Although *proportionate* in all regards to their own size, it was clear that the giants had had no impact *at all* upon their *environment*; for there were no signs of any kind of *cultivation* or *pastoralism*; nor of any permanent *human settlement*, or even *temporary construction*...

As I mused once more on the *tragic hopelessness* of my hosts, we finally stopped, having, it seemed, reached our destination —— a small cave puncturing the side of an *overgrown hillock* in the midst of this *wretched wilderness*...

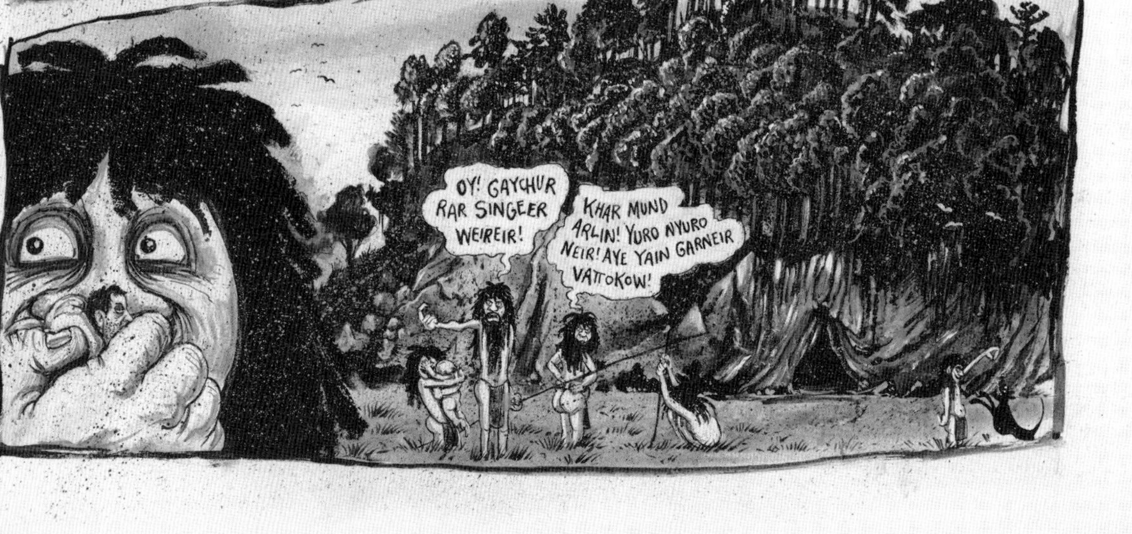
OY! GAYCHUR RAR SINGEER WEIREIR!
KHAR MUND ARLIN! YURO NYURO NEIR! AYE YAIN GARNEIR VATTOKOW!

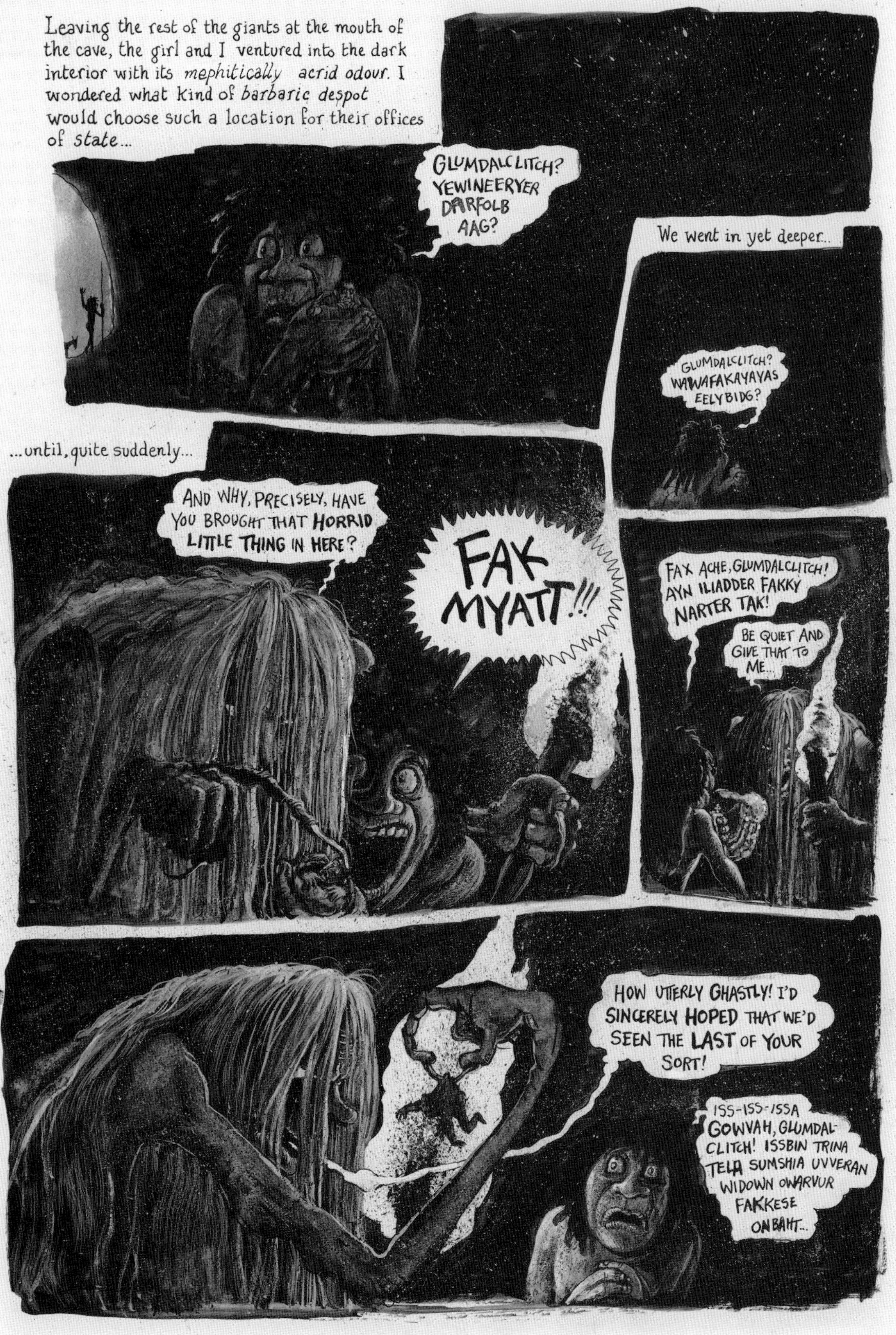
Leaving the rest of the giants at the mouth of the cave, the girl and I ventured into the dark interior with its *mephitically* acrid odour. I wondered what kind of *barbaric despot* would choose such a location for their offices of *state*...
GLUMDALCLITCH? YEWINEERYER DARFOLB AAG?
We went in yet deeper...
GLUMDALCLITCH? WAWAFAKAYAYAS EELYBIDG?
...until, quite suddenly...
AND WHY, PRECISELY, HAVE YOU BROUGHT THAT **HORRID LITTLE THING** IN HERE?
FAK MYATT!!!
FAX ACHE, GLUMDALCLITCH! AYN ILIADDER FAKKY NARTER TAK!
BE QUIET AND GIVE THAT TO ME...
HOW UTTERLY GHASTLY! I'D SINCERELY **HOPED** THAT WE'D SEEN THE **LAST** OF YOUR SORT!
ISS-ISS-ISSA GOWVAH, GLUMDAL-CLITCH! ISSBIN TRINA TELA SUMSHIA UVVERAN WIDOWN OWARVUR FAKKESE ONBAHT...

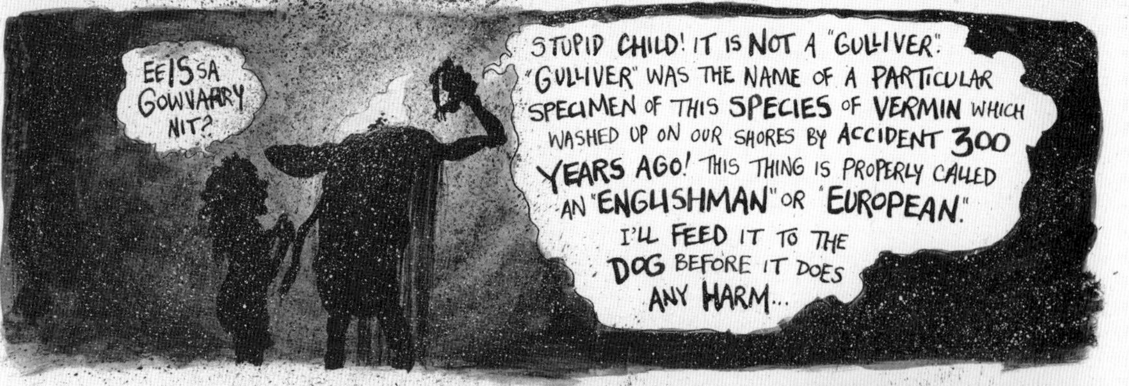
EE IS SA GOWVARRY NIT?
STUPID CHILD! IT IS NOT A "GULLIVER". "GULLIVER" WAS THE NAME OF A PARTICULAR SPECIMEN OF THIS SPECIES OF VERMIN WHICH WASHED UP ON OUR SHORES BY ACCIDENT 300 YEARS AGO! THIS THING IS PROPERLY CALLED AN "ENGLISHMAN" OR "EUROPEAN". I'LL FEED IT TO THE DOG BEFORE IT DOES ANY HARM...

For reasons beyond my *understanding*, the old crone's words were easily comprehensible to me, and thus I was able, with *considerable alarm*, to learn the immediate fate she planned for me.

Having already decided the old woman was a *shaman* or *witch* – and therefore a figure of *power* and *influence* among the giants, I suddenly realised that *simply by telling the truth* I should be able, through the mere *fact of my surname*, so astound her *simple mind* by this extraordinary co-incidence of nomenclature, that she would stay her hand...

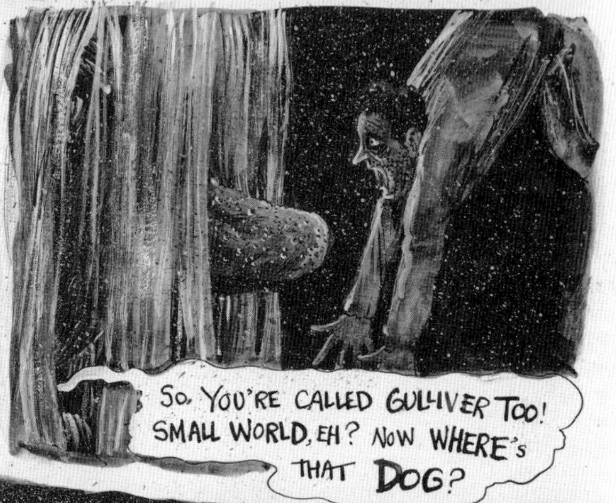
SO, YOU'RE CALLED GULLIVER TOO! SMALL WORLD, EH? NOW WHERE'S THAT DOG?

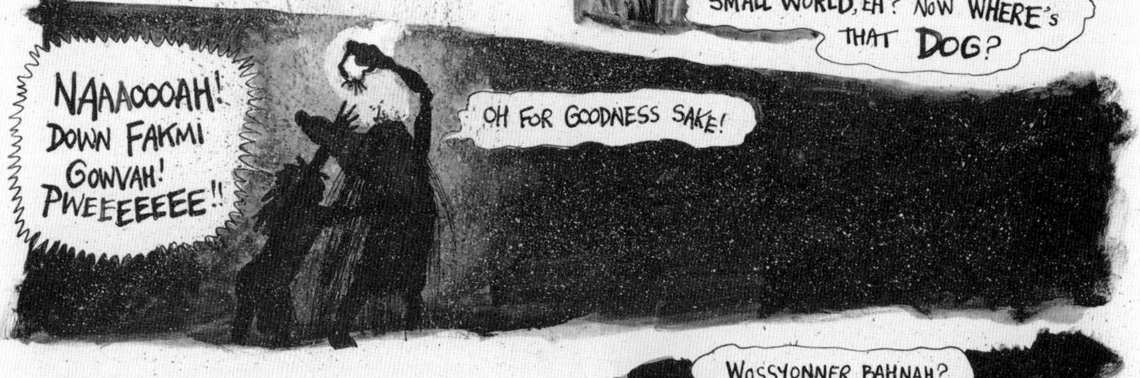
NAAAOOOAH! DOWN FAKMI GOWVAH! PWEEEEEEE!!
OH FOR GOODNESS SAKE!

The hag finally placed me on a rock.
I now *bowed low*, introduced myself formally, requested of the old woman the name of this country and begged her humbly if it was the giants' *queen* whom I had the *privilege* of addressing. As she made no answer, I thought she had not understood me...

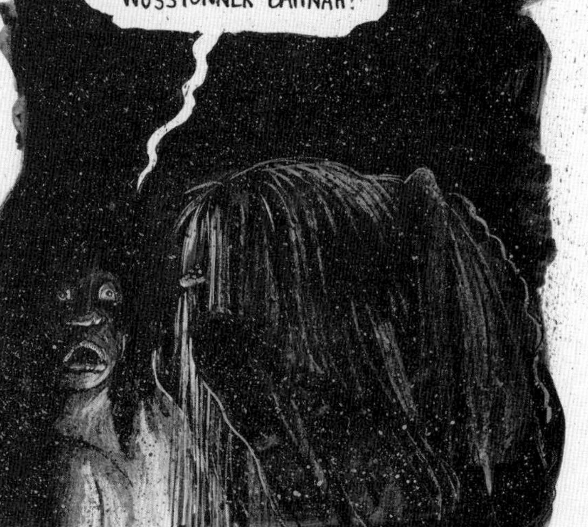
WOSSYONNER BAHNAH?
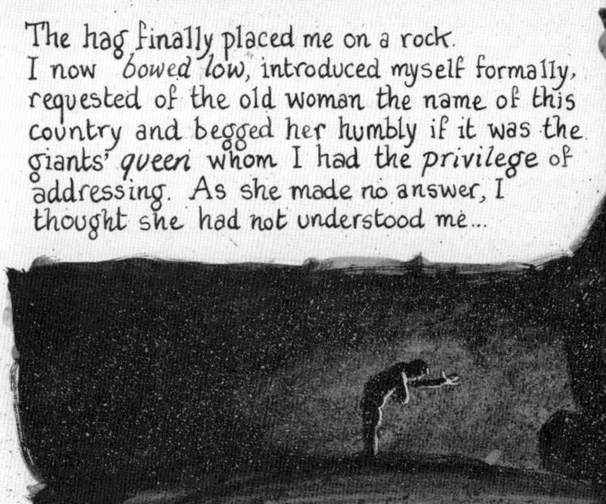

... and so I repeated myself, *more slowly...*

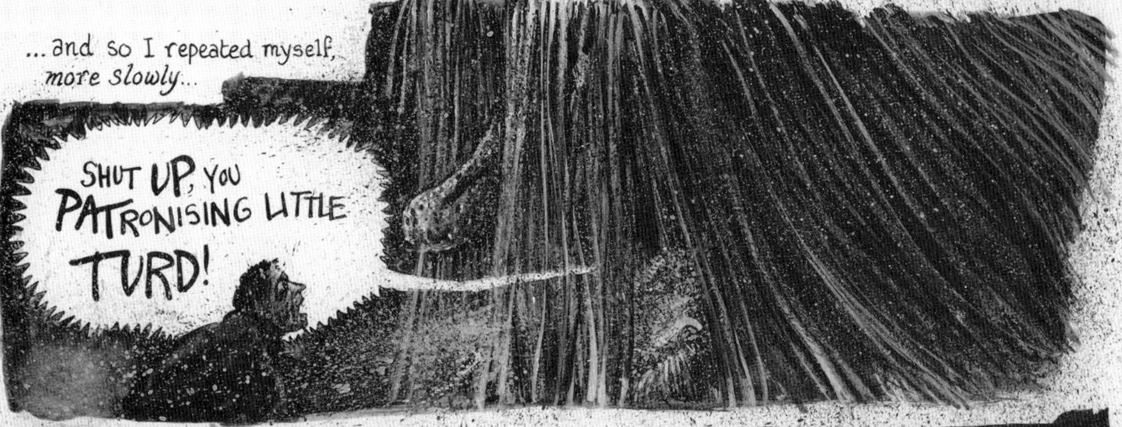
SHUT UP, YOU PATRONISING LITTLE TURD!

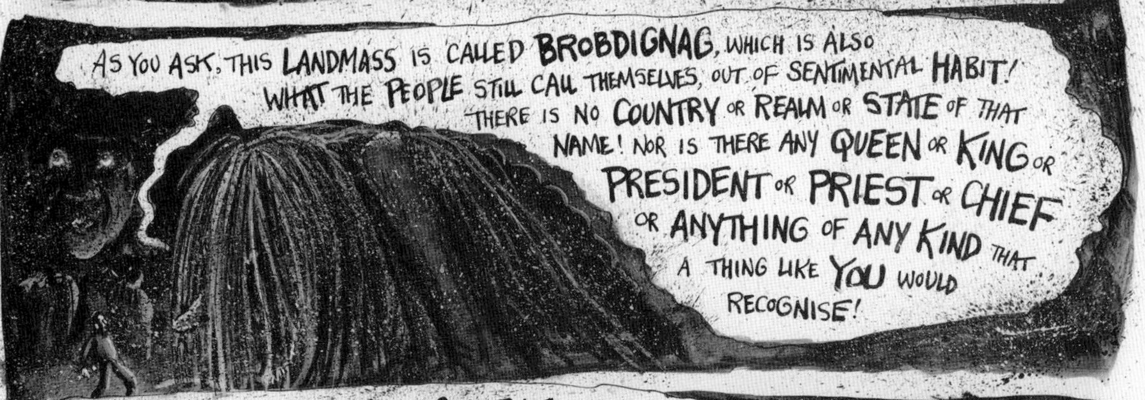
AS YOU ASK, THIS LANDMASS IS CALLED BROBDIGNAG, WHICH IS ALSO WHAT THE PEOPLE STILL CALL THEMSELVES, OUT OF SENTIMENTAL HABIT! THERE IS NO COUNTRY OR REALM OR STATE OF THAT NAME! NOR IS THERE ANY QUEEN OR KING OR PRESIDENT OR PRIEST OR CHIEF OR ANYTHING OF ANY KIND THAT A THING LIKE YOU WOULD RECOGNISE!

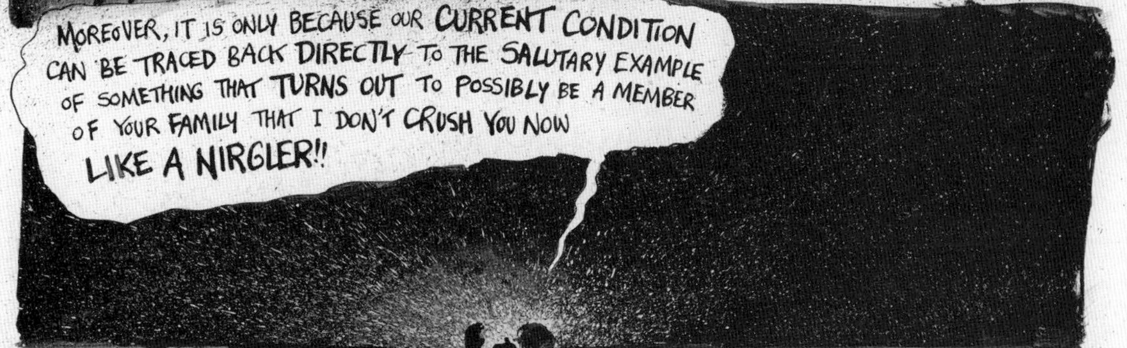
MOREOVER, IT IS ONLY BECAUSE OUR CURRENT CONDITION CAN BE TRACED BACK DIRECTLY TO THE SALUTARY EXAMPLE OF SOMETHING THAT TURNS OUT TO POSSIBLY BE A MEMBER OF YOUR FAMILY THAT I DON'T CRUSH YOU NOW LIKE A NIRGLER!!

The old woman was so enraged I began to stutter an apology; for if my ancestor had played any part in reducing the race of giants to their present straits of *savage ignominy*, then – albeit by the most *tenuous* of *associations* – I felt a terrible sense of *personal culpability*...

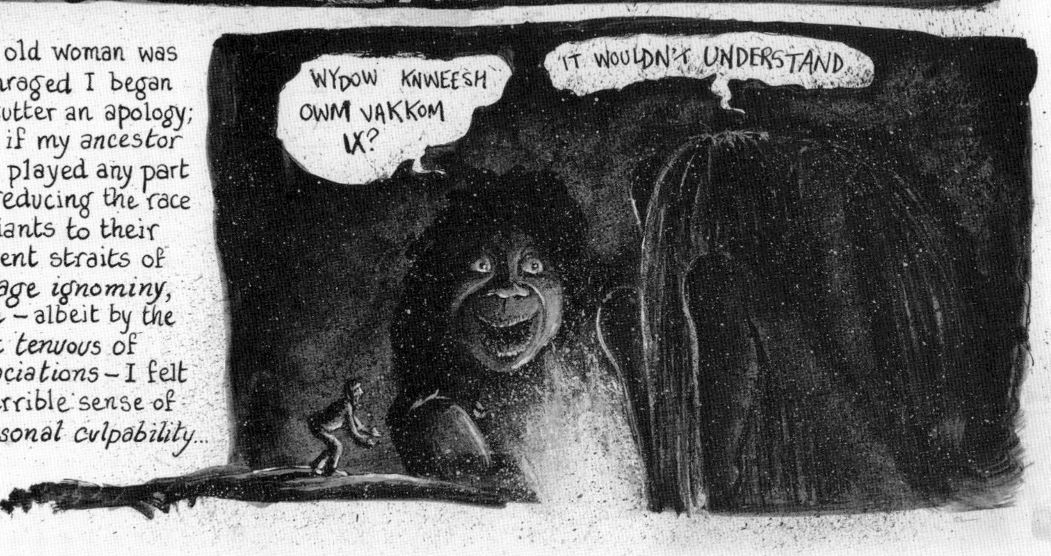
WYDOW KNWEESH OWM VAKKOM IX?
IT WOULDN'T UNDERSTAND.

But then...

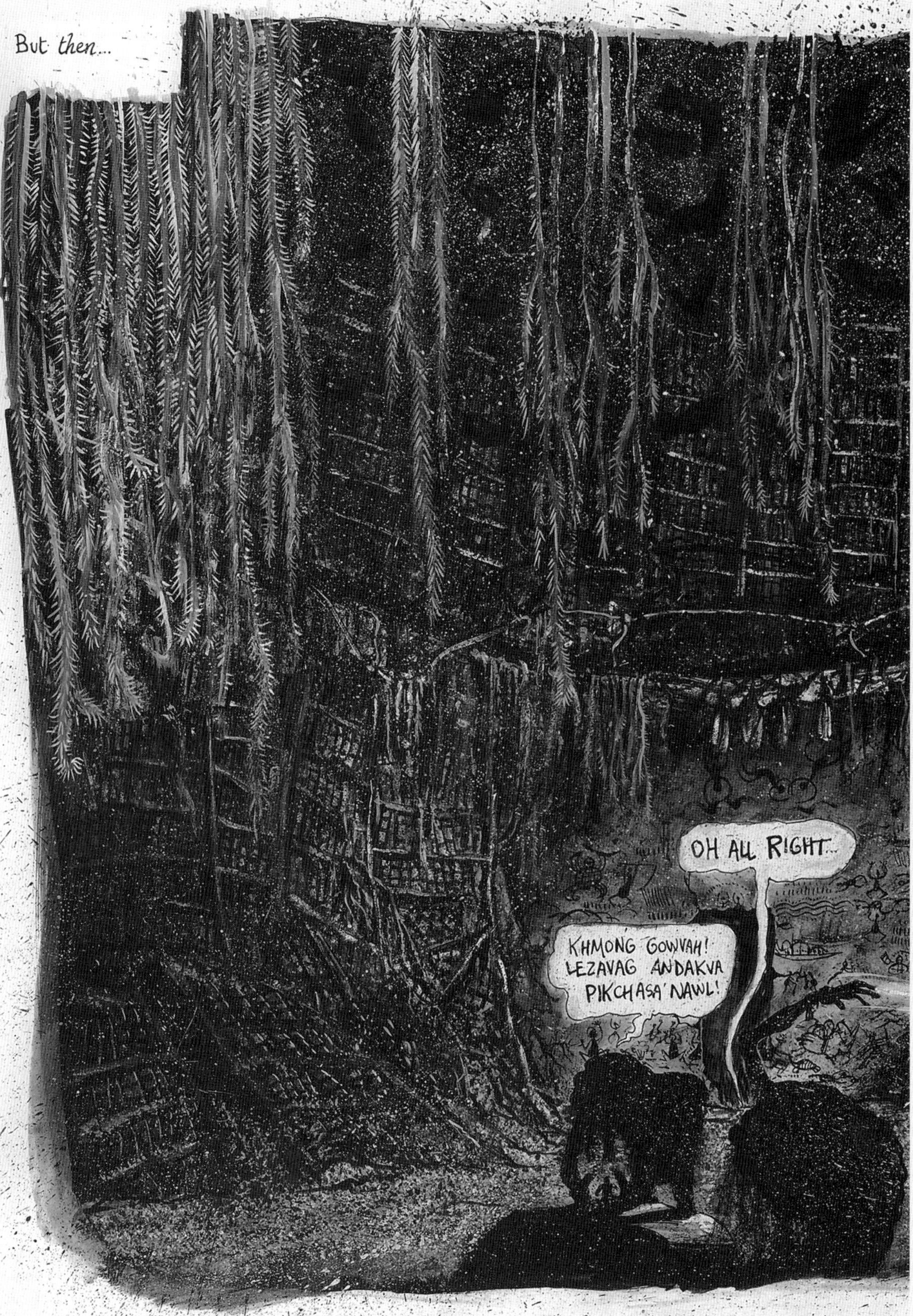

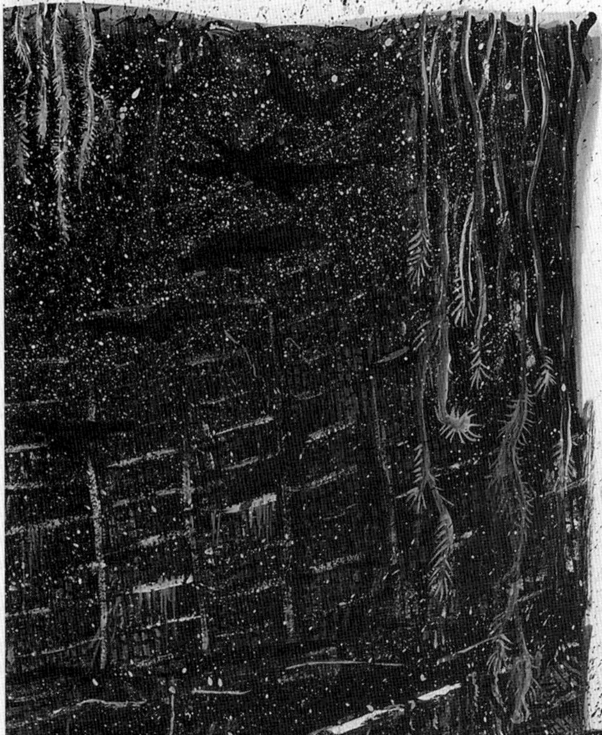

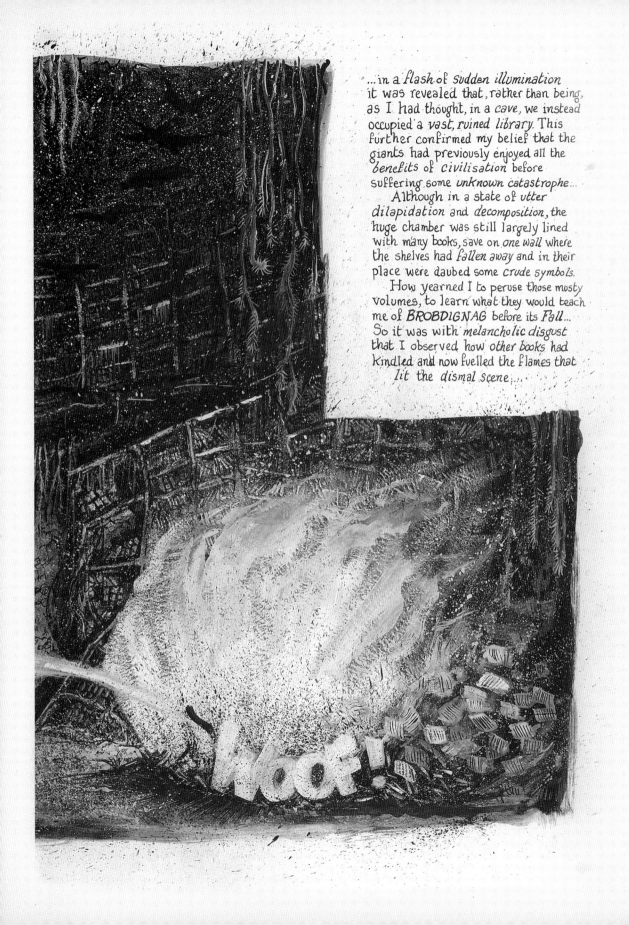

...in a *flash* of *sudden illumination* it was revealed that, rather than being, as I had thought, in a *cave*, we instead occupied a *vast, ruined library*. This further confirmed my belief that the giants had previously enjoyed all the *benefits* of *civilisation* before suffering some *unknown catastrophe*...

Although in a state of *utter dilapidation* and *decomposition*, the huge chamber was still largely lined with many books, save on *one wall* where the shelves had *fallen away* and in their place were daubed some *crude symbols*.

How yearned I to peruse those musty volumes, to learn what they would teach me of **BROBDIGNAG** before its *Fall*... So it was with *melancholic disgust* that I observed how *other books* had kindled and now fuelled the flames that *lit* the *dismal scene*...

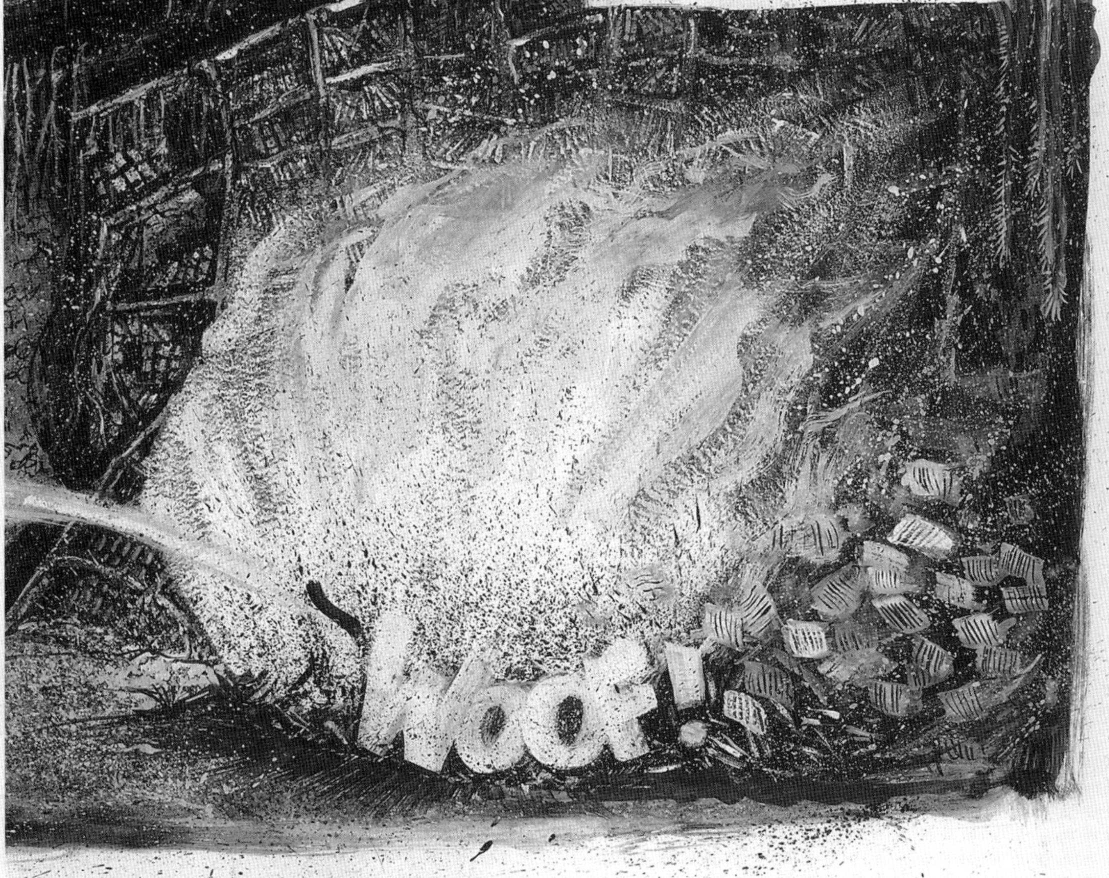
WOOF!

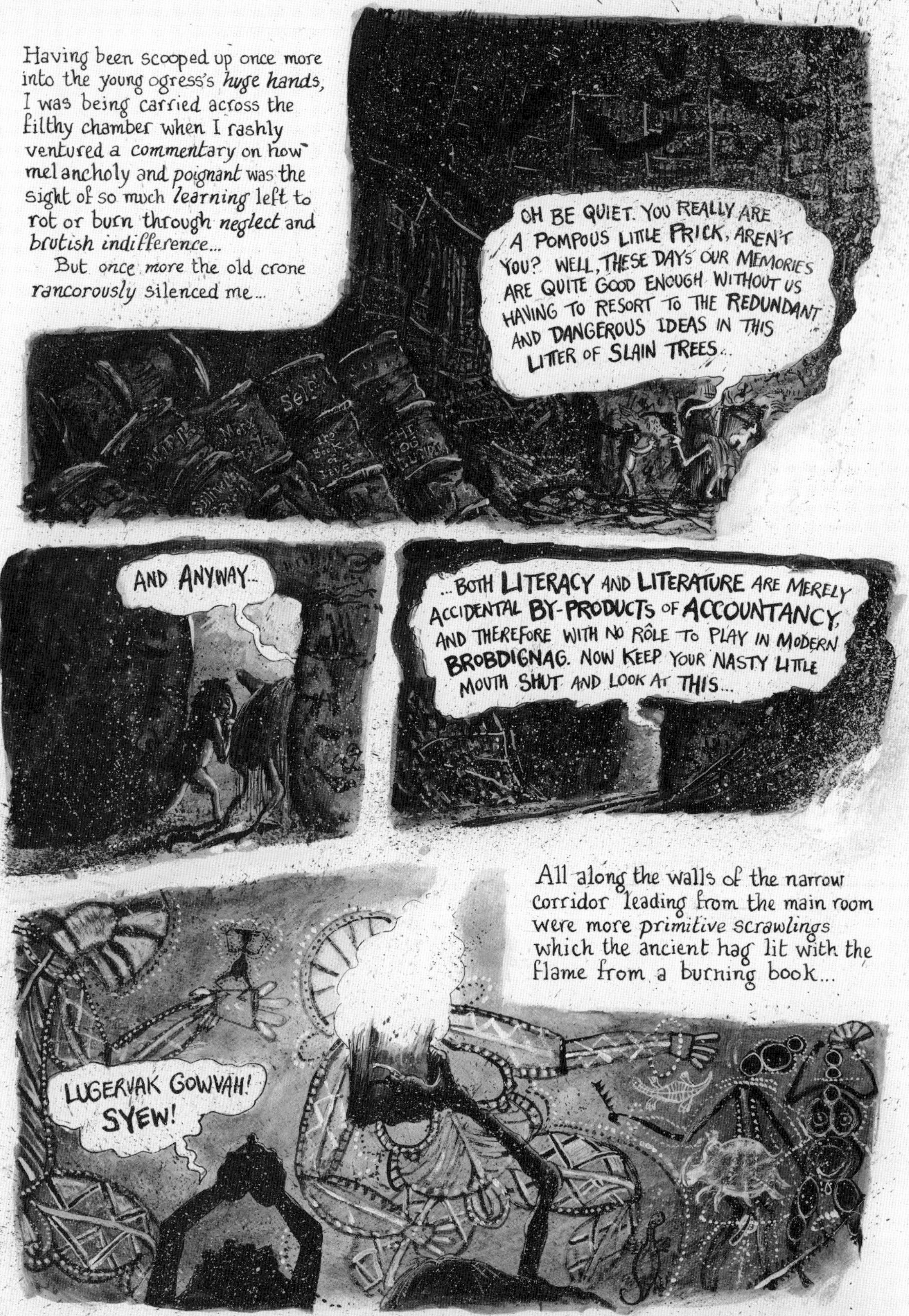
Having been scooped up once more into the young ogress's *huge hands*, I was being carried across the filthy chamber when I rashly ventured a *commentary* on how melancholy and *poignant* was the sight of so much *learning* left to rot or burn through *neglect* and *brutish indifference*...
But once more the old crone *rancorously* silenced me...
OH BE QUIET. YOU REALLY ARE A POMPOUS LITTLE PRICK, AREN'T YOU? WELL, THESE DAYS OUR MEMORIES ARE QUITE GOOD ENOUGH WITHOUT US HAVING TO RESORT TO THE REDUNDANT AND DANGEROUS IDEAS IN THIS LITTER OF SLAIN TREES...
AND ANYWAY...
...BOTH LITERACY AND LITERATURE ARE MERELY ACCIDENTAL BY-PRODUCTS OF ACCOUNTANCY, AND THEREFORE WITH NO RÔLE TO PLAY IN MODERN BROBDIGNAG. NOW KEEP YOUR NASTY LITTLE MOUTH SHUT AND LOOK AT THIS...
All along the walls of the narrow corridor leading from the main room were more *primitive scrawlings* which the ancient hag lit with the flame from a burning book...
LUGERVAK GOWVAH! SYEW!

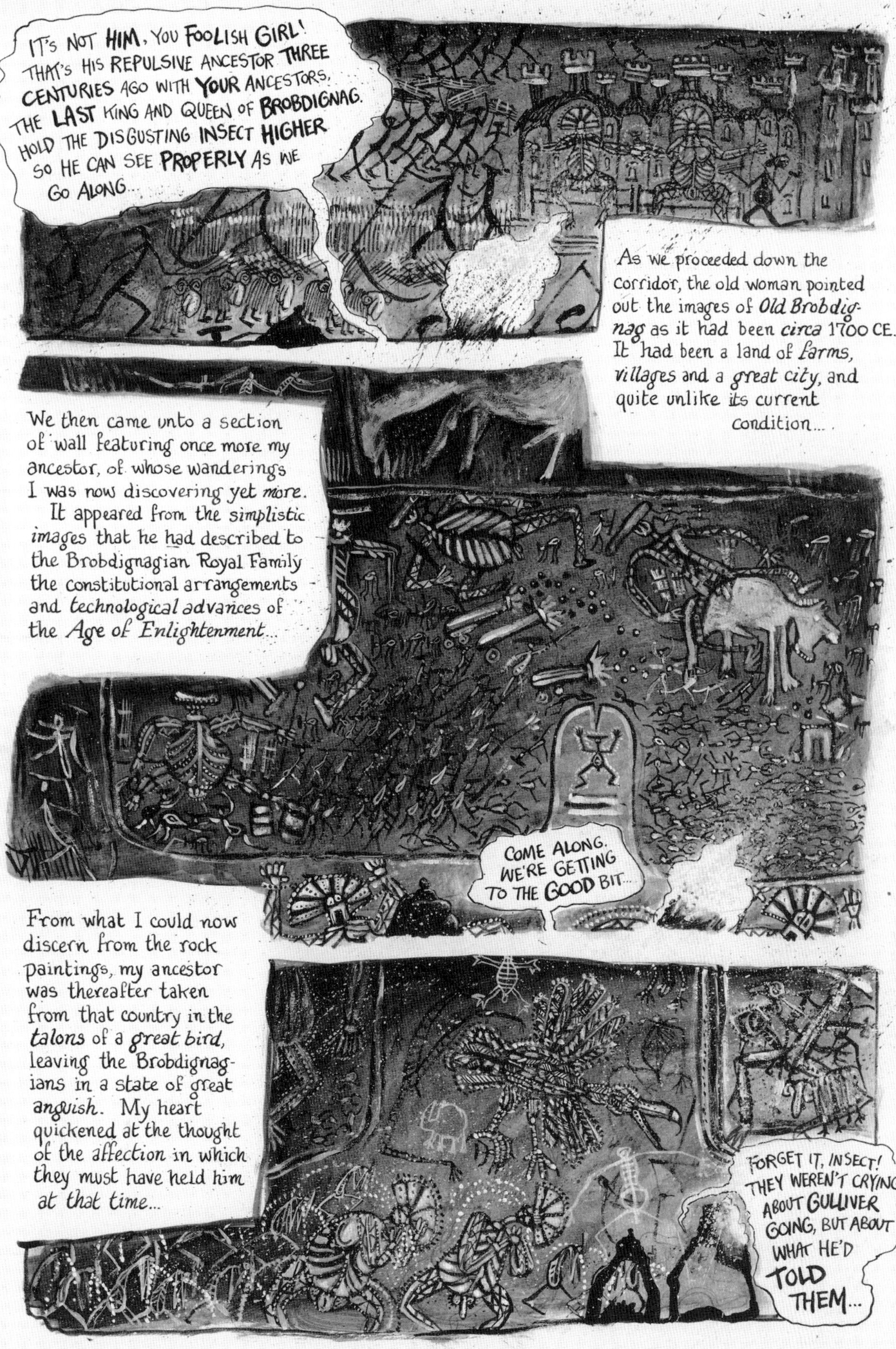
IT'S NOT HIM, YOU FOOLISH GIRL! THAT'S HIS REPULSIVE ANCESTOR THREE CENTURIES AGO WITH YOUR ANCESTORS, THE LAST KING AND QUEEN OF BROBDIGNAG. HOLD THE DISGUSTING INSECT HIGHER SO HE CAN SEE PROPERLY AS WE GO ALONG...
As we proceeded down the corridor, the old woman pointed out the images of Old Brobdignag as it had been circa 1700 CE. It had been a land of farms, villages and a great city, and quite unlike its current condition...
We then came unto a section of wall featuring once more my ancestor, of whose wanderings I was now discovering yet more. It appeared from the simplistic images that he had described to the Brobdignagian Royal Family the constitutional arrangements and technological advances of the Age of Enlightenment...
COME ALONG. WE'RE GETTING TO THE GOOD BIT...
From what I could now discern from the rock paintings, my ancestor was thereafter taken from that country in the talons of a great bird, leaving the Brobdignagians in a state of great anguish. My heart quickened at the thought of the affection in which they must have held him at that time...
FORGET IT, INSECT! THEY WEREN'T CRYING ABOUT GULLIVER GOING, BUT ABOUT WHAT HE'D TOLD THEM...

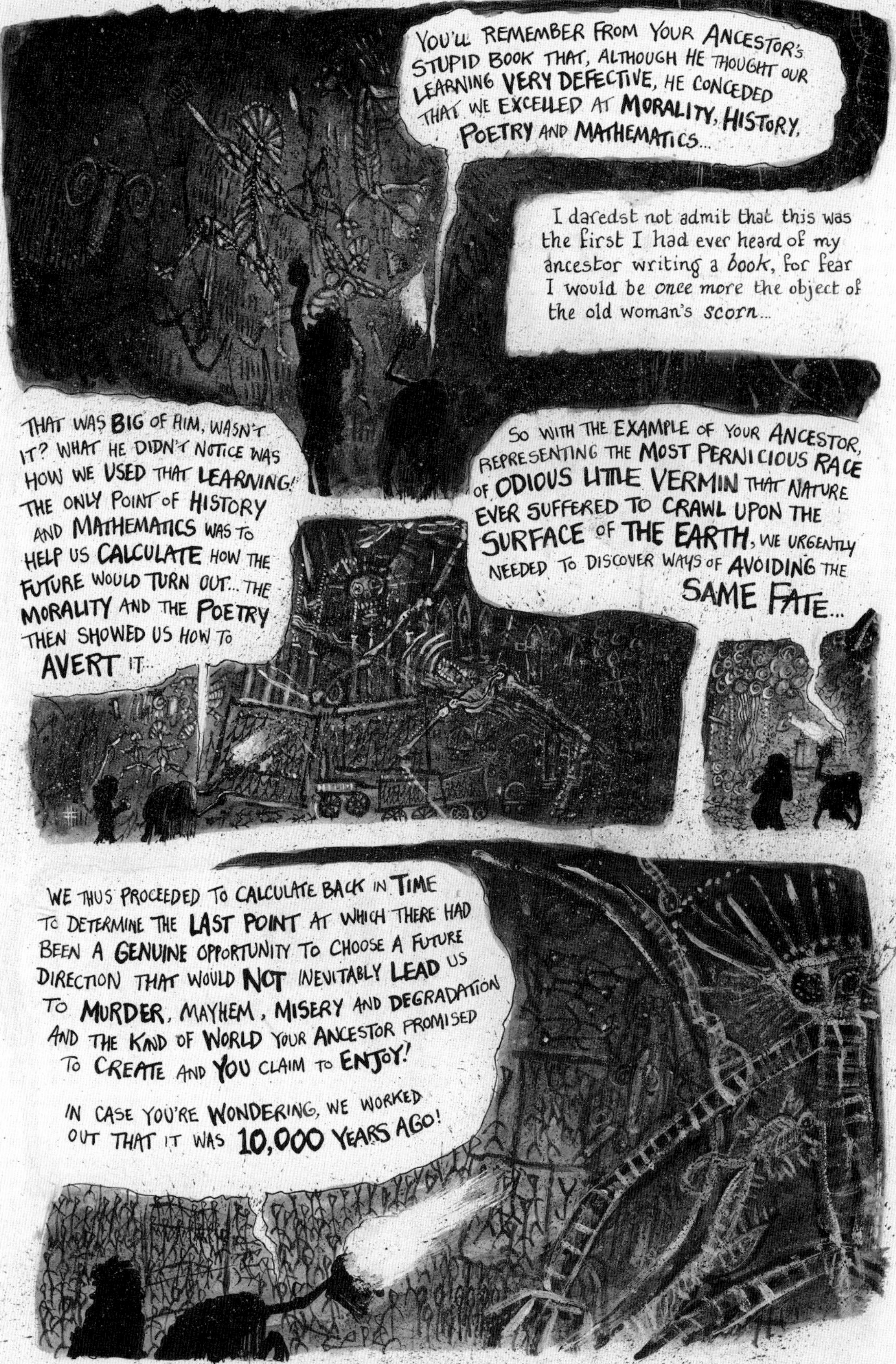

YOU'LL REMEMBER FROM YOUR ANCESTOR'S STUPID BOOK THAT, ALTHOUGH HE THOUGHT OUR LEARNING VERY DEFECTIVE, HE CONCEDED THAT WE EXCELLED AT MORALITY, HISTORY, POETRY AND MATHEMATICS...
I daredst not admit that this was the first I had ever heard of my ancestor writing a book, for fear I would be once more the object of the old woman's scorn...
THAT WAS BIG OF HIM, WASN'T IT? WHAT HE DIDN'T NOTICE WAS HOW WE USED THAT LEARNING! THE ONLY POINT OF HISTORY AND MATHEMATICS WAS TO HELP US CALCULATE HOW THE FUTURE WOULD TURN OUT... THE MORALITY AND THE POETRY THEN SHOWED US HOW TO AVERT IT...
SO WITH THE EXAMPLE OF YOUR ANCESTOR, REPRESENTING THE MOST PERNICIOUS RACE OF ODIOUS LITTLE VERMIN THAT NATURE EVER SUFFERED TO CRAWL UPON THE SURFACE OF THE EARTH, WE URGENTLY NEEDED TO DISCOVER WAYS OF AVOIDING THE SAME FATE...
WE THUS PROCEEDED TO CALCULATE BACK IN TIME TO DETERMINE THE LAST POINT AT WHICH THERE HAD BEEN A GENUINE OPPORTUNITY TO CHOOSE A FUTURE DIRECTION THAT WOULD NOT INEVITABLY LEAD US TO MURDER, MAYHEM, MISERY AND DEGRADATION AND THE KIND OF WORLD YOUR ANCESTOR PROMISED TO CREATE AND YOU CLAIM TO ENJOY!
IN CASE YOU'RE WONDERING, WE WORKED OUT THAT IT WAS 10,000 YEARS AGO!

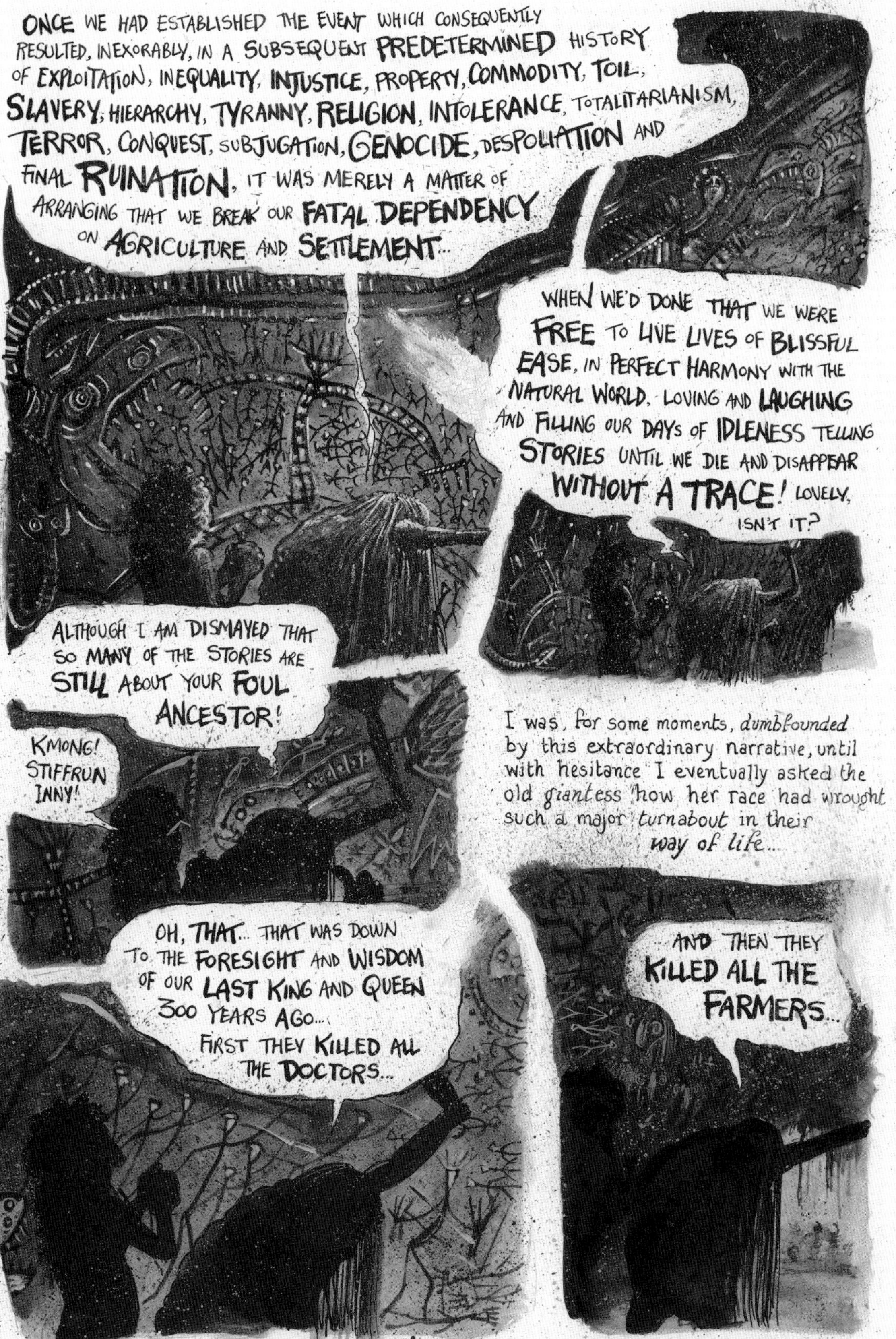
ONCE WE HAD ESTABLISHED THE EVENT WHICH CONSEQUENTLY RESULTED, INEXORABLY, IN A SUBSEQUENT PREDETERMINED HISTORY OF EXPLOITATION, INEQUALITY, INJUSTICE, PROPERTY, COMMODITY, TOIL, SLAVERY, HIERARCHY, TYRANNY, RELIGION, INTOLERANCE, TOTALITARIANISM, TERROR, CONQUEST, SUBJUGATION, GENOCIDE, DESPOLIATION AND FINAL RUINATION, IT WAS MERELY A MATTER OF ARRANGING THAT WE BREAK OUR FATAL DEPENDENCY ON AGRICULTURE AND SETTLEMENT...
WHEN WE'D DONE THAT WE WERE FREE TO LIVE LIVES OF BLISSFUL EASE, IN PERFECT HARMONY WITH THE NATURAL WORLD, LOVING AND LAUGHING AND FILLING OUR DAYS OF IDLENESS TELLING STORIES UNTIL WE DIE AND DISAPPEAR WITHOUT A TRACE! LOVELY, ISN'T IT?
ALTHOUGH I AM DISMAYED THAT SO MANY OF THE STORIES ARE STILL ABOUT YOUR FOUL ANCESTOR!
KMONG! STIFFRUN INNY!
I was, for some moments, dumbfounded by this extraordinary narrative, until with hesitance I eventually asked the old giantess how her race had wrought such a major turnabout in their way of life...
OH, THAT... THAT WAS DOWN TO THE FORESIGHT AND WISDOM OF OUR LAST KING AND QUEEN 300 YEARS AGO...
FIRST THEY KILLED ALL THE DOCTORS...
...AND THEN THEY KILLED ALL THE FARMERS...

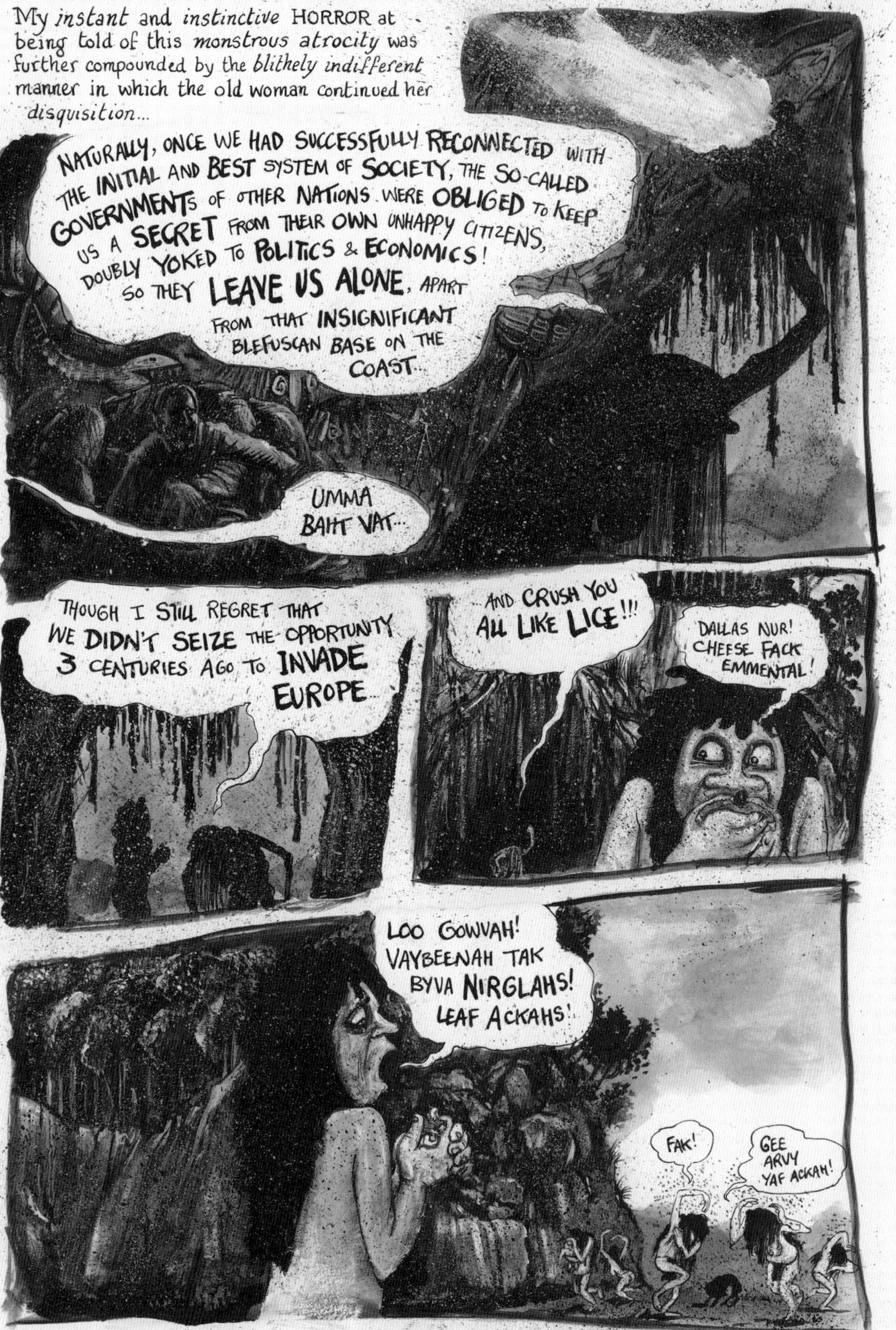
My *instant* and *instinctive* HORROR at being told of this *monstrous atrocity* was further compounded by the *blithely indifferent* manner in which the old woman continued her *disquisition*...
NATURALLY, ONCE WE HAD SUCCESSFULLY RECONNECTED WITH THE INITIAL AND BEST SYSTEM OF SOCIETY, THE SO-CALLED GOVERNMENTS OF OTHER NATIONS WERE OBLIGED TO KEEP US A SECRET FROM THEIR OWN UNHAPPY CITIZENS, DOUBLY YOKED TO POLITICS & ECONOMICS! SO THEY LEAVE US ALONE, APART FROM THAT INSIGNIFICANT BLEFUSCAN BASE ON THE COAST.
UMMA BAHT VAT...
THOUGH I STILL REGRET THAT WE DIDN'T SEIZE THE OPPORTUNITY 3 CENTURIES AGO TO INVADE EUROPE...
...AND CRUSH YOU ALL LIKE LICE!!!
DALLAS NUR! CHEESE FACK EMMENTAL!
LOO GOWVAH! VAYBEENAH TAK BYVA NIRGLAHS! LEAF ACKAHS!
FAK!
GEE ARVY YAF ACKAH!

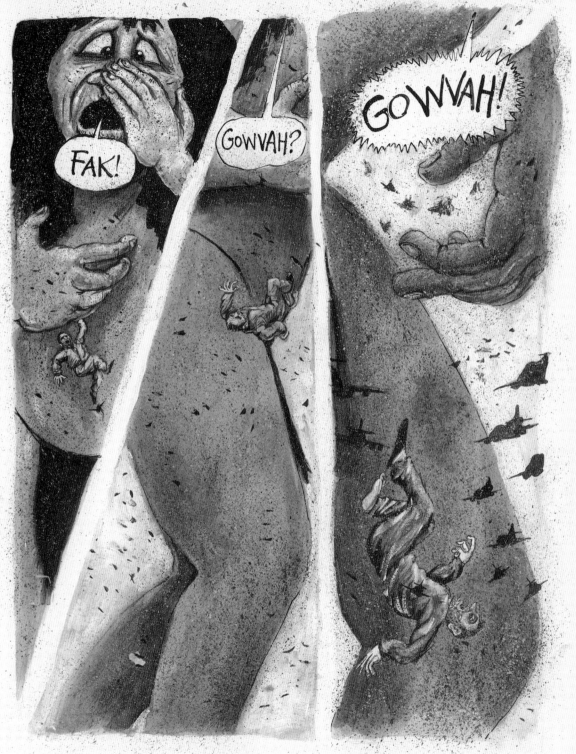

I was by now more determined than ever to escape from the captivity of these monsters who had, with such *heartless calculation*, barbarously reduced themselves to lives of *bestial discomfort* and *deprivation*. Then the girl, believing herself *"stung"* by a *"nirglah"*, loosened her grip on me, and I soon ascertained the *"nirglah"* infestation to be, in truth, a *retaliatory Blefuscan air strike*, avenging the destruction of their camp on the coast...

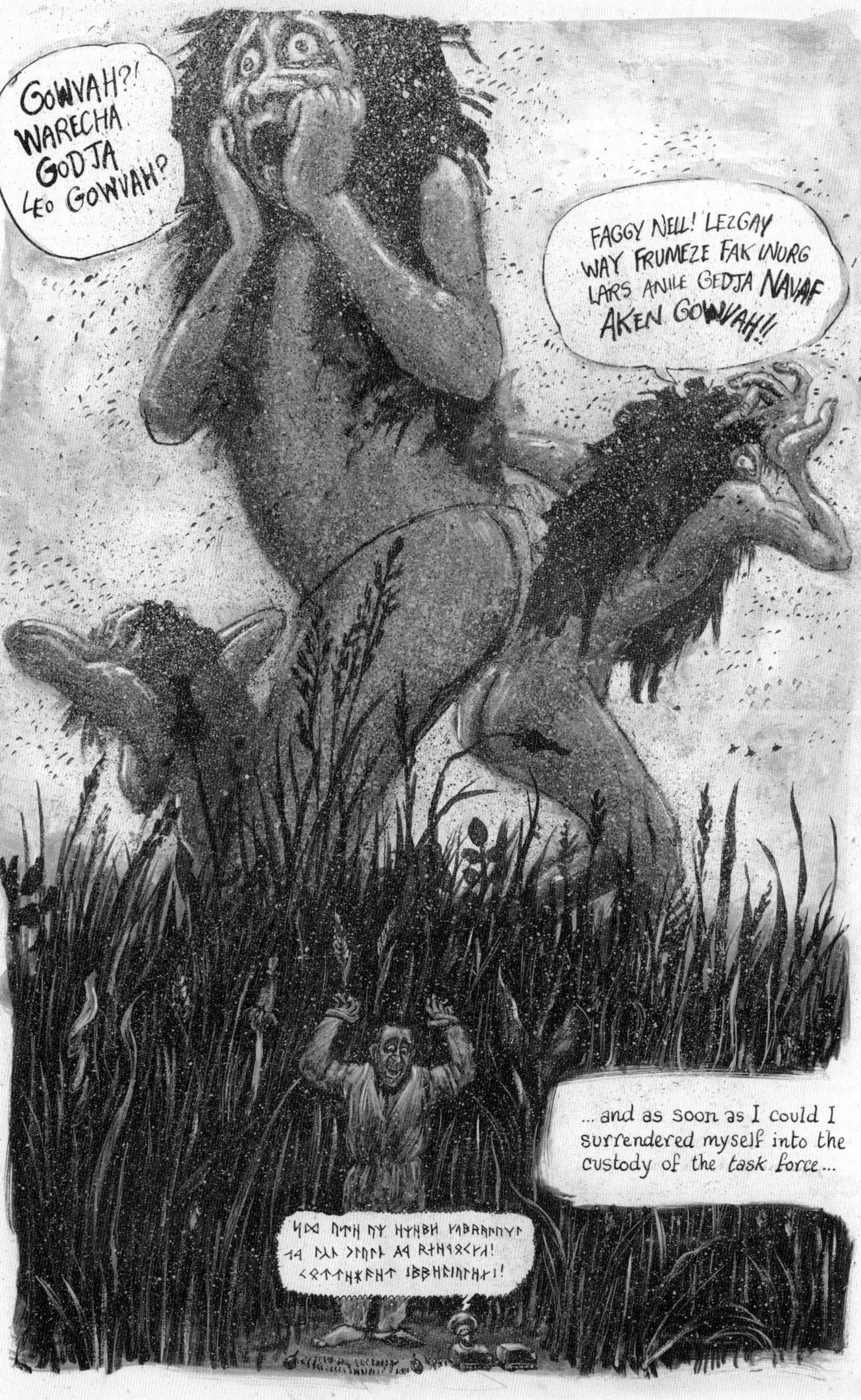
GOWVAH?! WARECHA GODJA LEO GOWVAH?
FAGGY NELL! LEZGAY WAY FRUMEZE FAK INURG LARS ANILE GEDJA NAVAF AKEN GOWVAH!!
...and as soon as I could I surrendered myself into the custody of the *task force*...

A VOYAGE TO LAPUTA

BALNIBARBI, LUGGNAGG, GLUBBDUBDRIB

AND Japan

It saddens me to confess that the Blefuscans' *hospitality* remained very much *wanting*. For several days I was again required to endure the complete deprivation of my *senses*, although nonetheless conscious that I had been transported considerable *distances* by the time *hearing* and then *sight* were restored to me, each in their *turn*...

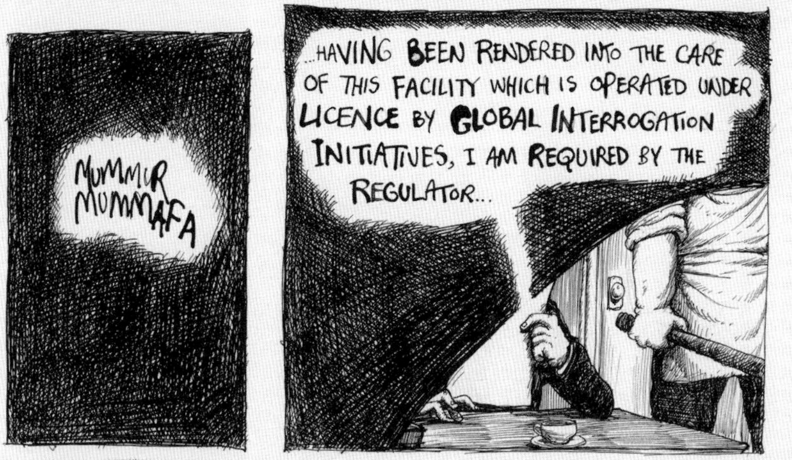
MUMMUR MUMMAFA
...HAVING BEEN RENDERED INTO THE CARE OF THIS FACILITY WHICH IS OPERATED UNDER LICENCE BY GLOBAL INTERROGATION INITIATIVES, I AM REQUIRED BY THE REGULATOR...

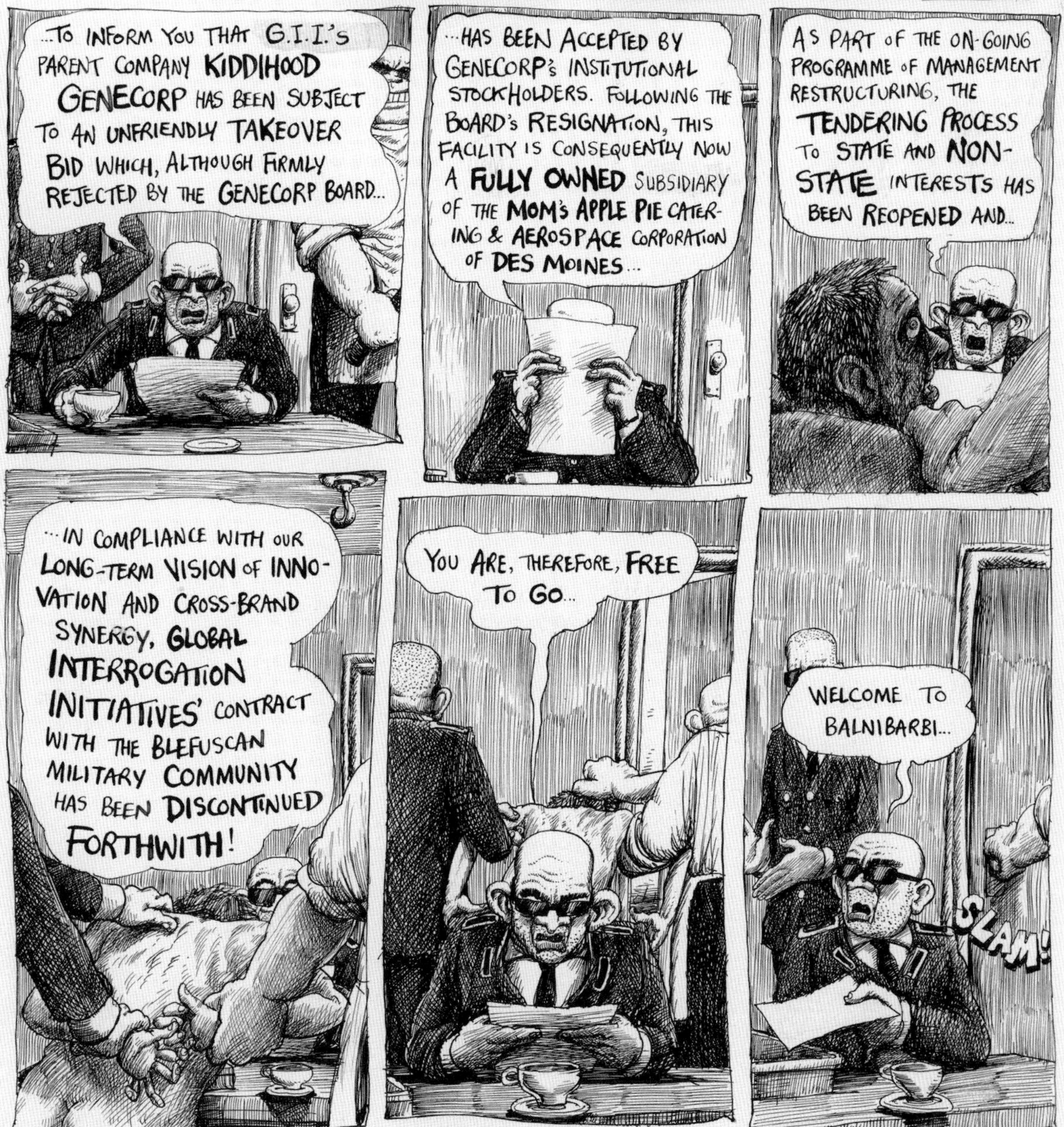
...TO INFORM YOU THAT G.I.I.'s PARENT COMPANY KIDDIHOOD GENECORP HAS BEEN SUBJECT TO AN UNFRIENDLY TAKEOVER BID WHICH, ALTHOUGH FIRMLY REJECTED BY THE GENECORP BOARD...
...HAS BEEN ACCEPTED BY GENECORP's INSTITUTIONAL STOCKHOLDERS. FOLLOWING THE BOARD's RESIGNATION, THIS FACILITY IS CONSEQUENTLY NOW A FULLY OWNED SUBSIDIARY OF THE MOM's APPLE PIE CATERING & AEROSPACE CORPORATION OF DES MOINES...
AS PART OF THE ON-GOING PROGRAMME OF MANAGEMENT RESTRUCTURING, THE TENDERING PROCESS TO STATE AND NON-STATE INTERESTS HAS BEEN REOPENED AND...
...IN COMPLIANCE WITH OUR LONG-TERM VISION OF INNOVATION AND CROSS-BRAND SYNERGY, GLOBAL INTERROGATION INITIATIVES' CONTRACT WITH THE BLEFUSCAN MILITARY COMMUNITY HAS BEEN DISCONTINUED FORTHWITH!
YOU ARE, THEREFORE, FREE TO GO...
WELCOME TO BALNIBARBI...
SLAM!

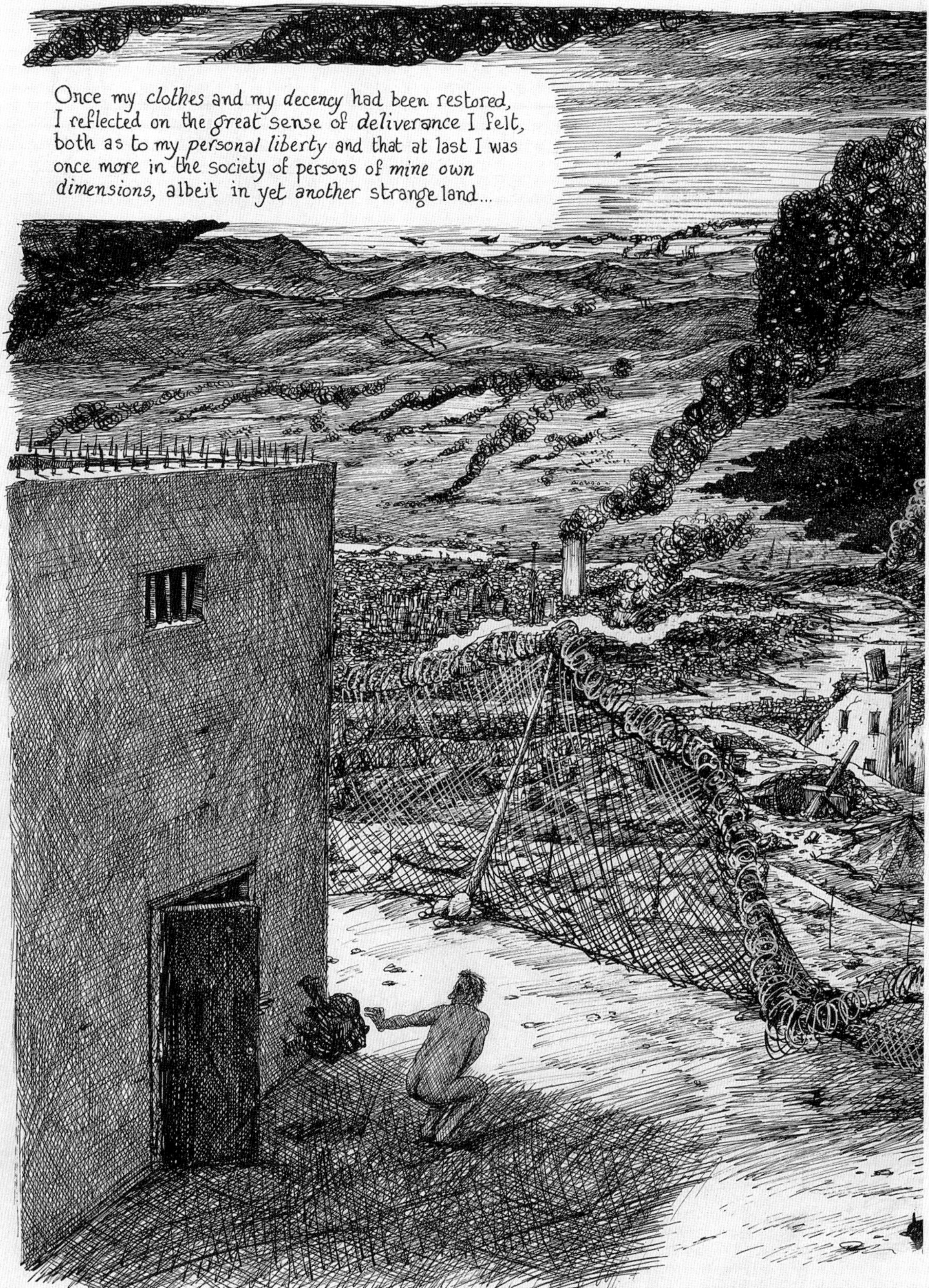
Once my clothes and my decency had been restored, I reflected on the great sense of deliverance I felt, both as to my personal liberty and that at last I was once more in the society of persons of mine own dimensions, albeit in yet another strange land...

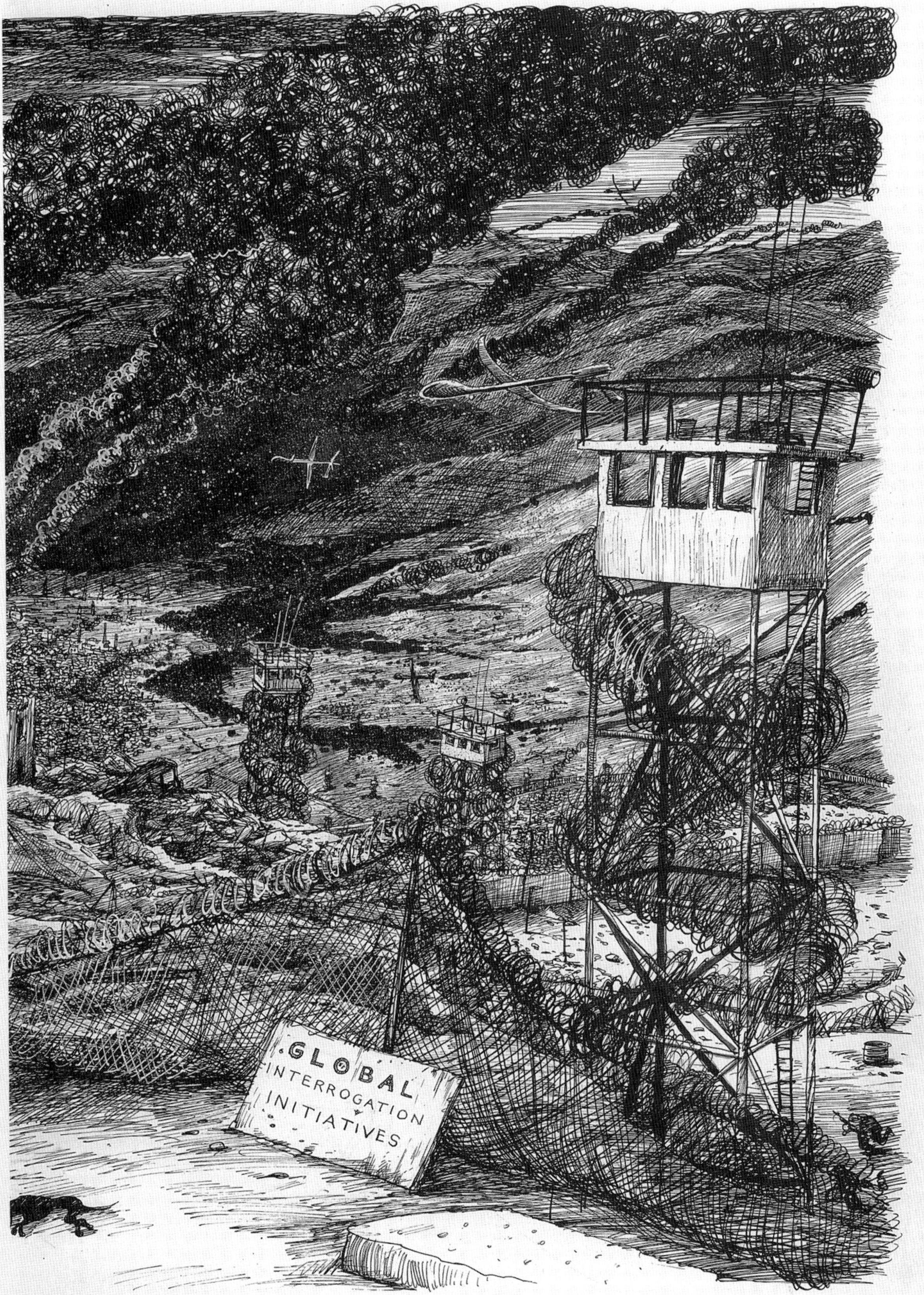
GLOBAL
INTERROGATION
INITIATIVES

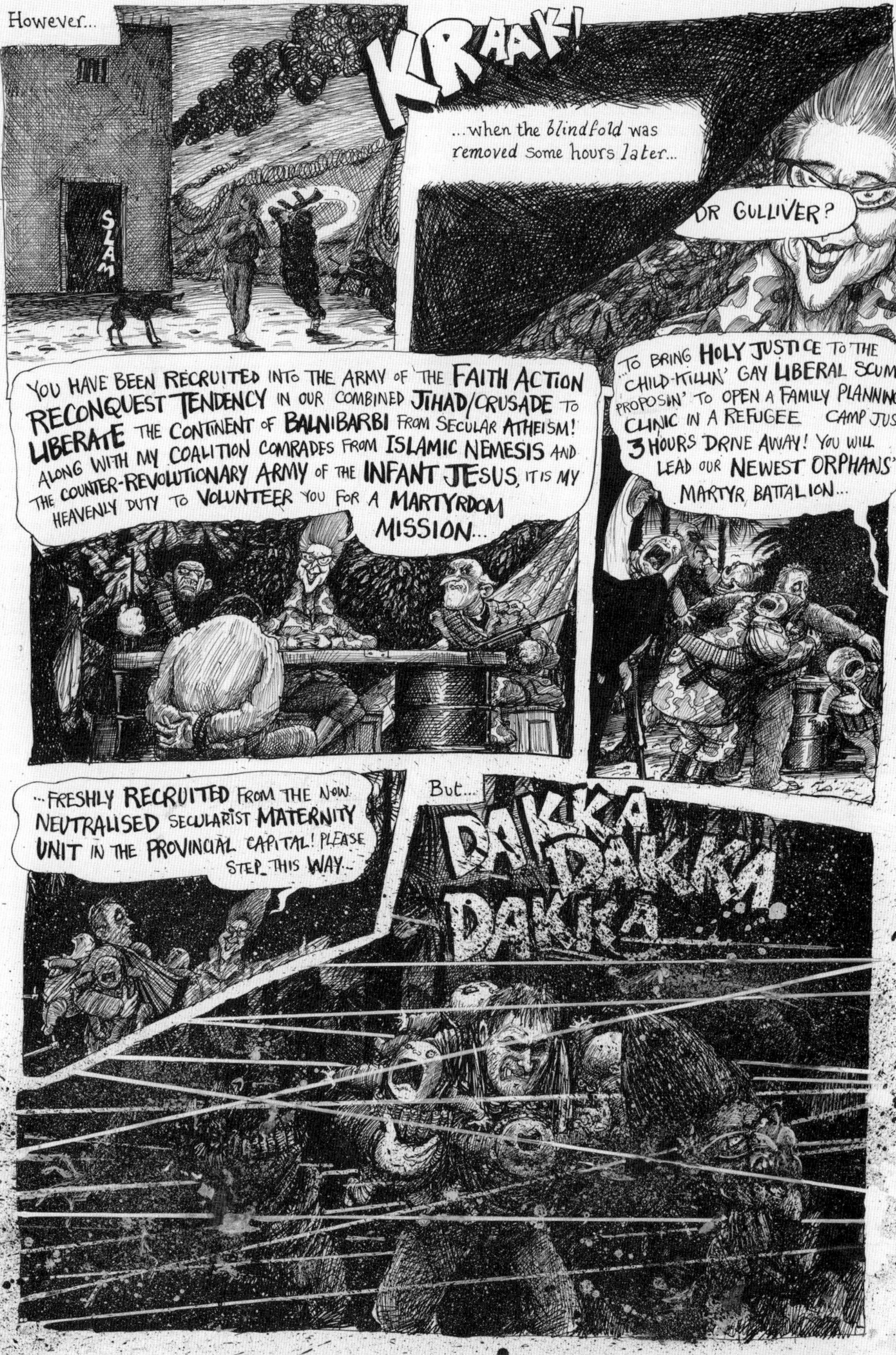
However...
KRAAK!
SLAM
...when the blindfold was removed some hours later...
DR GULLIVER?
YOU HAVE BEEN RECRUITED INTO THE ARMY OF THE FAITH ACTION RECONQUEST TENDENCY IN OUR COMBINED JIHAD/CRUSADE TO LIBERATE THE CONTINENT OF BALNIBARBI FROM SECULAR ATHEISM! ALONG WITH MY COALITION COMRADES FROM ISLAMIC NEMESIS AND THE COUNTER-REVOLUTIONARY ARMY OF THE INFANT JESUS, IT IS MY HEAVENLY DUTY TO VOLUNTEER YOU FOR A MARTYRDOM MISSION...
...TO BRING HOLY JUSTICE TO THE 'CHILD-KILLIN' GAY LIBERAL SCUM' PROPOSIN' TO OPEN A FAMILY PLANNING CLINIC IN A REFUGEE CAMP JUST 3 HOURS DRIVE AWAY! YOU WILL LEAD OUR NEWEST ORPHANS' MARTYR BATTALION...
...FRESHLY RECRUITED FROM THE NOW NEUTRALISED SECULARIST MATERNITY UNIT IN THE PROVINCIAL CAPITAL! PLEASE STEP THIS WAY...
But...
DAKKA DAKKA DAKKA

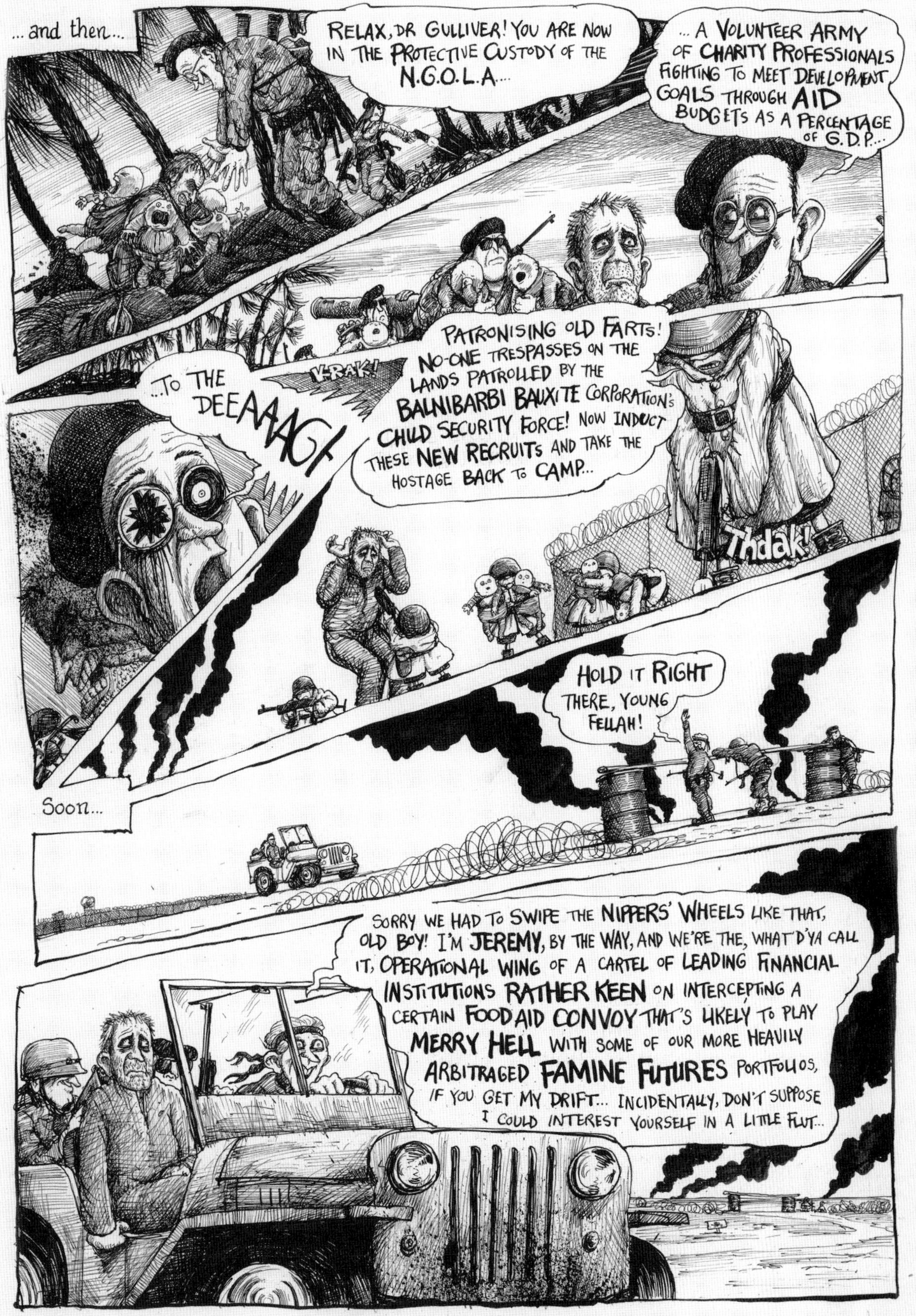
...and then...
RELAX, DR GULLIVER! YOU ARE NOW IN THE PROTECTIVE CUSTODY OF THE N.G.O.L.A...
... A VOLUNTEER ARMY OF CHARITY PROFESSIONALS FIGHTING TO MEET DEVELOPMENT GOALS THROUGH AID BUDGETS AS A PERCENTAGE OF G.D.P...
...TO THE DEEAAAGH!
K-RAK!
PATRONISING OLD FARTS! NO-ONE TRESPASSES ON THE LANDS PATROLLED BY THE BALNIBARBI BAUXITE CORPORATION'S CHILD SECURITY FORCE! NOW INDUCT THESE NEW RECRUITS AND TAKE THE HOSTAGE BACK TO CAMP...
Thdak!
HOLD IT RIGHT THERE, YOUNG FELLAH!
Soon...
SORRY WE HAD TO SWIPE THE NIPPERS' WHEELS LIKE THAT, OLD BOY! I'M JEREMY, BY THE WAY, AND WE'RE THE, WHAT D'YA CALL IT, OPERATIONAL WING OF A CARTEL OF LEADING FINANCIAL INSTITUTIONS RATHER KEEN ON INTERCEPTING A CERTAIN FOOD AID CONVOY THAT'S LIKELY TO PLAY MERRY HELL WITH SOME OF OUR MORE HEAVILY ARBITRAGED FAMINE FUTURES PORTFOLIOS, IF YOU GET MY DRIFT... INCIDENTALLY, DON'T SUPPOSE I COULD INTEREST YOURSELF IN A LITTLE FLUT...

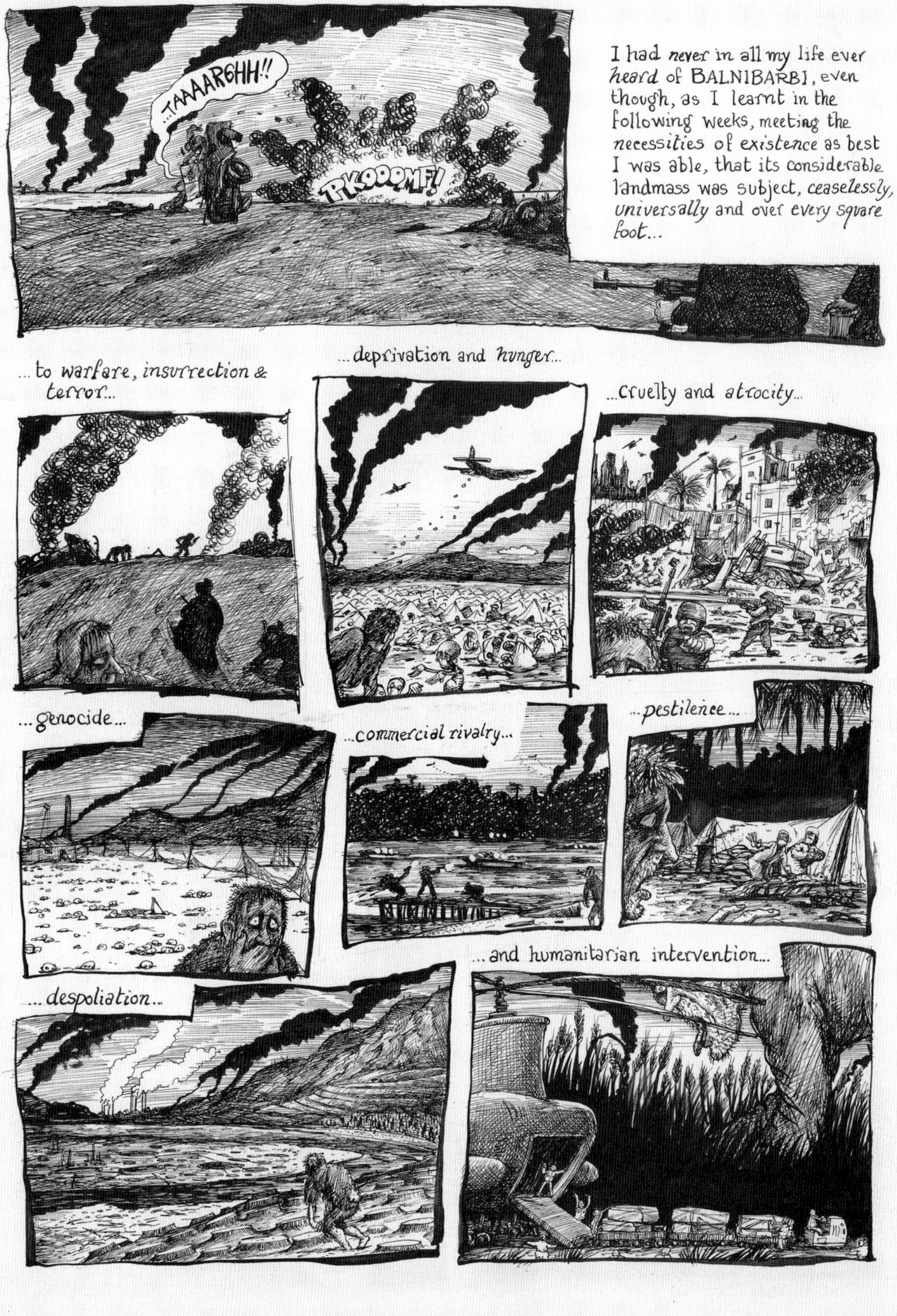

...TAAAARGHH!!
PKOOOMF!
I had never in all my life ever heard of BALNIBARBI, even though, as I learnt in the following weeks, meeting the necessities of existence as best I was able, that its considerable landmass was subject, ceaselessly, universally and over every square foot...
...to warfare, insurrection & terror...
...deprivation and hunger...
...cruelty and atrocity...
...genocide...
...commercial rivalry...
...pestilence...
...despoliation...
...and humanitarian intervention...

...until I eventually sought refuge from the chaos & carnage by climbing a high mountain, atop of which I found myself both over-shadowed and addressed by name from high above where I sat...

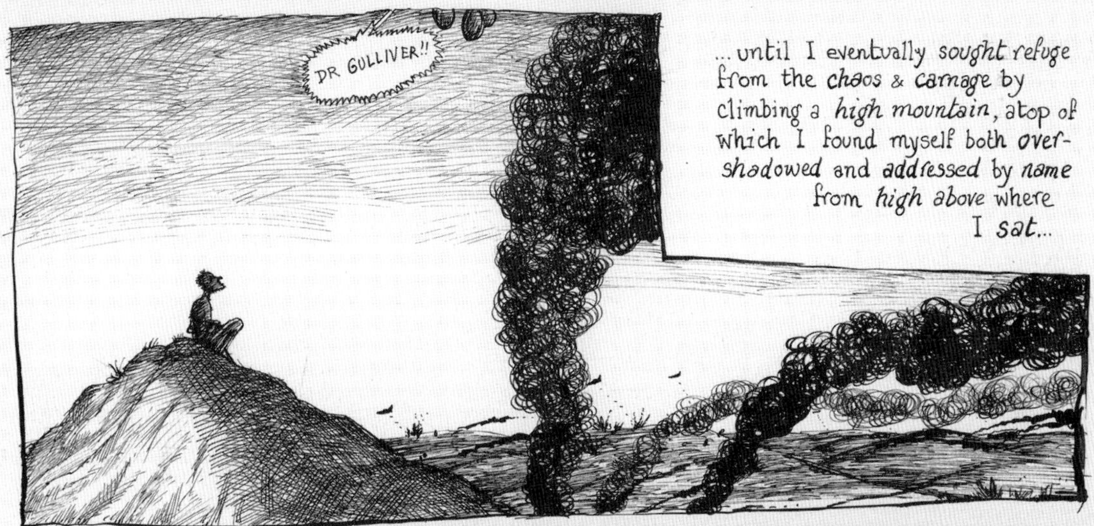
DR GULLIVER!!

Looking up, I beheld a *large floating island*...

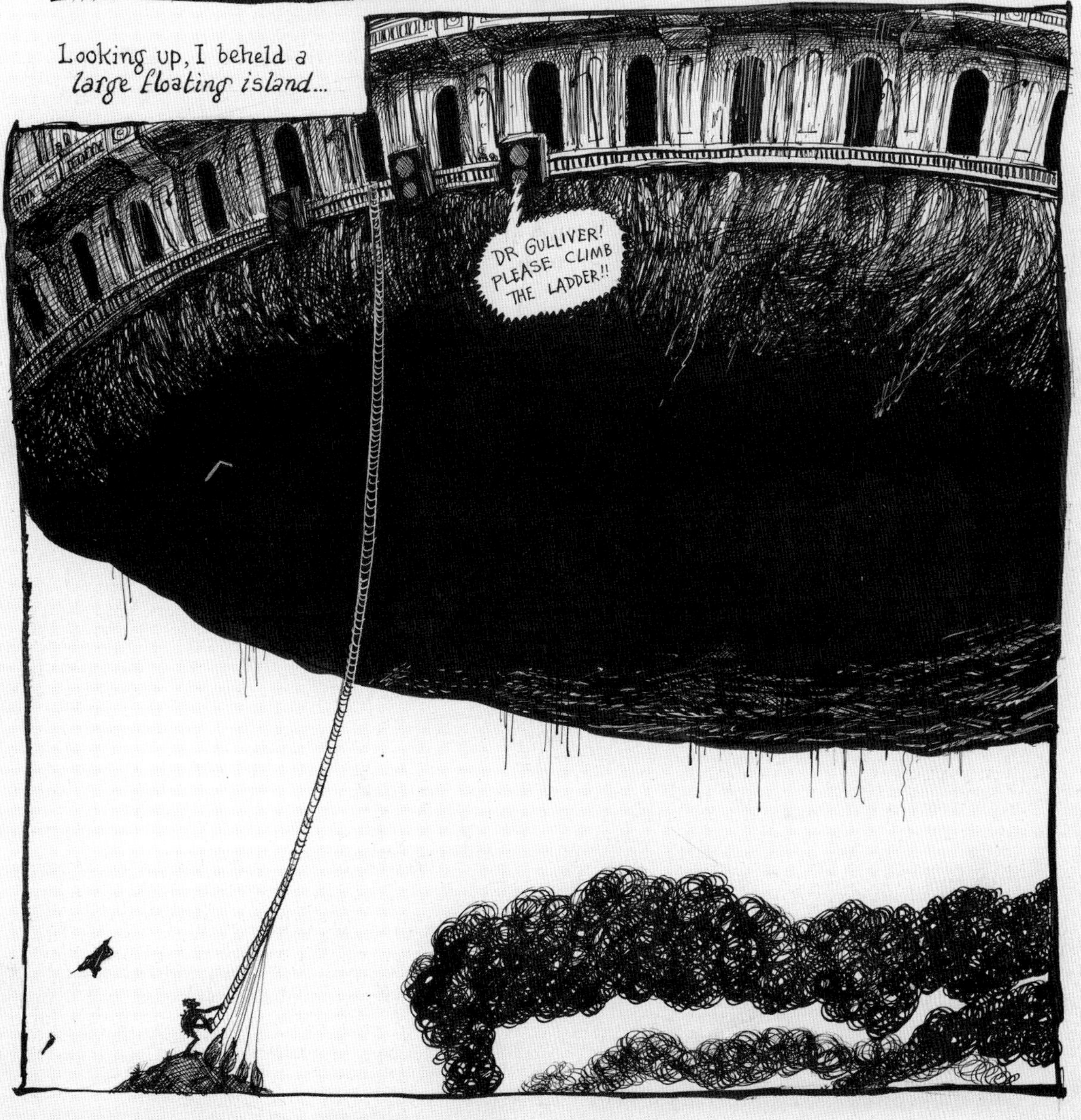
DR GULLIVER! PLEASE CLIMB THE LADDER!!

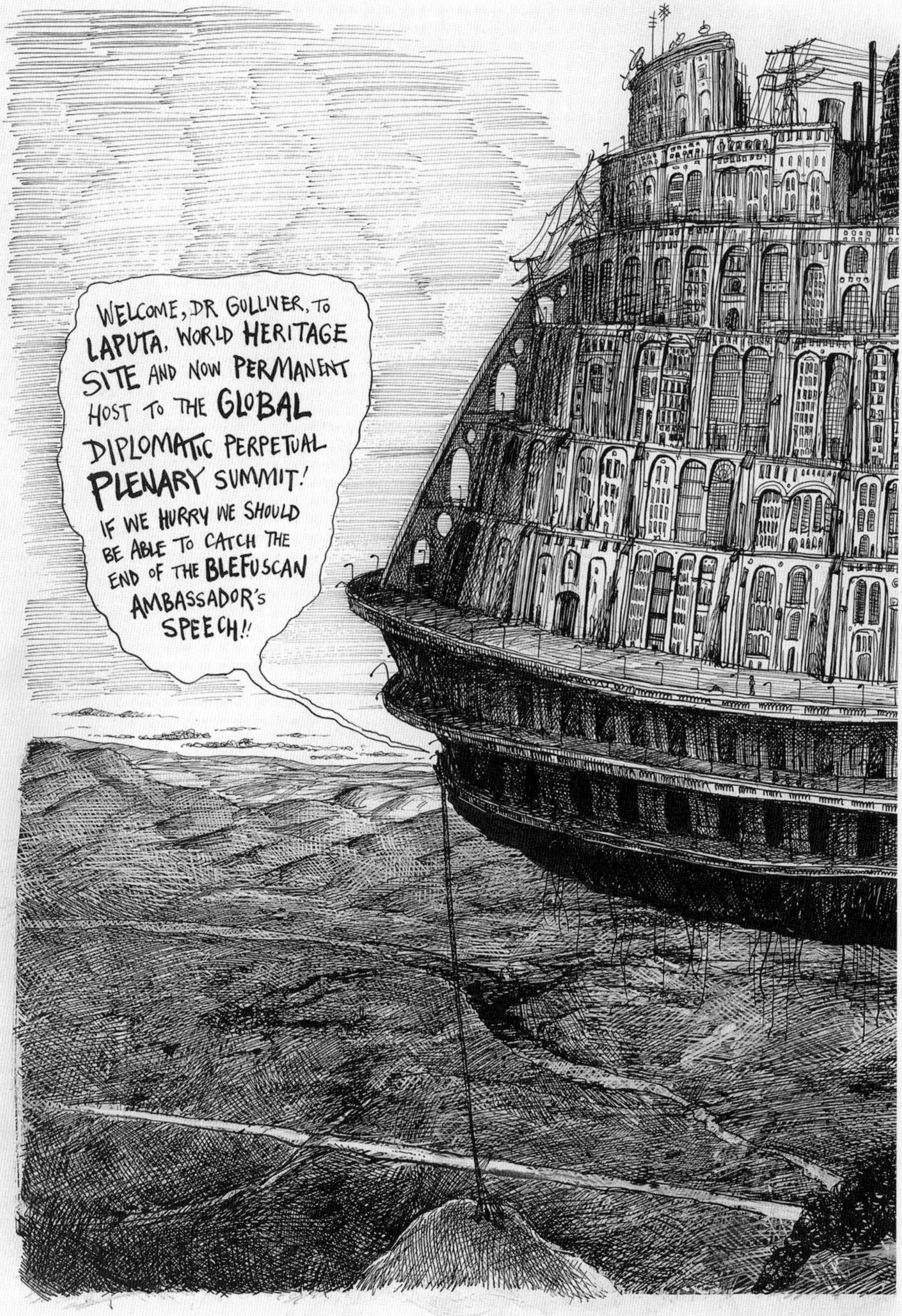
WELCOME, DR GULLIVER, TO LAPUTA, WORLD HERITAGE SITE AND NOW PERMANENT HOST TO THE GLOBAL DIPLOMATIC PERPETUAL PLENARY SUMMIT! IF WE HURRY WE SHOULD BE ABLE TO CATCH THE END OF THE BLEFUSCAN AMBASSADOR'S SPEECH!!

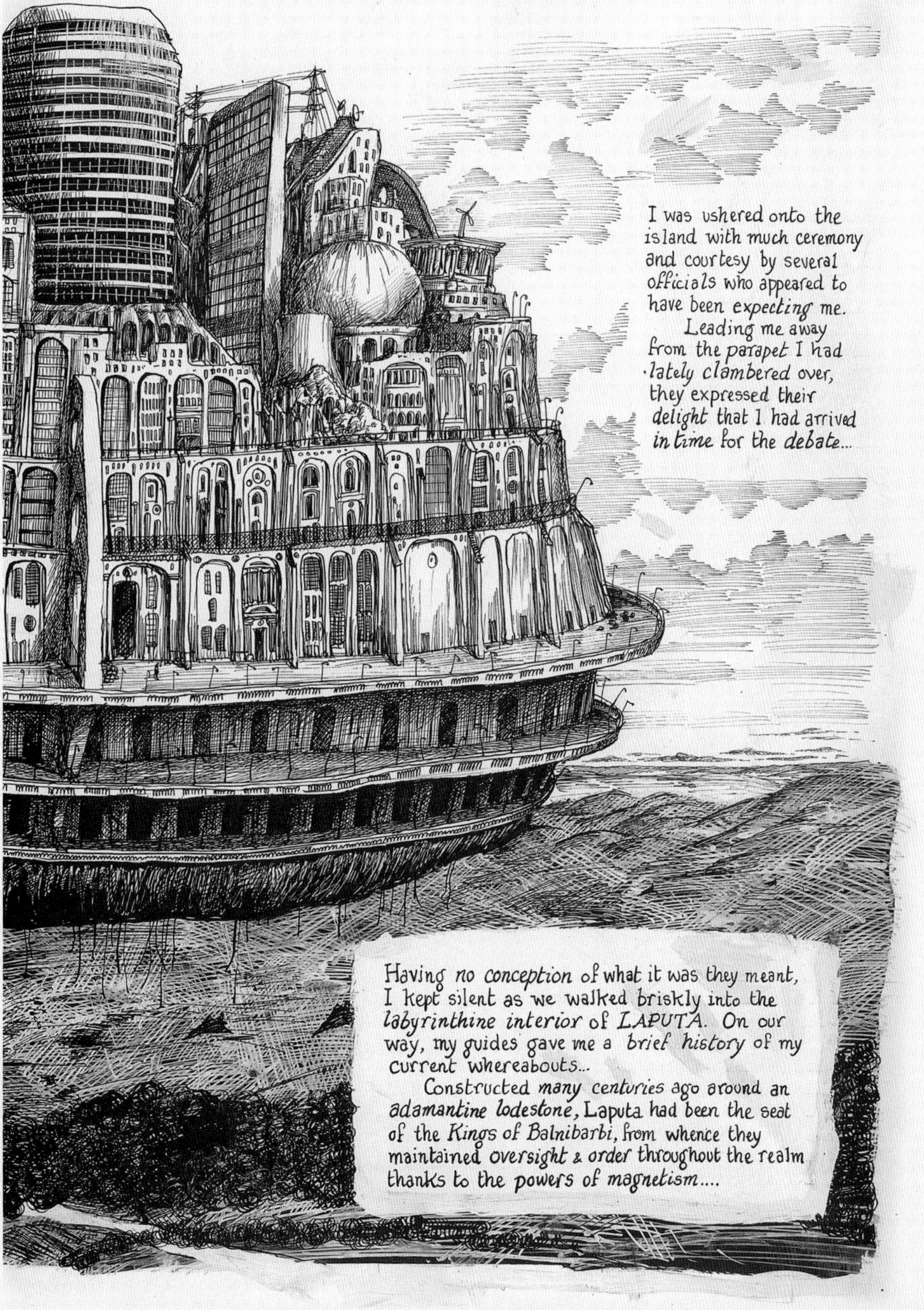
I was ushered onto the island with much ceremony and courtesy by several officials who appeared to have been expecting me. Leading me away from the parapet I had lately clambered over, they expressed their delight that I had arrived in time for the debate...
Having no conception of what it was they meant, I kept silent as we walked briskly into the labyrinthine interior of LAPUTA. On our way, my guides gave me a brief history of my current whereabouts... Constructed many centuries ago around an adamantine lodestone, Laputa had been the seat of the Kings of Balnibarbi, from whence they maintained oversight & order throughout the realm thanks to the powers of magnetism....

It was further explained that in the *olden days* Laputa had been able to *rise* and *sink* at will through an *arcane manipulation* of the *magnetic lodestone.*

However, during the *long decadence* of their *Monarchy*, this technology had become totally and *inexorably lost* to them, and without Laputa's *deterrent power* to overawe and ultimately *crush* its subjects, *things on the ground* quickly collapsed into the *parlous condition* which endured to this day...

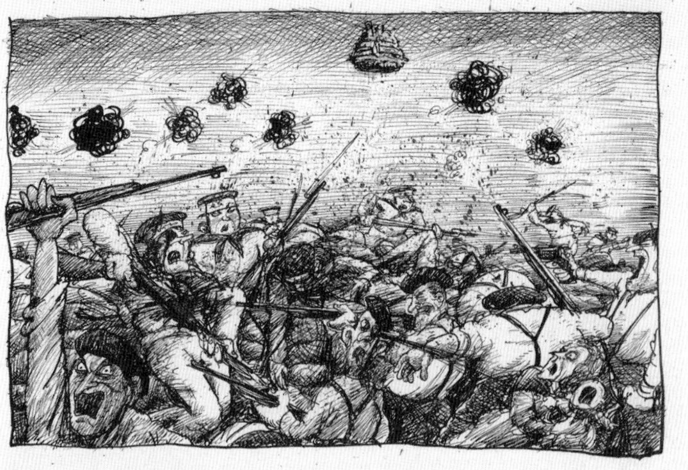

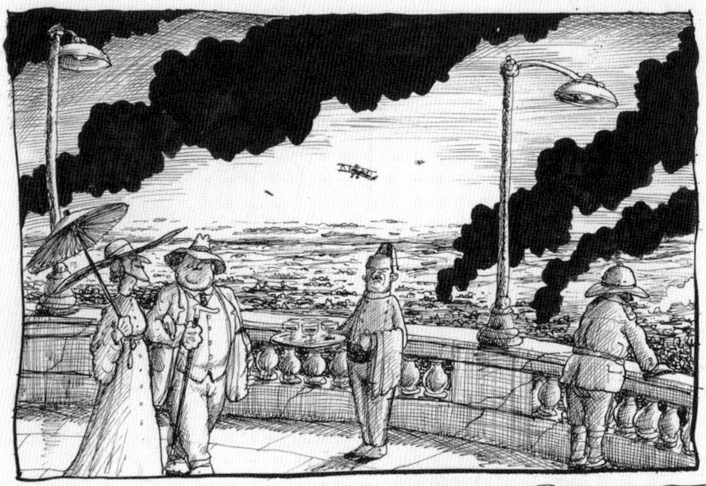

While Laputa, thanks to its *curious history*, charming architecture and *excellent views*, had for many years enjoyed a reputation as the ideal destination for the more *discerning tourist*, the state of *Balnibarbi* had greatly vexed the *International Community*, so much so that *talks* to *resolve* the *manifold crises below* were soon being convened in Laputa *in permanent emergency session*. After several years this situation had been formalised and *institutionalised...*

We had by now reached the *Grand Debating Chamber*, where I was shown into a *sound-proof booth* and provided a *suit of clothes* more fitting to my surroundings...

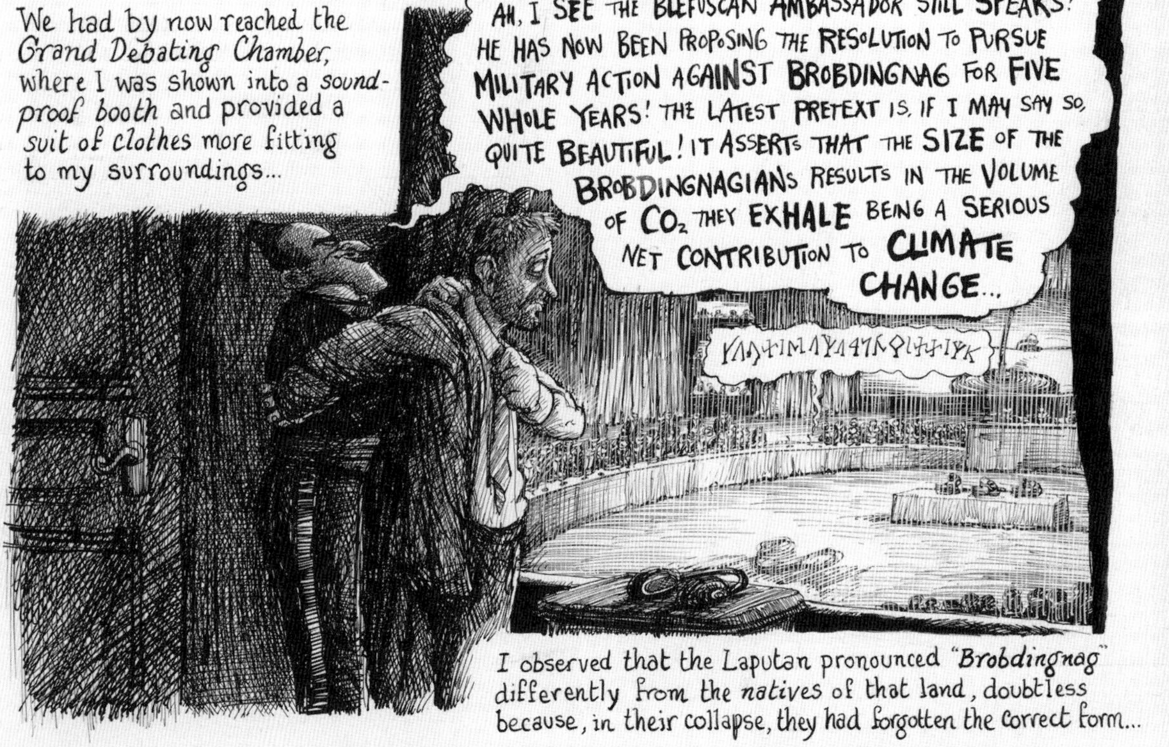
AH, I SEE THE BLEFUSCAN AMBASSADOR STILL SPEAKS! HE HAS NOW BEEN PROPOSING THE RESOLUTION TO PURSUE MILITARY ACTION AGAINST BROBDINGNAG FOR FIVE WHOLE YEARS! THE LATEST PRETEXT IS, IF I MAY SAY SO, QUITE BEAUTIFUL! IT ASSERTS THAT THE SIZE OF THE BROBDINGNAGIANS RESULTS IN THE VOLUME OF CO_2 THEY EXHALE BEING A SERIOUS NET CONTRIBUTION TO CLIMATE CHANGE...

I observed that the Laputan pronounced *"Brobdingnag"* differently from the *natives* of that land, doubtless because, in their collapse, they had forgotten the correct form...

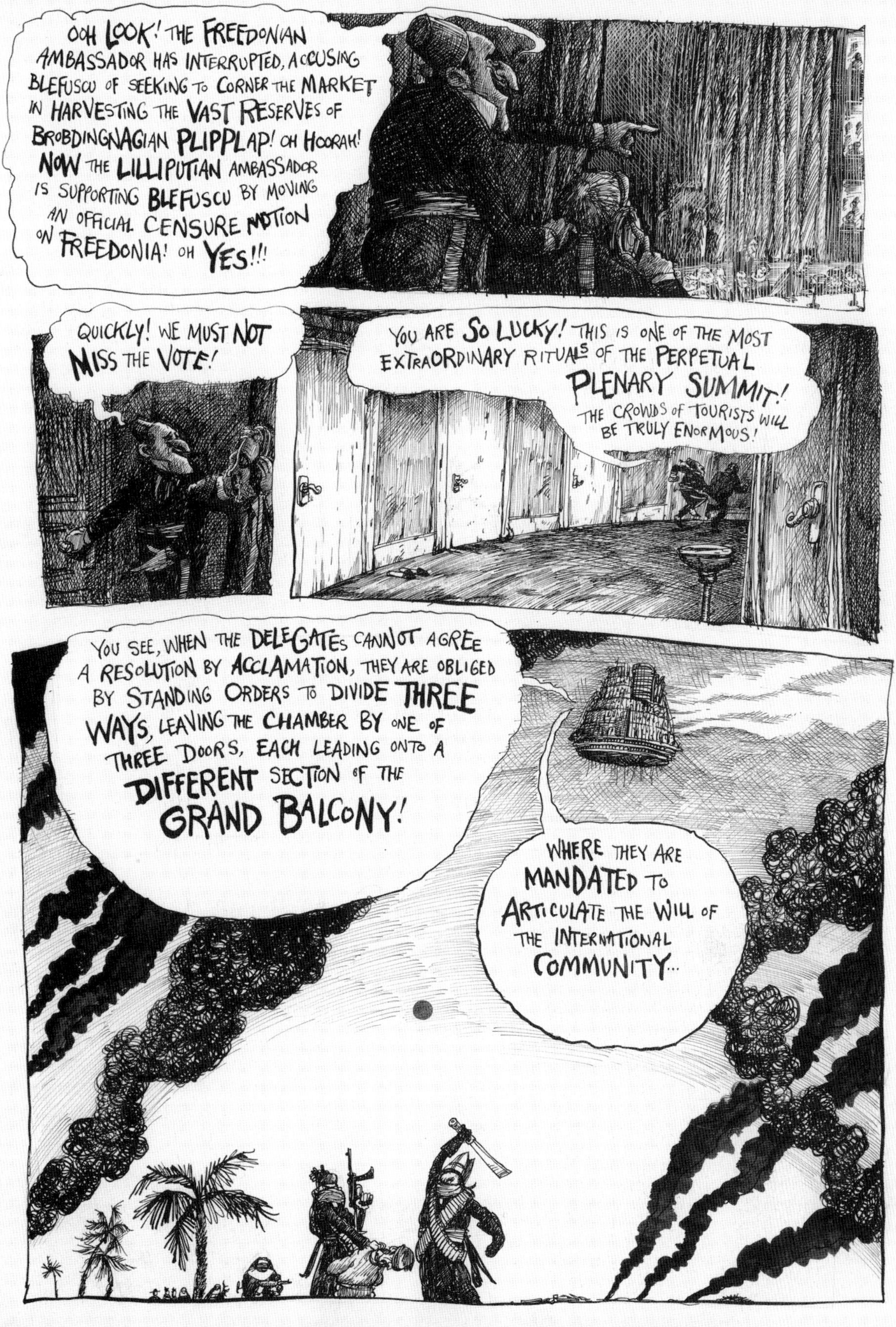
OOH LOOK! THE FREEDONIAN AMBASSADOR HAS INTERRUPTED, ACCUSING BLEFUSCU OF SEEKING TO CORNER THE MARKET IN HARVESTING THE VAST RESERVES OF BROBDINGNAGIAN PLIPPLAP! OH HOORAH! NOW THE LILLIPUTIAN AMBASSADOR IS SUPPORTING BLEFUSCU BY MOVING AN OFFICIAL CENSURE MOTION ON FREEDONIA! OH YES!!!
QUICKLY! WE MUST NOT MISS THE VOTE!
YOU ARE SO LUCKY! THIS IS ONE OF THE MOST EXTRAORDINARY RITUALS OF THE PERPETUAL PLENARY SUMMIT! THE CROWDS OF TOURISTS WILL BE TRULY ENORMOUS!
YOU SEE, WHEN THE DELEGATES CANNOT AGREE A RESOLUTION BY ACCLAMATION, THEY ARE OBLIGED BY STANDING ORDERS TO DIVIDE THREE WAYS, LEAVING THE CHAMBER BY ONE OF THREE DOORS, EACH LEADING ONTO A DIFFERENT SECTION OF THE GRAND BALCONY!
WHERE THEY ARE MANDATED TO ARTICULATE THE WILL OF THE INTERNATIONAL COMMUNITY...

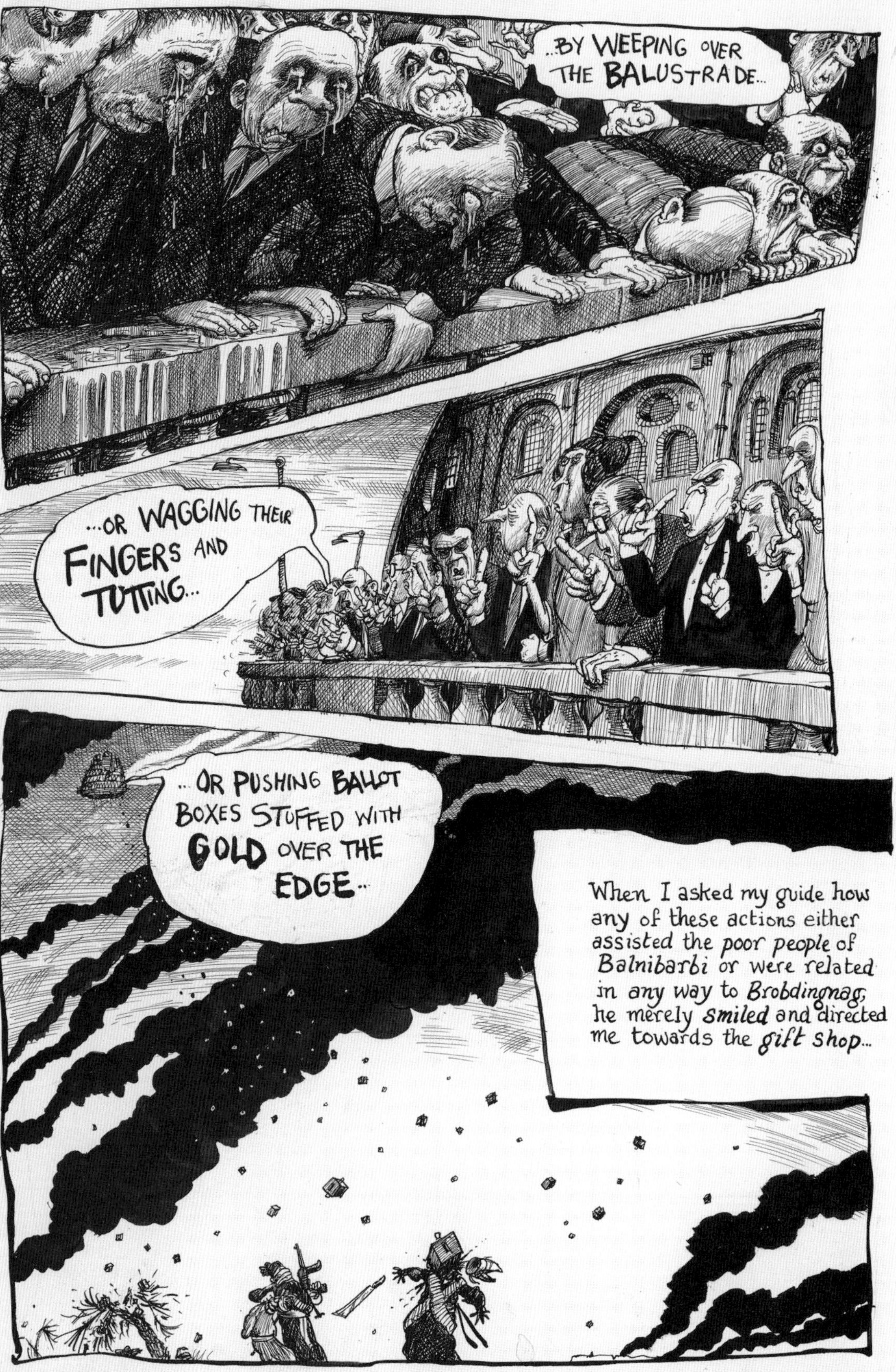
...BY WEEPING OVER THE BALUSTRADE...
...OR WAGGING THEIR FINGERS AND TUTTING...
...OR PUSHING BALLOT BOXES STUFFED WITH GOLD OVER THE EDGE...
When I asked my guide how any of these actions either assisted the poor people of Balnibarbi or were related in any way to Brobdingnag, he merely smiled and directed me towards the gift shop...

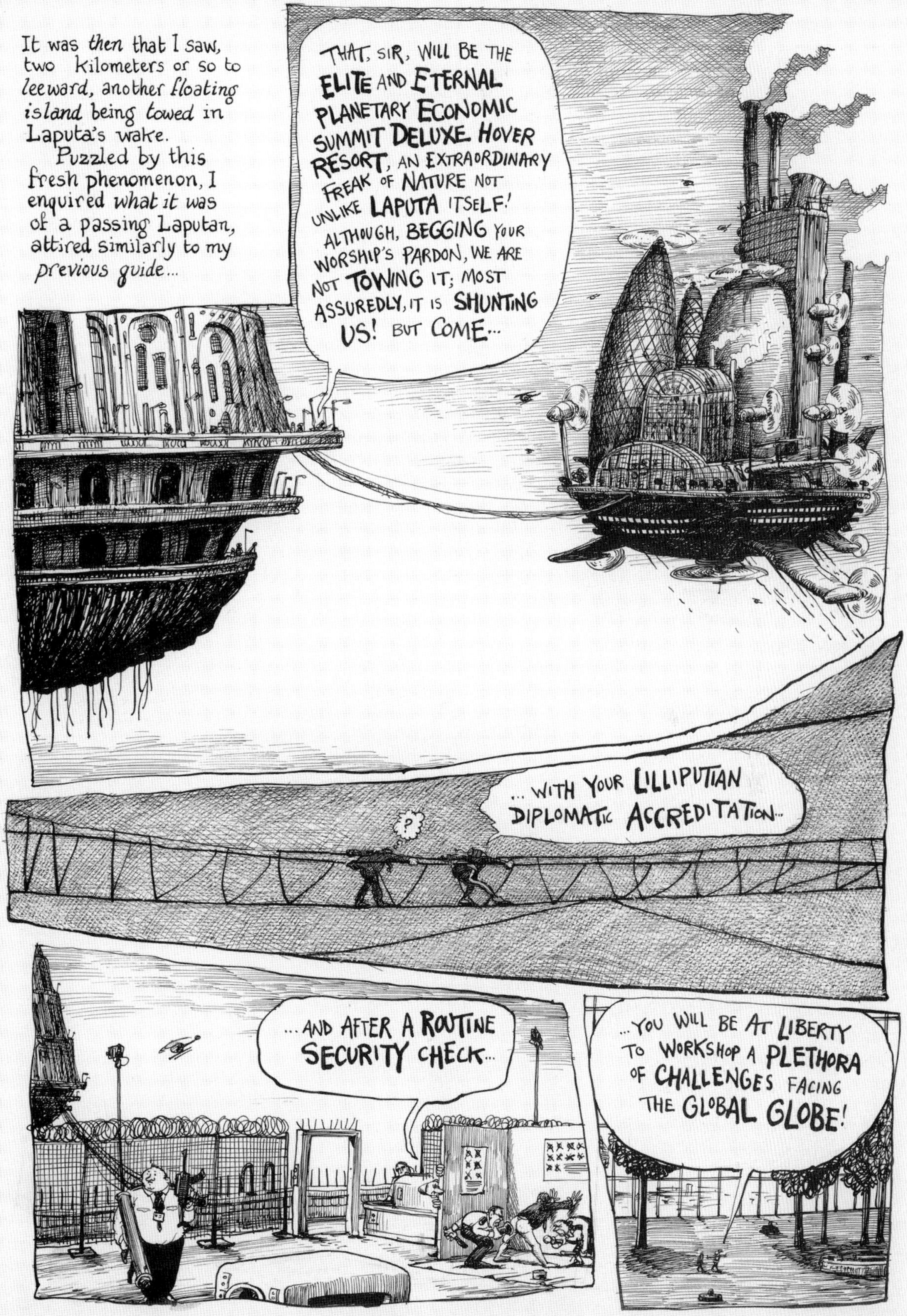
It was then that I saw, two kilometers or so to leeward, another floating island being towed in Laputa's wake. Puzzled by this fresh phenomenon, I enquired what it was of a passing Laputan, attired similarly to my previous guide...
THAT, SIR, WILL BE THE ELITE AND ETERNAL PLANETARY ECONOMIC SUMMIT DELUXE HOVER RESORT, AN EXTRAORDINARY FREAK OF NATURE NOT UNLIKE LAPUTA ITSELF! ALTHOUGH, BEGGING YOUR WORSHIP'S PARDON, WE ARE NOT TOWING IT; MOST ASSUREDLY, IT IS SHUNTING US! BUT COME...
... WITH YOUR LILLIPUTIAN DIPLOMATIC ACCREDITATION...
?
...AND AFTER A ROUTINE SECURITY CHECK...
...YOU WILL BE AT LIBERTY TO WORKSHOP A PLETHORA OF CHALLENGES FACING THE GLOBAL GLOBE!

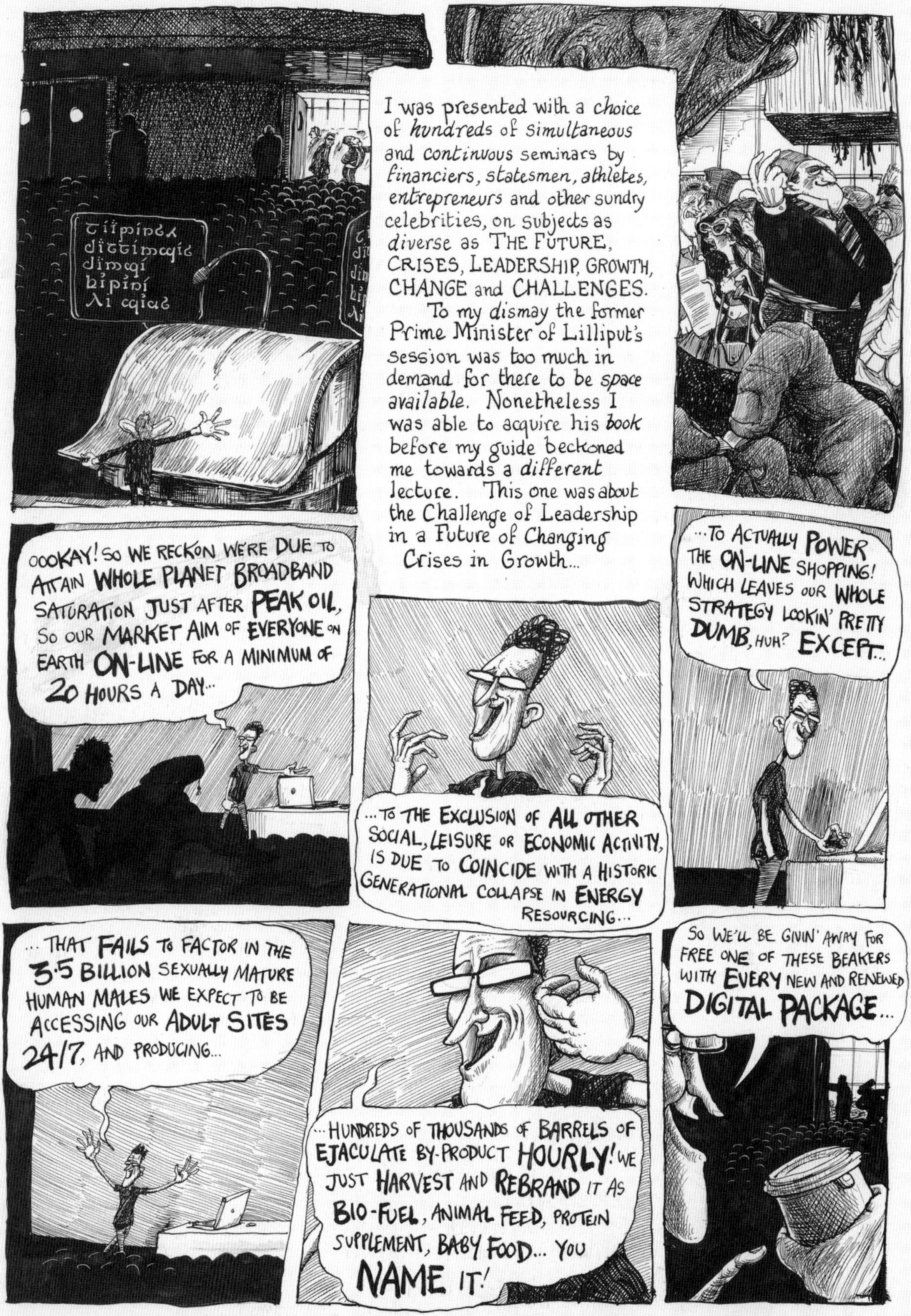

I was presented with a choice of hundreds of simultaneous and continuous seminars by financiers, statesmen, athletes, entrepreneurs and other sundry celebrities, on subjects as diverse as THE FUTURE, CRISES, LEADERSHIP, GROWTH, CHANGE and CHALLENGES.
To my dismay the former Prime Minister of Lilliput's session was too much in demand for there to be space available. Nonetheless I was able to acquire his book before my guide beckoned me towards a different lecture. This one was about the Challenge of Leadership in a Future of Changing Crises in Growth...
OOOKAY! SO WE RECKON WE'RE DUE TO ATTAIN WHOLE PLANET BROADBAND SATURATION JUST AFTER PEAK OIL, SO OUR MARKET AIM OF EVERYONE ON EARTH ON-LINE FOR A MINIMUM OF 20 HOURS A DAY...
...TO THE EXCLUSION OF ALL OTHER SOCIAL, LEISURE OR ECONOMIC ACTIVITY, IS DUE TO COINCIDE WITH A HISTORIC GENERATIONAL COLLAPSE IN ENERGY RESOURCING...
...TO ACTUALLY POWER THE ON-LINE SHOPPING! WHICH LEAVES OUR WHOLE STRATEGY LOOKIN' PRETTY DUMB, HUH? EXCEPT...
...THAT FAILS TO FACTOR IN THE 3·5 BILLION SEXUALLY MATURE HUMAN MALES WE EXPECT TO BE ACCESSING OUR ADULT SITES 24/7, AND PRODUCING...
...HUNDREDS OF THOUSANDS OF BARRELS OF EJACULATE BY-PRODUCT HOURLY! WE JUST HARVEST AND REBRAND IT AS BIO-FUEL, ANIMAL FEED, PROTEIN SUPPLEMENT, BABY FOOD... YOU NAME IT!
SO WE'LL BE GIVIN' AWAY FOR FREE ONE OF THESE BEAKERS WITH EVERY NEW AND RENEWED DIGITAL PACKAGE...

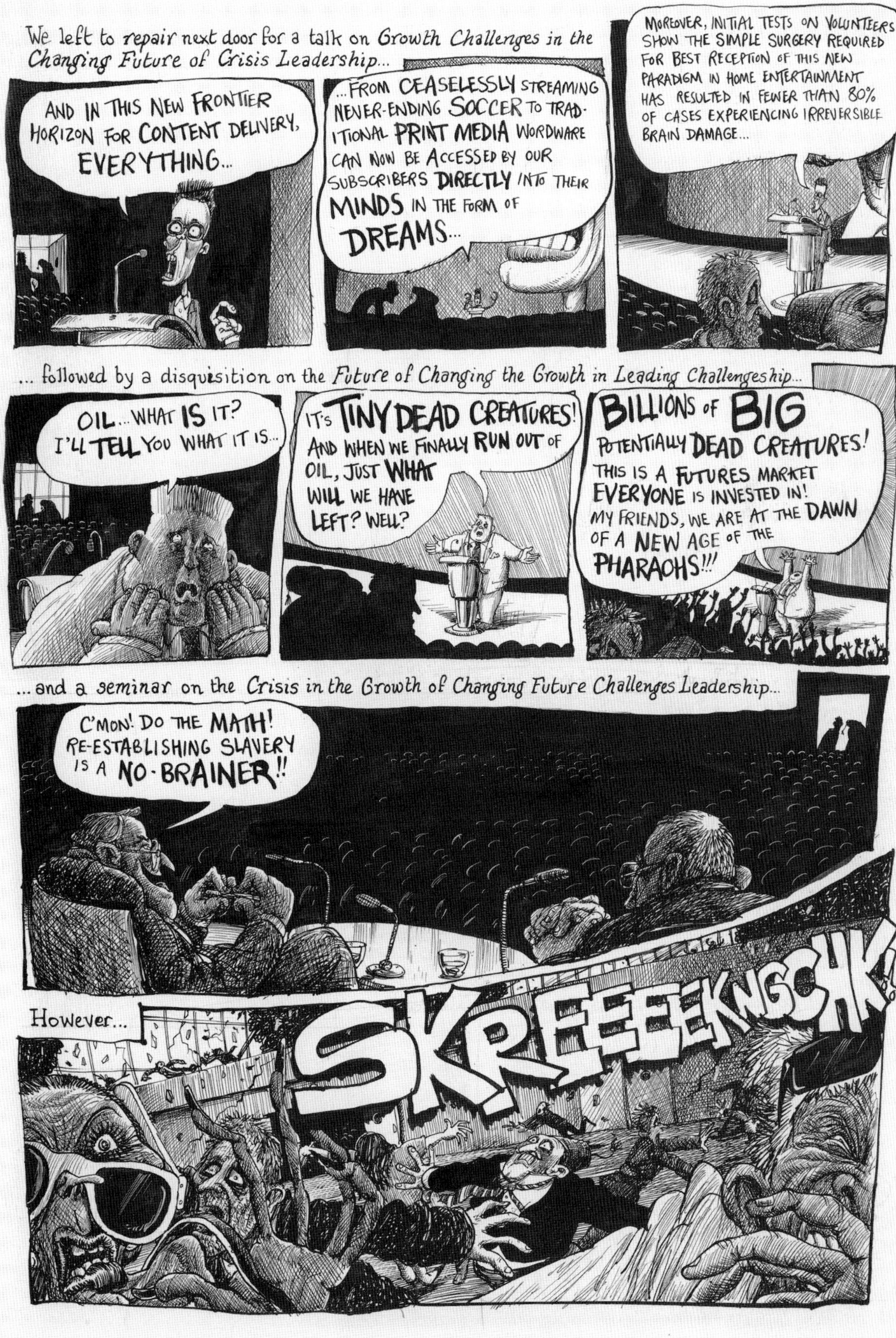
We left to repair next door for a talk on Growth Challenges in the Changing Future of Crisis Leadership...
AND IN THIS NEW FRONTIER HORIZON FOR CONTENT DELIVERY, EVERYTHING...
...FROM CEASELESSLY STREAMING NEVER-ENDING SOCCER TO TRADITIONAL PRINT MEDIA WORDWARE CAN NOW BE ACCESSED BY OUR SUBSCRIBERS DIRECTLY INTO THEIR MINDS IN THE FORM OF DREAMS...
MOREOVER, INITIAL TESTS ON VOLUNTEERS SHOW THE SIMPLE SURGERY REQUIRED FOR BEST RECEPTION OF THIS NEW PARADIGM IN HOME ENTERTAINMENT HAS RESULTED IN FEWER THAN 80% OF CASES EXPERIENCING IRREVERSIBLE BRAIN DAMAGE...
... followed by a disquisition on the Future of Changing the Growth in Leading Challengeship...
OIL... WHAT IS IT? I'LL TELL YOU WHAT IT IS...
IT'S TINY DEAD CREATURES! AND WHEN WE FINALLY RUN OUT OF OIL, JUST WHAT WILL WE HAVE LEFT? WELL?
BILLIONS OF BIG POTENTIALLY DEAD CREATURES! THIS IS A FUTURES MARKET EVERYONE IS INVESTED IN! MY FRIENDS, WE ARE AT THE DAWN OF A NEW AGE OF THE PHARAOHS!!!
... and a seminar on the Crisis in the Growth of Changing Future Challenges Leadership...
C'MON! DO THE MATH! RE-ESTABLISHING SLAVERY IS A NO-BRAINER!!
However...
SKREEEEKNGCHK!!!

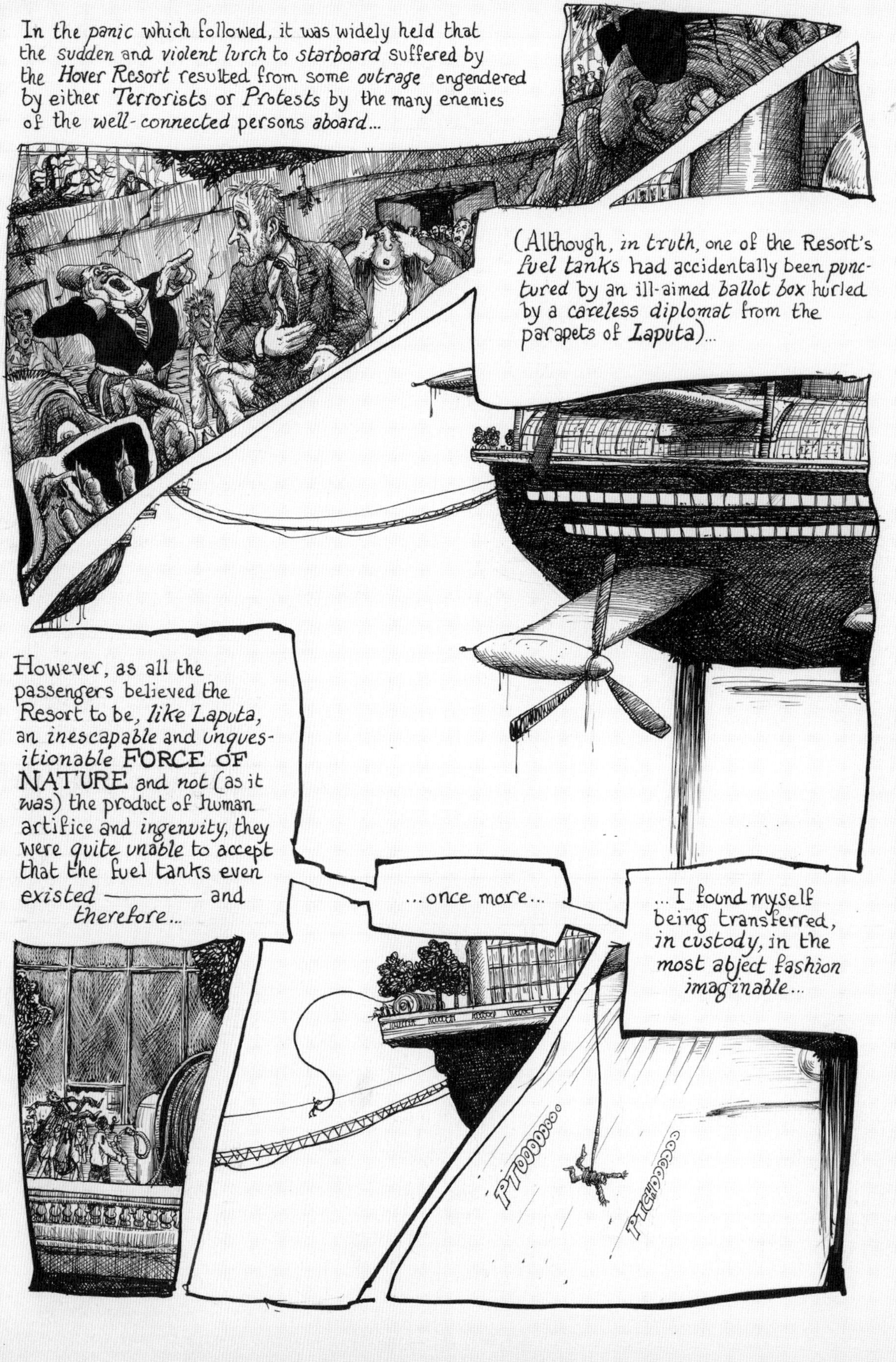
In the panic which followed, it was widely held that the sudden and violent lurch to starboard suffered by the Hover Resort resulted from some outrage engendered by either Terrorists or Protests by the many enemies of the well-connected persons aboard...
(Although, in truth, one of the Resort's fuel tanks had accidentally been punctured by an ill-aimed ballot box hurled by a careless diplomat from the parapets of Laputa)...
However, as all the passengers believed the Resort to be, like Laputa, an inescapable and unquesitionable FORCE OF NATURE and not (as it was) the product of human artifice and ingenuity, they were quite unable to accept that the fuel tanks even existed —— and therefore...
...once more...
...I found myself being transferred, in custody, in the most abject fashion imaginable...
PTOOOOooo
PTCHOOOOooo

...to the ground, by which time I was happily *well beyond* the range of the *pot shots* taken at me from the decks of the *Floating Resort*, either for *sport* or as part of some sophisticated form of *wager* or *investment*...

The place I had landed was a *ruined* urban landscape, the surface littered with *debris*, spattered with oil from the Resort's *ruptured hull* and peppered with *spent bullets* fallen from the sky...

As the spillage worsened I sought shelter beneath an *enormous classical* façade, fronted by a badly damaged monument to what appeared to be a *cucumber*...

Beyond the columns was a small *hut* with a scrap of tattered paper affixed to its door... Thus enjoined, I *knocked*...

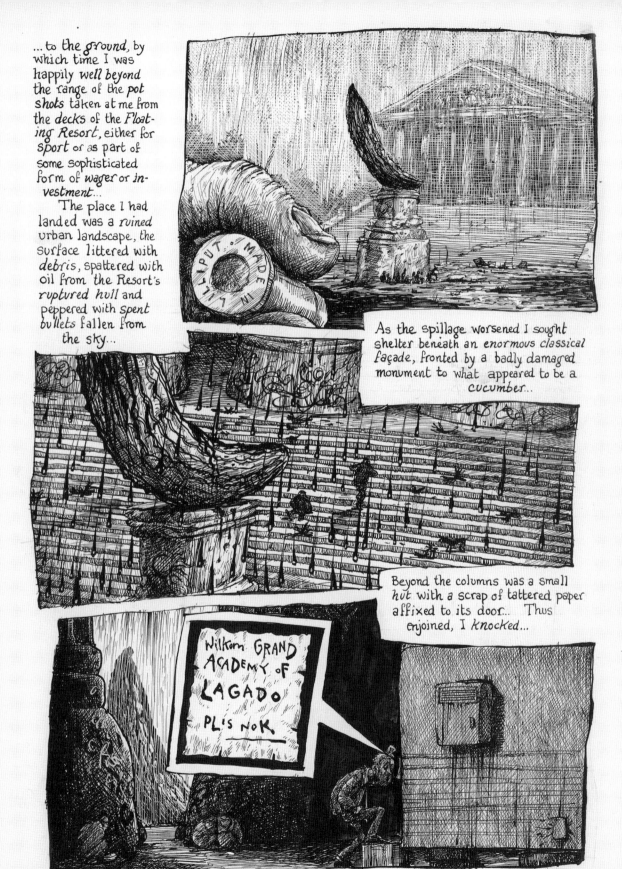

Wilkorn GRAND ACADEMY OF LAGADO PL'S NoK

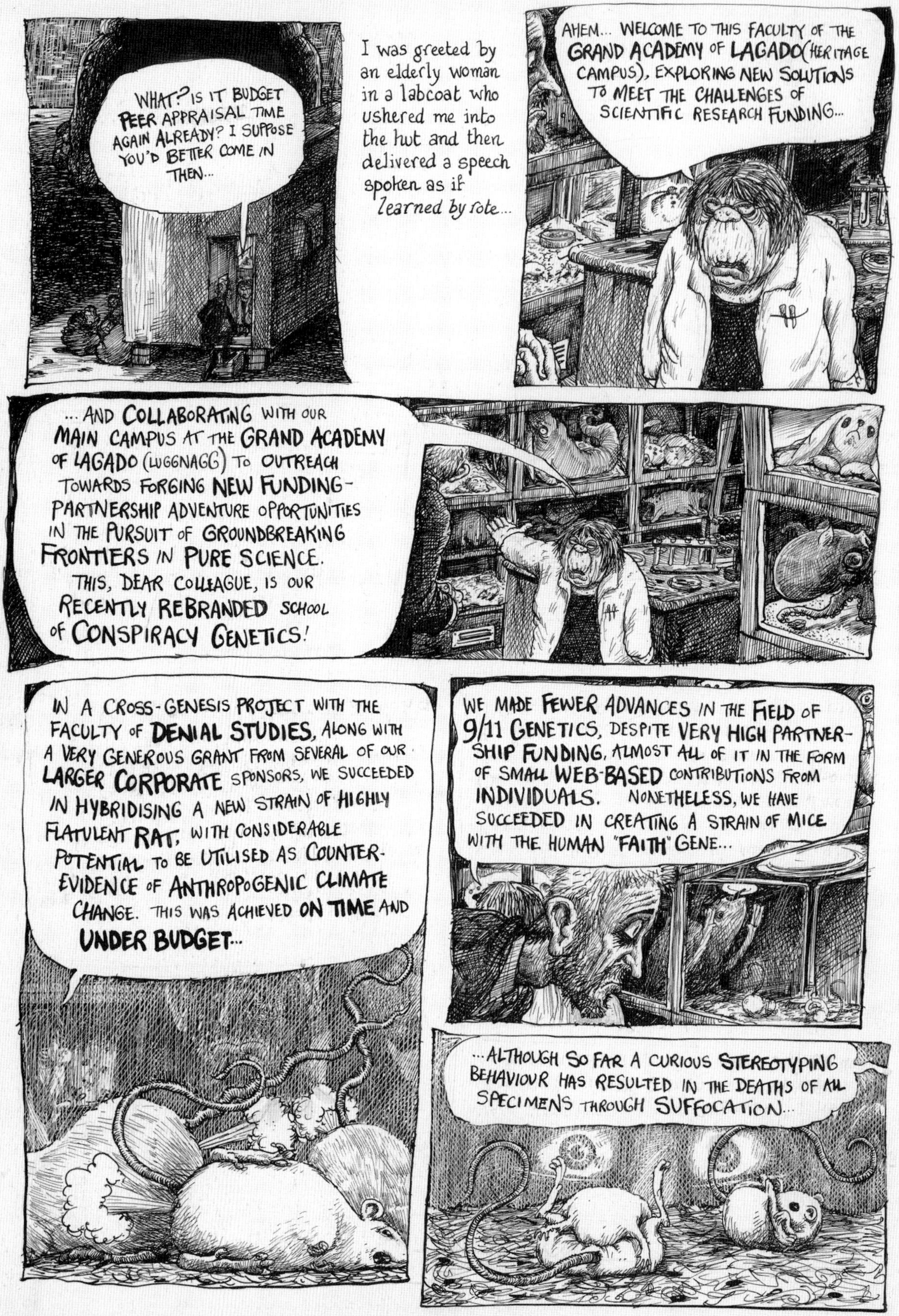
WHAT? IS IT BUDGET PEER APPRAISAL TIME AGAIN ALREADY? I SUPPOSE YOU'D BETTER COME IN THEN...
I was greeted by an elderly woman in a labcoat who ushered me into the hut and then delivered a speech spoken as if learned by rote...
AHEM... WELCOME TO THIS FACULTY OF THE GRAND ACADEMY OF LAGADO (HERITAGE CAMPUS), EXPLORING NEW SOLUTIONS TO MEET THE CHALLENGES OF SCIENTIFIC RESEARCH FUNDING...
...AND COLLABORATING WITH OUR MAIN CAMPUS AT THE GRAND ACADEMY OF LAGADO (LUGGNAGG) TO OUTREACH TOWARDS FORGING NEW FUNDING-PARTNERSHIP ADVENTURE OPPORTUNITIES IN THE PURSUIT OF GROUNDBREAKING FRONTIERS IN PURE SCIENCE. THIS, DEAR COLLEAGUE, IS OUR RECENTLY REBRANDED SCHOOL OF CONSPIRACY GENETICS!
IN A CROSS-GENESIS PROJECT WITH THE FACULTY OF DENIAL STUDIES, ALONG WITH A VERY GENEROUS GRANT FROM SEVERAL OF OUR LARGER CORPORATE SPONSORS, WE SUCCEEDED IN HYBRIDISING A NEW STRAIN OF HIGHLY FLATULENT RAT, WITH CONSIDERABLE POTENTIAL TO BE UTILISED AS COUNTER-EVIDENCE OF ANTHROPOGENIC CLIMATE CHANGE. THIS WAS ACHIEVED ON TIME AND UNDER BUDGET...
WE MADE FEWER ADVANCES IN THE FIELD OF 9/11 GENETICS, DESPITE VERY HIGH PARTNERSHIP FUNDING, ALMOST ALL OF IT IN THE FORM OF SMALL WEB-BASED CONTRIBUTIONS FROM INDIVIDUALS. NONETHELESS, WE HAVE SUCCEEDED IN CREATING A STRAIN OF MICE WITH THE HUMAN "FAITH" GENE...
...ALTHOUGH SO FAR A CURIOUS STEREOTYPING BEHAVIOUR HAS RESULTED IN THE DEATHS OF ALL SPECIMENS THROUGH SUFFOCATION...

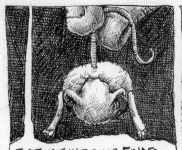

OH, AND COULD YOU GIVE THEM THIS REPORT ON THE SPECIES REASSIGNMENT PROGRAMME WHEN YOU GET BACK TO LUGGNAGG? AND TELL THEM THE CENTRIFUGE GOT BROKEN IN THE LAST ROCKET ATTACK...

CLOSE THE DOOR ON YOUR WAY OUT. OTHERWISE THE JOURNALISTS GET IN AND TRY TO EAT THE ANIMALS...

FORTUNATELY FOR OUR **FUNDED** PARTNERSHIP PROJECT SEQUENCING THE **CREATION** GENOME, WE HAVE BEEN ABLE TO OBSERVE SIMILAR FUNDAMENTING TRAITS IN A **CONTROL POPULATION** OF **ATHEIST MICE**...

Her comments made more sense once I established that the *pitiful* creatures huddled together for shelter outside the Academy were the remnants of several *TV* crews, sent originally to report on the tragic turmoil of Balnibarbi, but long since abandoned by the vicissitudes of the *twenty-four hour* News Cycle. I asked them how to get to *Luggnagg*...

... and they told me I must travel via the coastal city of *Maldonada*, far to the *South-East*, begging me to take them *with* me...
Sadly, when the bus for the coast eventually arrived a week or so later, its driver insisted that he was unable to allow the unhappy journalists to board, as this could seriously compromise his *freelance* rôle in the *Global War on Drugs*, as he explained further on the journey...

HONESTLY, M'SIEUR, IT'S SIMPLE, THOUGH THE PRESS ALWAYS GET IT WRONG. NOW I GET PAID TO BURN ALL THE CROPS ON MY ROUTE IN ORDER TO REMOVE FROM THE SUPPLY CHAIN MATERIAL POTENTIALLY OF CONSUMABILITY DURING AN ATTACK OF THE MUNCHIES! THAT'S WHAT THE EXPERT FROM LUGGNAGG TOLD ME. THEIR RESEARCH, SPONSORED BY BLEFUSCU, HAS PROVED THAT THE MUNCHIES ARE THE CRITICAL STAGE IN THE DOWNWARD SPIRAL OF ADDICTION! SO ANYWAY...

...although I comprehended *little* of what he said...

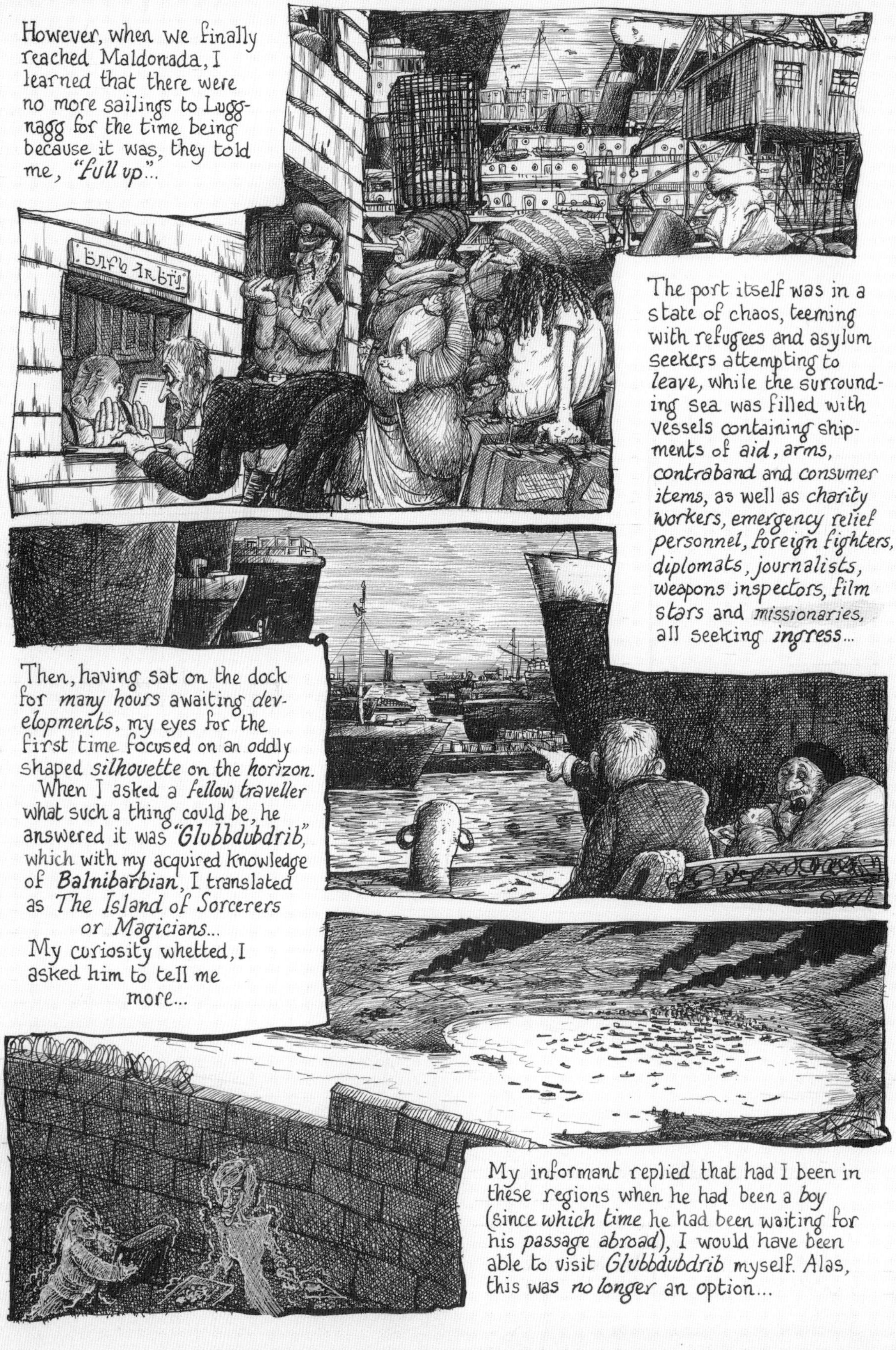
However, when we finally reached Maldonada, I learned that there were no more sailings to Luggnagg for the time being because it was, they told me, *"full up"*...
The port itself was in a state of chaos, teeming with refugees and asylum seekers attempting to *leave*, while the surrounding sea was filled with vessels containing shipments of *aid*, *arms*, *contraband* and *consumer items*, as well as *charity workers*, *emergency relief personnel*, *foreign fighters*, *diplomats*, *journalists*, *weapons inspectors*, *film stars* and *missionaries*, all seeking *ingress*...
Then, having sat on the dock for *many hours* awaiting *developments*, my eyes for the first time focused on an oddly shaped *silhouette* on the *horizon*.
When I asked a *fellow traveller* what such a thing could be, he answered it was *"Glubbdubdrib"*, which with my acquired knowledge of *Balnibarbian*, I translated as *The Island of Sorcerers or Magicians*...
My curiosity whetted, I asked him to tell me more...
My informant replied that had I been in these regions when he had been a *boy* (since *which time* he had been waiting for his *passage abroad*), I would have been able to visit *Glubbdubdrib* myself. Alas, this was *no longer* an option...

Back then, the old man continued, the island was still, as it had been for *centuries*, inhabited by a community of *necromancers* who, through their secret knowledge of certain *arcane* rites, were able to *summon up* the *spirits of the dead* to serve them with all their worldly desires for a term of 24 hours each. The income from *tourism* was *not inconsiderable*, he said...

Then, about **40** years ago...

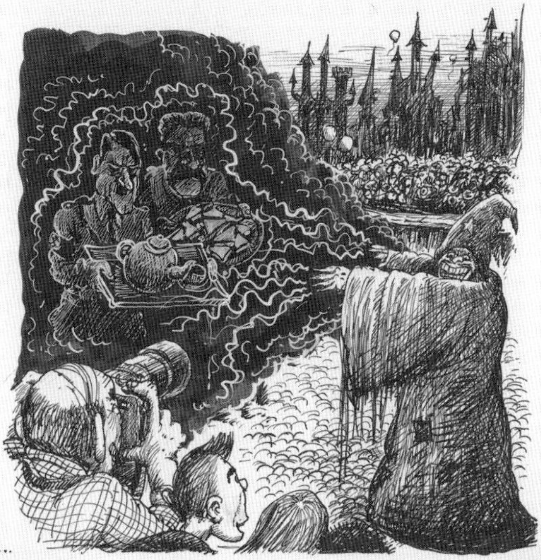

...magicians from all around the world began to settle on the *island*, claiming it to be a *refuge* from the *persecution* their kind had been suffering for *millennia*.

Moreover, now practising the dark art of *necromancy* too, the settlers began to *summon up* their *own ancestors'* shades who, it was thereafter claimed, asserted that the island, *historically*, was *rightfully* the *property of the settlers*. Naturally, this was *disputed*...

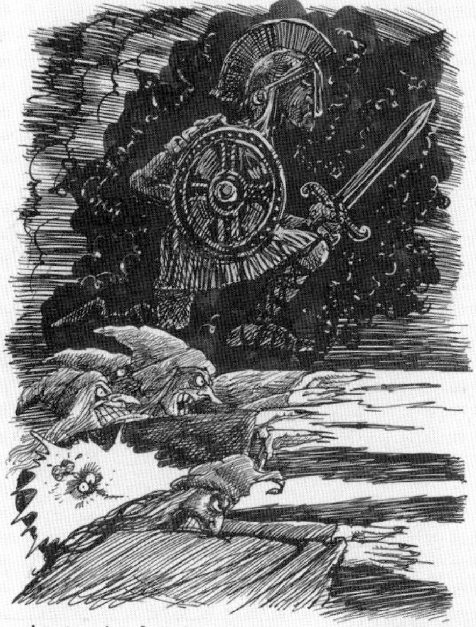

...by the *original inhabitants*, and for *decades* subsequently terrible wars, fought with *ferocity* and *magic*, had led to the deaths of *thousands*.

Worse, both sides summoned up great generals and strategists from throughout *History* to aid their cause (though never for longer than *24 hours*, when they would frequently be invoked by **the other side** – just as the dead on both sides were almost instantly conscripted, if only for a *day*, into the service of *their enemies*).

And all, as the old man observed, over a *small rock* of no *commercial*, *mineral*, *agricultural* or *strategic* significance *whatsoever*...

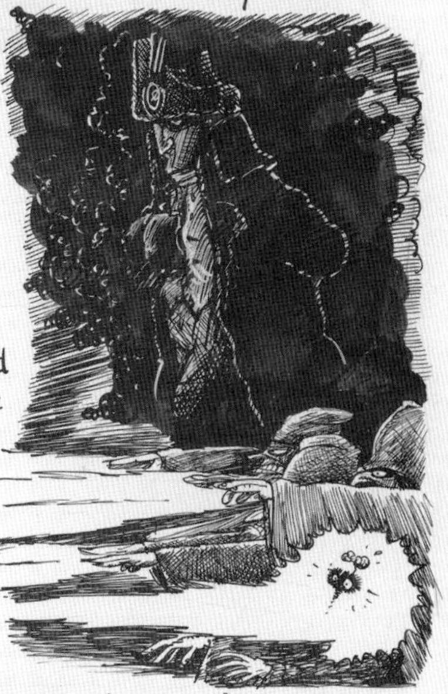

At last, thanks to the *diplomats* of *Laputa*, an uneasy *Peace* had been brokered between the *warring communities*, *both* still claiming the island as *entirely* their **exclusive homeland**.

This *peace* was maintained, albeit *precariously*, by the construction of a *Wall* to separate the populations, who nonetheless kept up *frequent* attacks over the barrier and attempted almost *daily* to encroach into the *other's territory*...

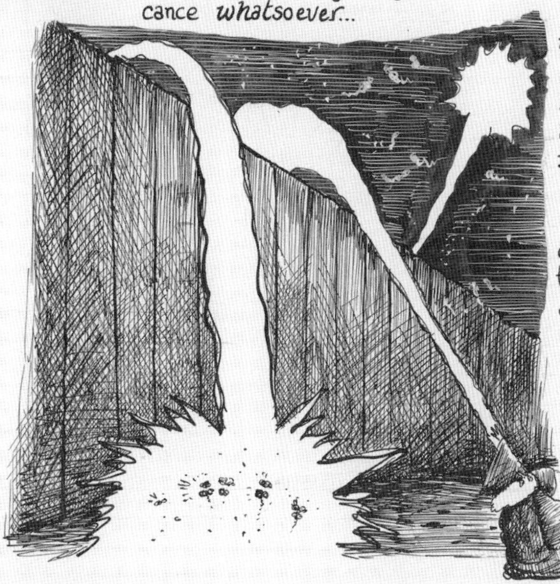

However, these *encroachments* were met with such *mutual savagery*, my new friend explained, that apart from the continuing *random acts of reprisal*, both sides now tacitly accepted the *impossibility* of settling their grievances through *conquest* or *annihilation*. And therefore they now expressed their *territorial ambitions* **vertically** instead...

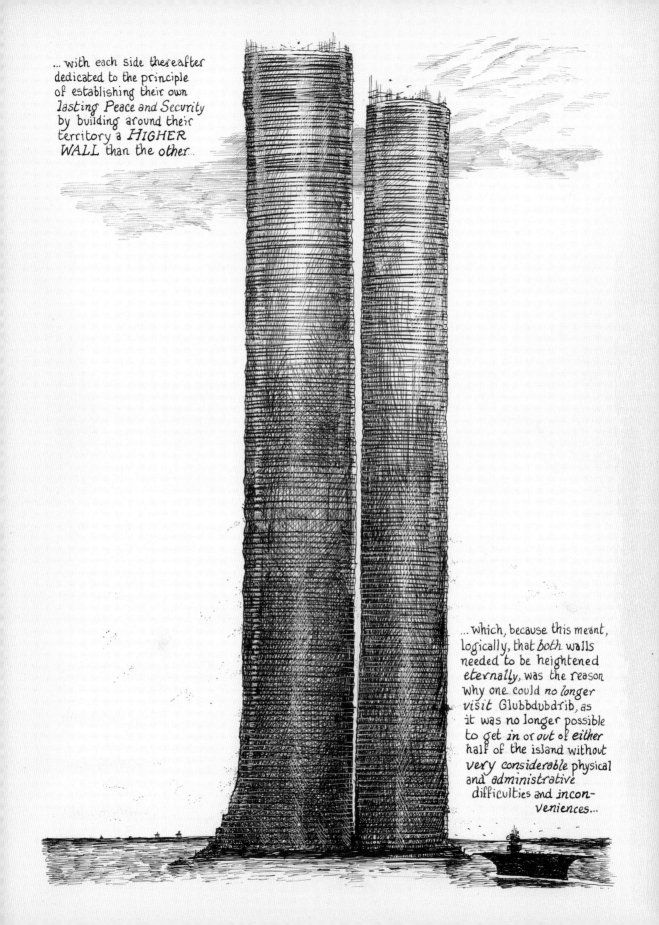

... with each side thereafter dedicated to the principle of establishing their own *lasting Peace and Security* by building around their territory a *HIGHER WALL* than the other...

... which, because this meant, logically, that *both* walls needed to be heightened *eternally*, was the reason why one could *no longer visit* Glubbdubdrib, as it was no longer possible to get *in* or *out* of *either* half of the island without *very considerable* physical and *administrative* difficulties and *inconveniences...*

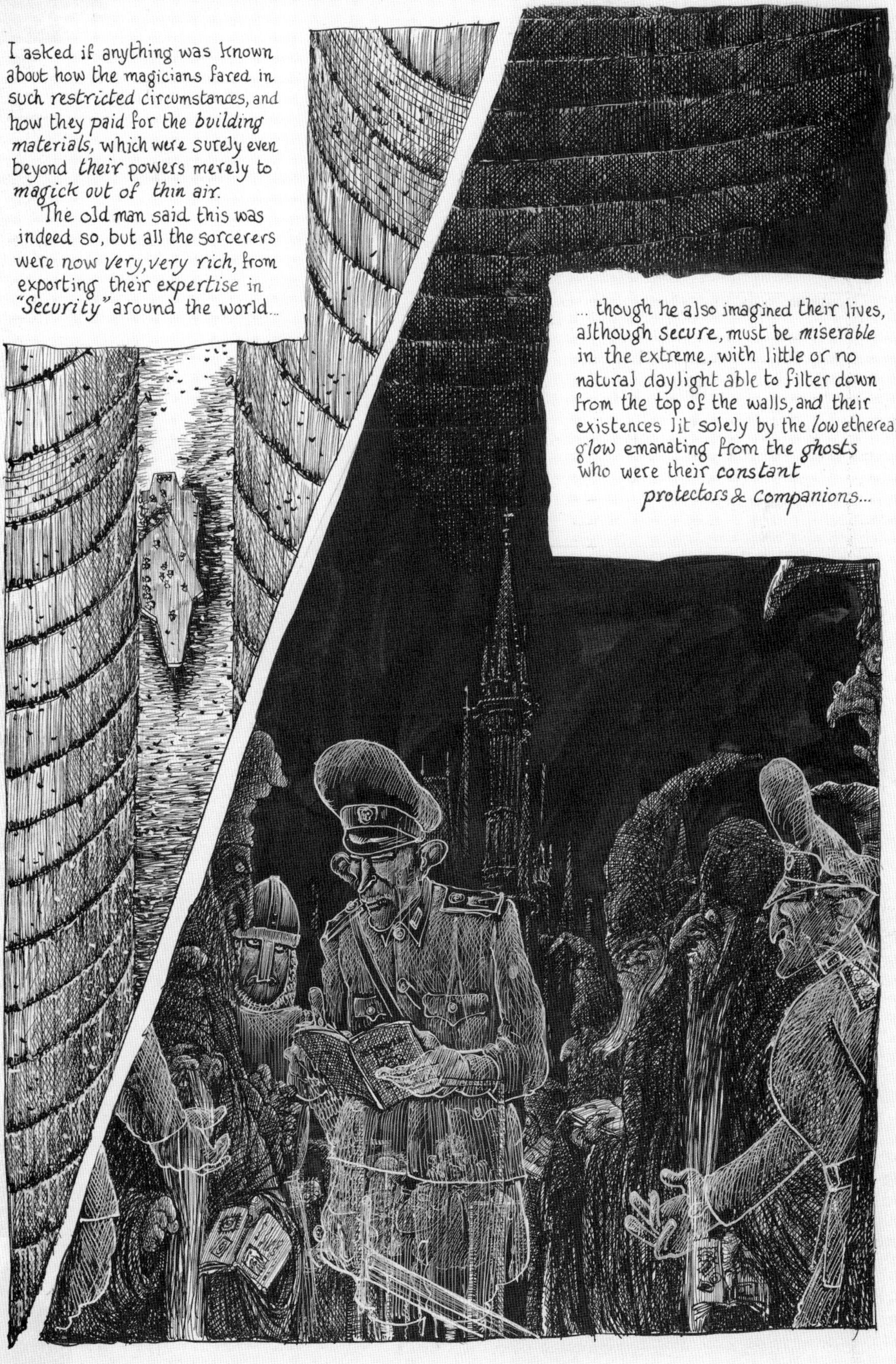
I asked if anything was known about how the magicians fared in such *restricted* circumstances, and how they *paid* for the *building materials*, which were surely even beyond *their* powers merely to *magick out of thin air.*
The old man said this was indeed so, but all the sorcerers were now *very, very rich*, from exporting their *expertise* in *"Security"* around the world...
... though he also imagined their lives, although *secure*, must be *miserable* in the extreme, with little or no natural daylight able to filter down from the top of the walls, and their existences lit solely by the *low* ethereal *glow* emanating from the *ghosts* who were their *constant* *protectors & companions*...

I believe that I might have *languished* in Maldonada — with or without a trip to *Glubbdubdrib* — for *many months* had it not been for the *Earthquake*...

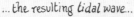
...the resulting *tidal wave*...

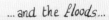
...and the *floods*...

...which, on top of the *outbreaks* of *looting* and *pestilence*, led directly to the delegation of *post-grief* consultants arriving to *survey* the ruins in preparation for the construction of a *memorial golf resort*, and who provided me with a *ride* to *Luggnagg*...

...which, *bizarrely*, boasts *no airports at all* of its own...

After a month's travel and the lengthy frustrations of *disembarkation*, I made my way with some difficulty to the *Grand Academy of Lagado* (*Luggnagg*)...

...and *thence* into the presence of the *Vice-Chancellor* himself...

...who was *not alone*...

DR GULLIVER! HOW **DELIGHTFUL!** WHEN WE **HEARD** YOU WERE COMING I **INVITED** SOME OF OUR SENIOR **STRULDBRUGGS** TO MEET YOU, THE ONES WHO **ALSO** MET **YOUR ANCESTOR!**

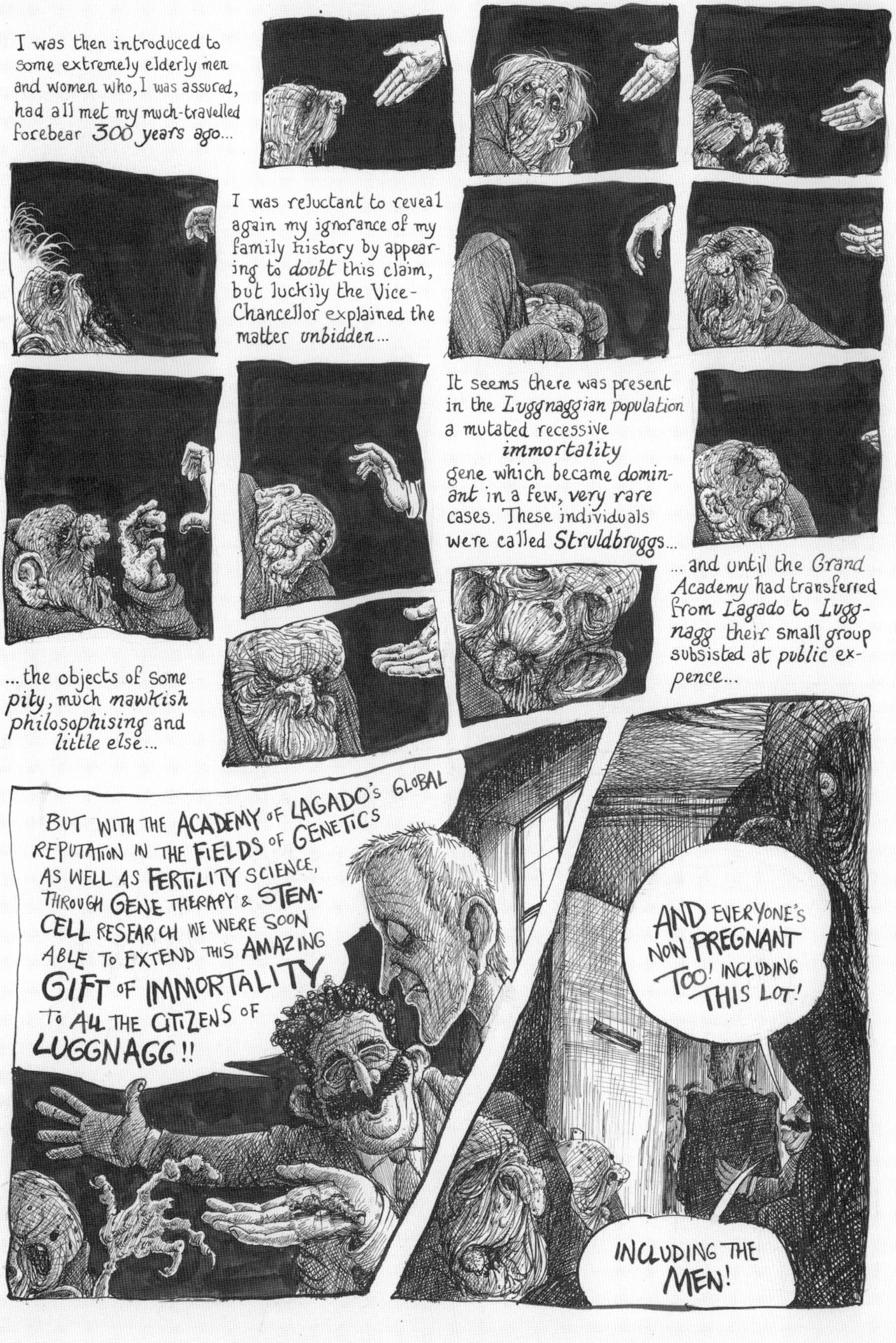
I was then introduced to some extremely elderly men and women who, I was assured, had all met my much-travelled forebear 300 years ago...
I was reluctant to reveal again my ignorance of my family history by appearing to doubt this claim, but luckily the Vice-Chancellor explained the matter unbidden...
It seems there was present in the Luggnaggian population a mutated recessive immortality gene which became dominant in a few, very rare cases. These individuals were called Struldbruggs...
... and until the Grand Academy had transferred from Lagado to Luggnagg their small group subsisted at public expence...
... the objects of some pity, much mawkish philosophising and little else...
BUT WITH THE ACADEMY OF LAGADO'S GLOBAL REPUTATION IN THE FIELDS OF GENETICS AS WELL AS FERTILITY SCIENCE, THROUGH GENE THERAPY & STEM-CELL RESEARCH WE WERE SOON ABLE TO EXTEND THIS AMAZING GIFT OF IMMORTALITY TO ALL THE CITIZENS OF LUGGNAGG!!
AND EVERYONE'S NOW PREGNANT TOO! INCLUDING THIS LOT!
INCLUDING THE MEN!

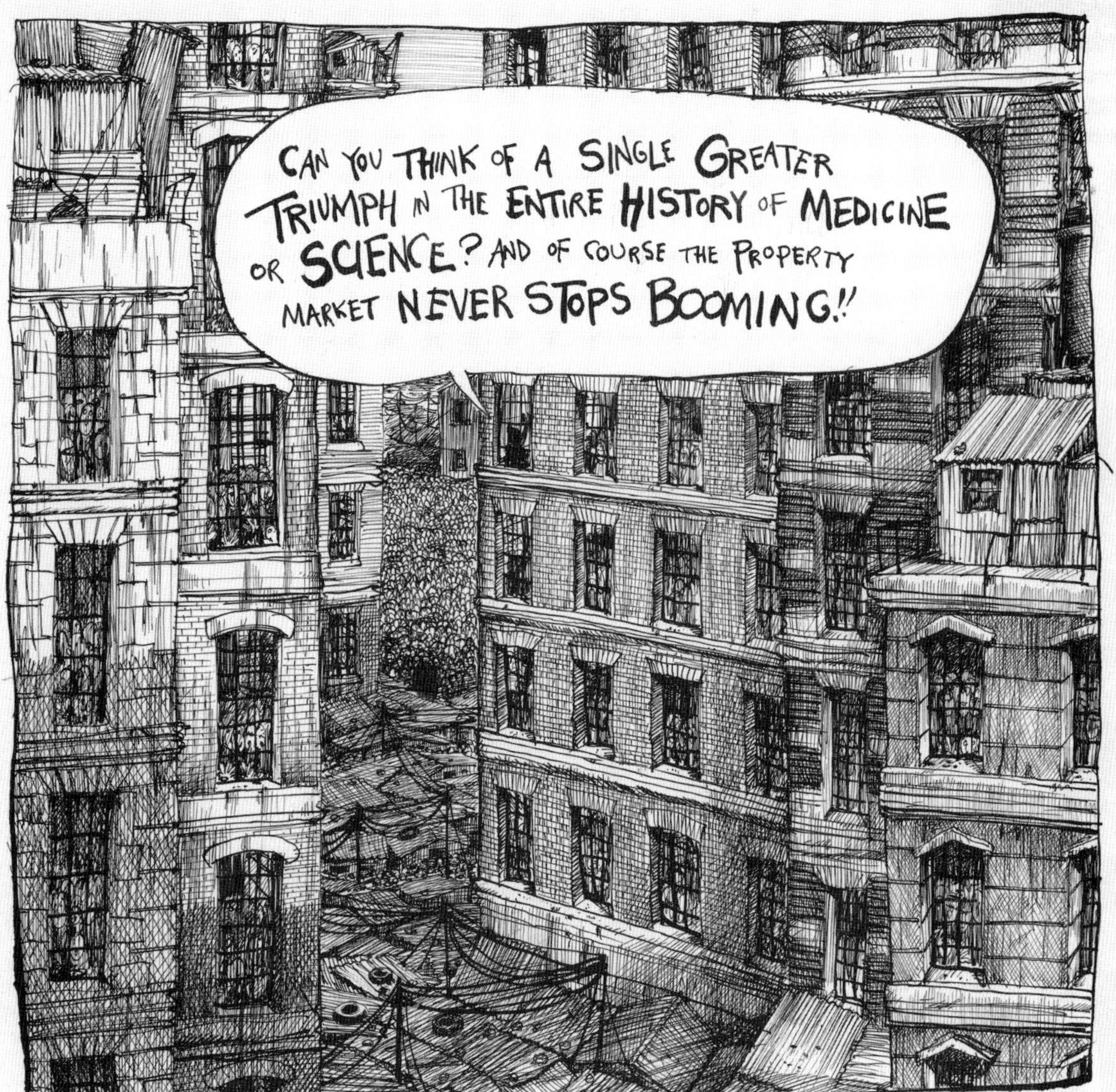
CAN YOU THINK OF A SINGLE GREATER TRIUMPH IN THE ENTIRE HISTORY OF MEDICINE OR SCIENCE? AND OF COURSE THE PROPERTY MARKET NEVER STOPS BOOMING!!

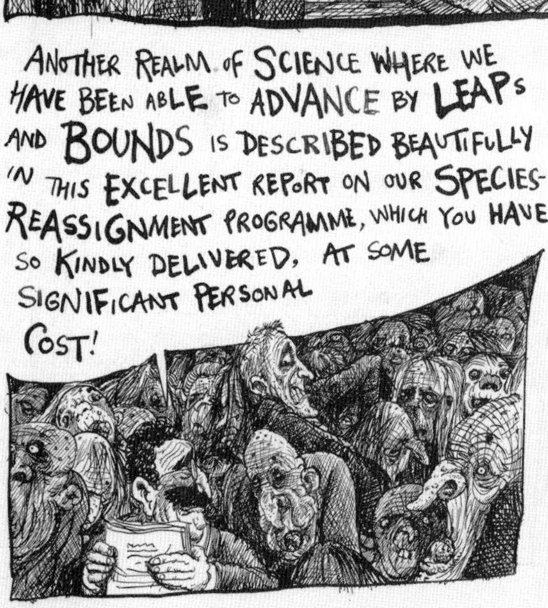
ANOTHER REALM OF SCIENCE WHERE WE HAVE BEEN ABLE TO ADVANCE BY LEAPS AND BOUNDS IS DESCRIBED BEAUTIFULLY IN THIS EXCELLENT REPORT ON OUR SPECIES-REASSIGNMENT PROGRAMME, WHICH YOU HAVE SO KINDLY DELIVERED, AT SOME SIGNIFICANT PERSONAL COST!

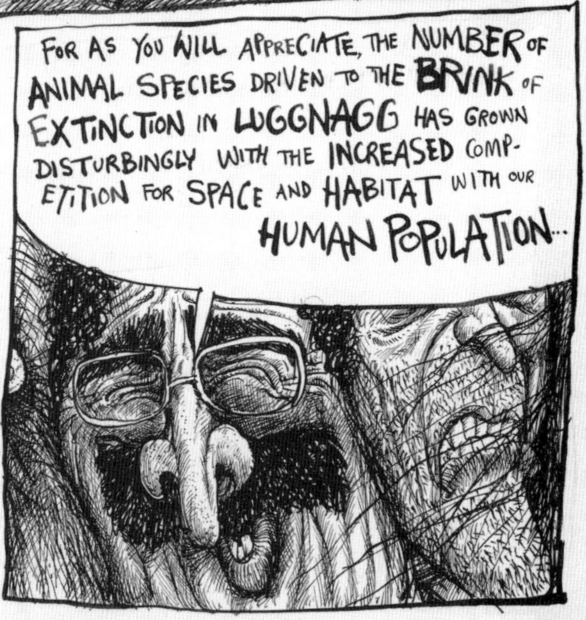
FOR AS YOU WILL APPRECIATE, THE NUMBER OF ANIMAL SPECIES DRIVEN TO THE BRINK OF EXTINCTION IN LUGGNAGG HAS GROWN DISTURBINGLY WITH THE INCREASED COMPETITION FOR SPACE AND HABITAT WITH OUR HUMAN POPULATION...

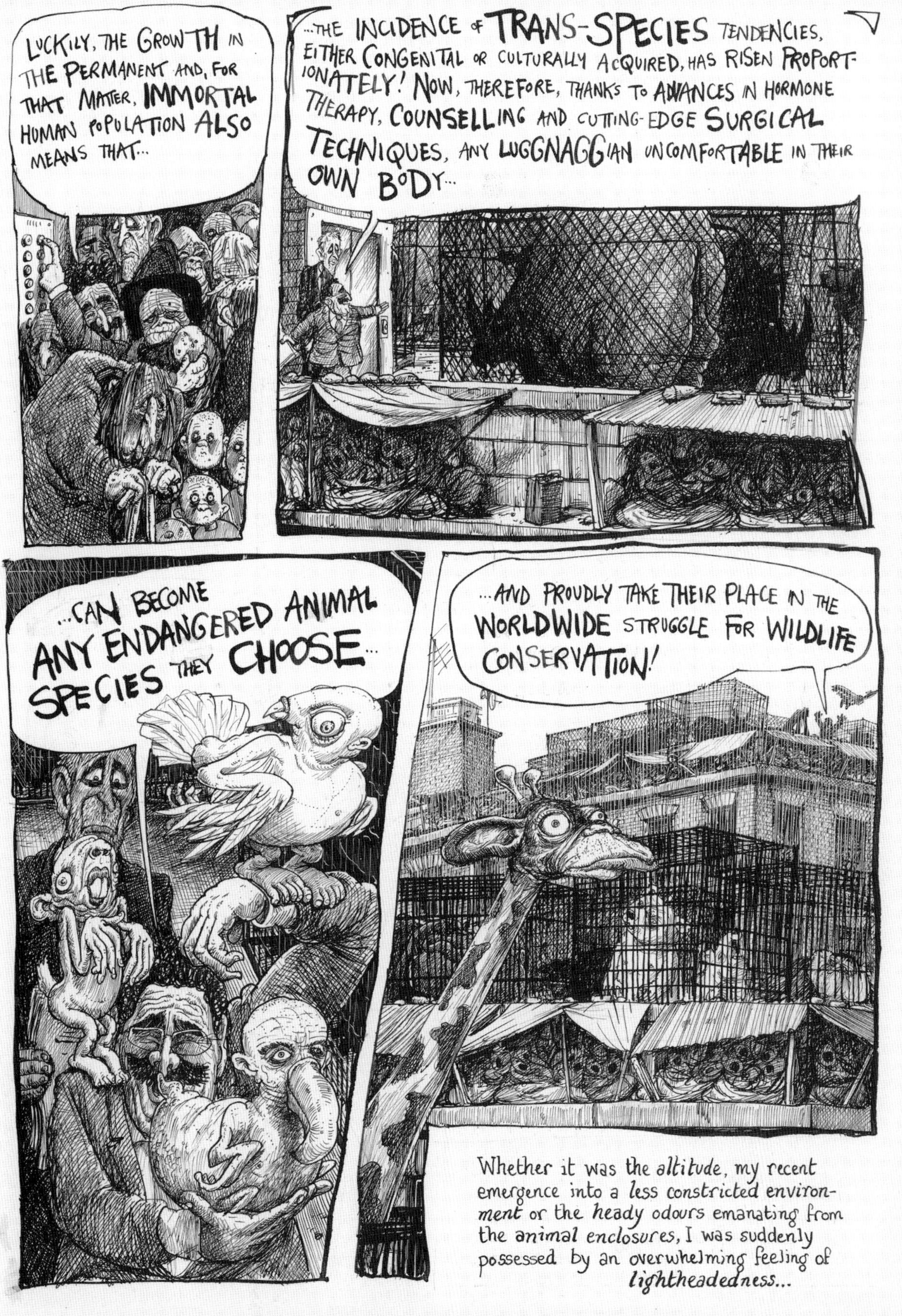
LUCKILY, THE GROWTH IN THE PERMANENT AND, FOR THAT MATTER, IMMORTAL HUMAN POPULATION ALSO MEANS THAT...
...THE INCIDENCE OF TRANS-SPECIES TENDENCIES, EITHER CONGENITAL OR CULTURALLY ACQUIRED, HAS RISEN PROPORTIONATELY! NOW, THEREFORE, THANKS TO ADVANCES IN HORMONE THERAPY, COUNSELLING AND CUTTING-EDGE SURGICAL TECHNIQUES, ANY LUGGNAGGIAN UNCOMFORTABLE IN THEIR OWN BODY...
...CAN BECOME ANY ENDANGERED ANIMAL SPECIES THEY CHOOSE...
...AND PROUDLY TAKE THEIR PLACE IN THE WORLDWIDE STRUGGLE FOR WILDLIFE CONSERVATION!
Whether it was the *altitude*, my recent emergence into a *less constricted* environment or the *heady* odours emanating from the *animal enclosures*, I was suddenly possessed by an overwhelming feeling of *lightheadedness*...

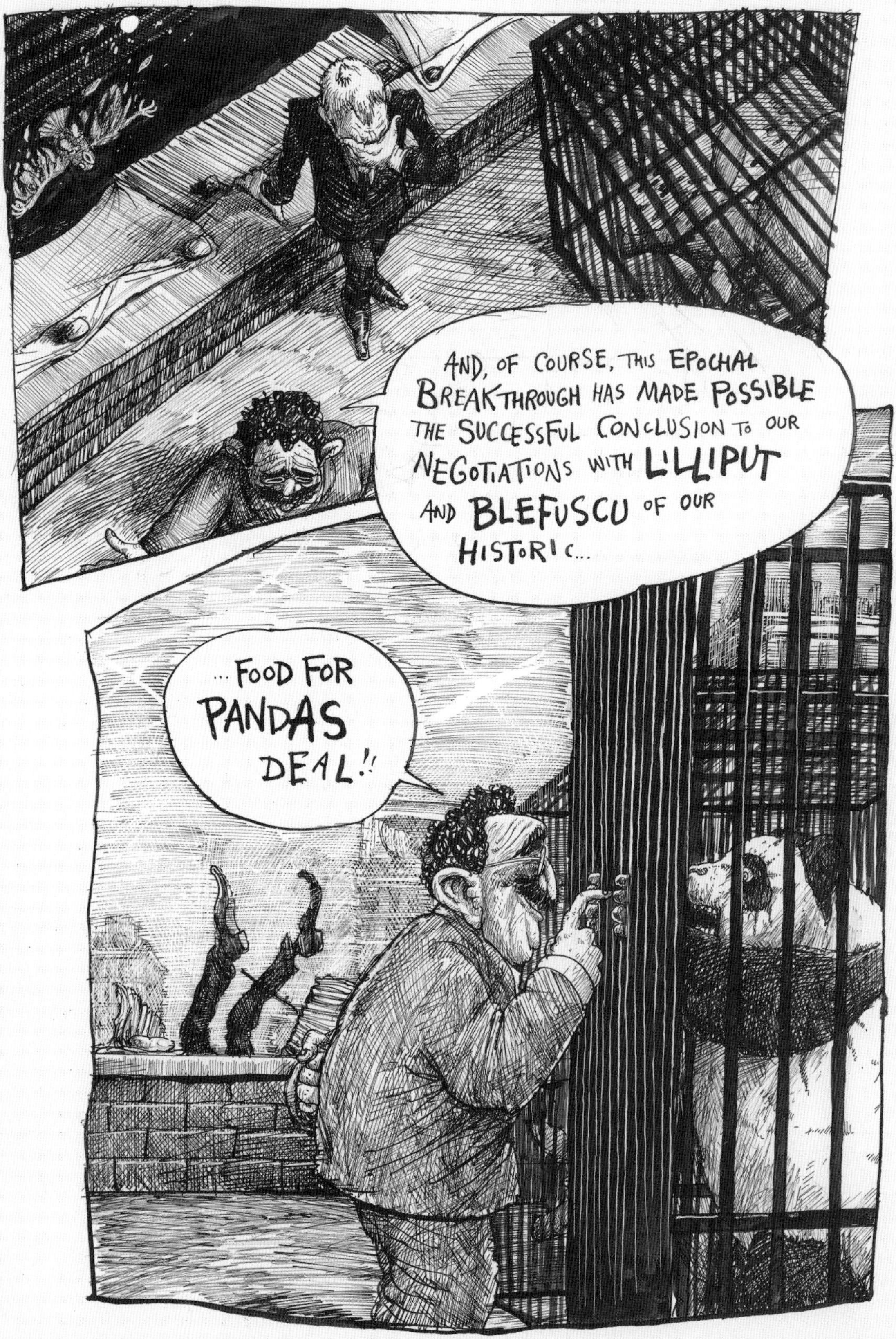
AND, OF COURSE, THIS EPOCHAL BREAKTHROUGH HAS MADE POSSIBLE THE SUCCESSFUL CONCLUSION TO OUR NEGOTIATIONS WITH LILLIPUT AND BLEFUSCU OF OUR HISTORIC...
...FOOD FOR PANDAS DEAL!!

A Voyage to the country of the HOUYHNHNMS

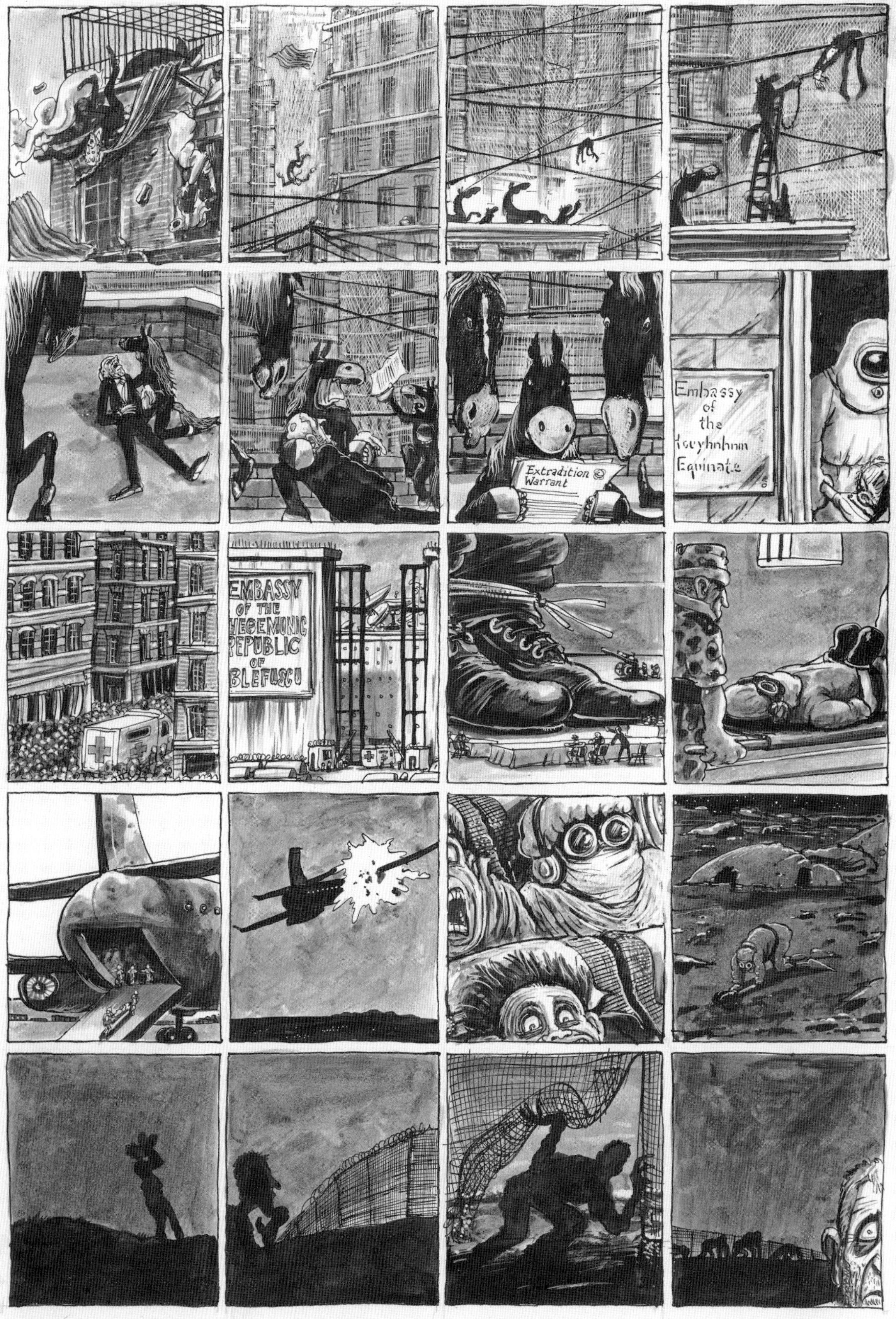

Extradition Warrant
Embassy of the Houyhnhnm Equinate
EMBASSY OF THE HEGEMONIC REPUBLIC OF BLEFUSCU

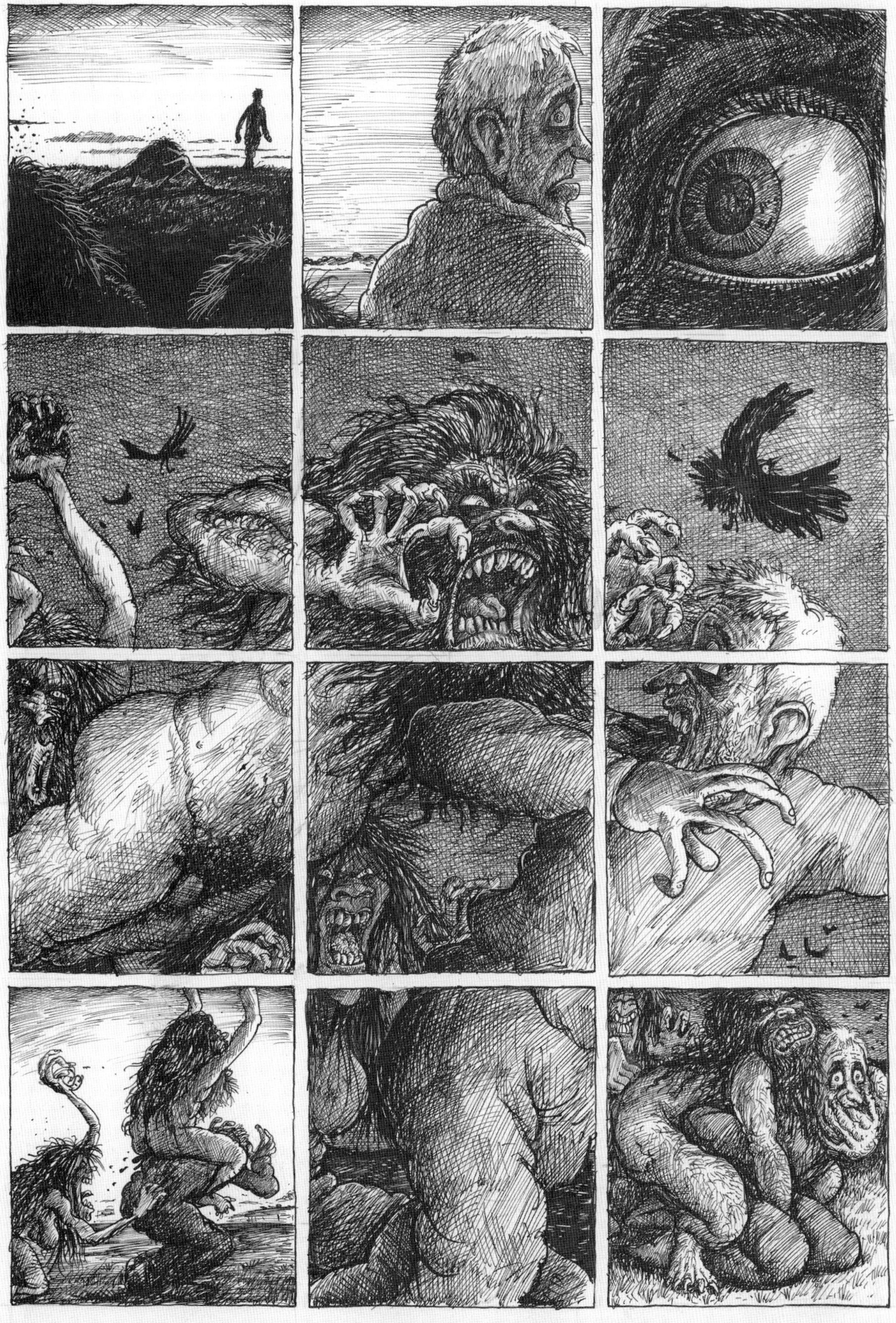

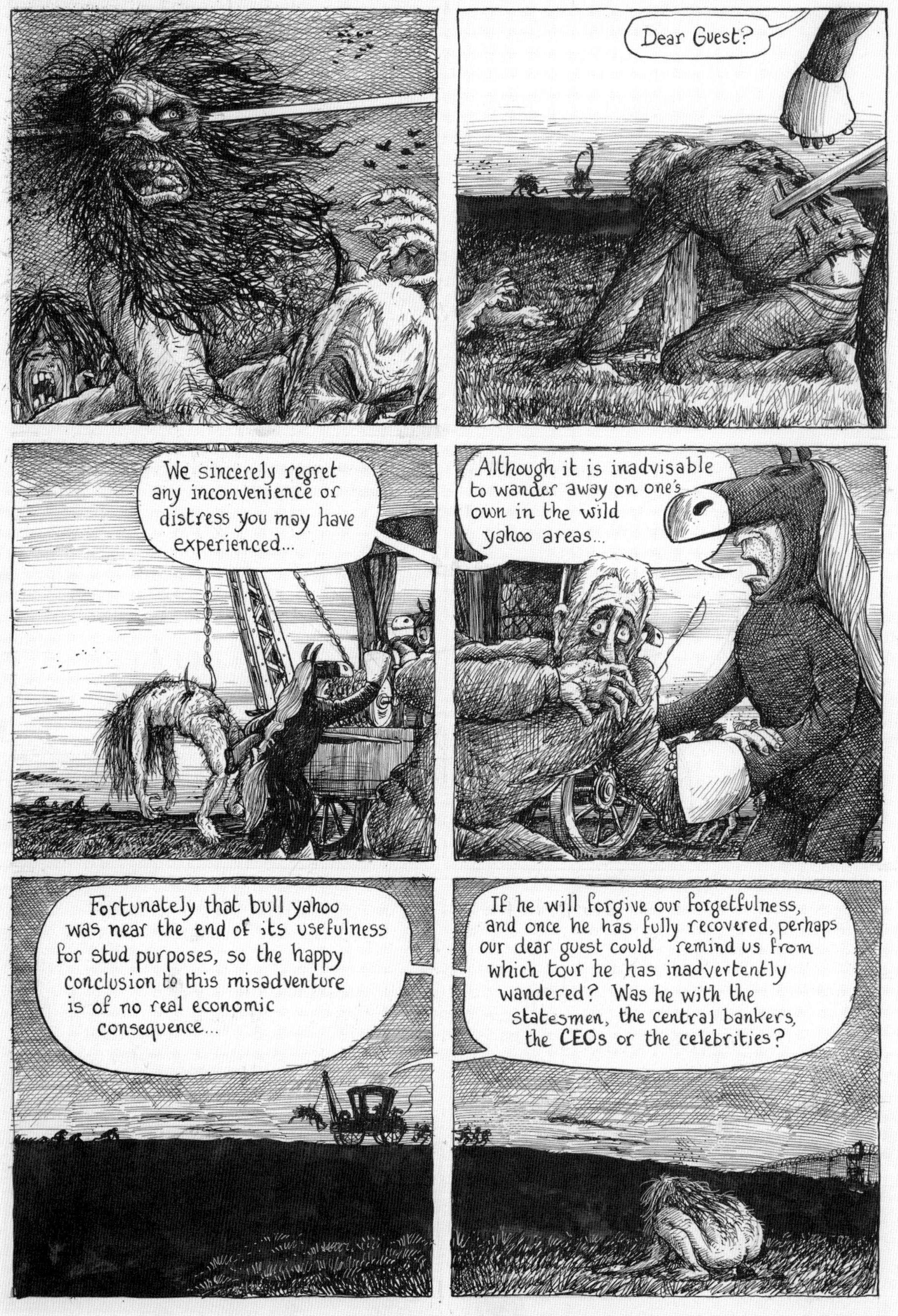
Dear Guest?
We sincerely regret any inconvenience or distress you may have experienced...
Although it is inadvisable to wander away on one's own in the wild yahoo areas...
Fortunately that bull yahoo was near the end of its usefulness for stud purposes, so the happy conclusion to this misadventure is of no real economic consequence...
If he will forgive our forgetfulness, and once he has fully recovered, perhaps our dear guest could remind us from which tour he has inadvertently wandered? Was he with the statesmen, the central bankers, the CEOs or the celebrities?

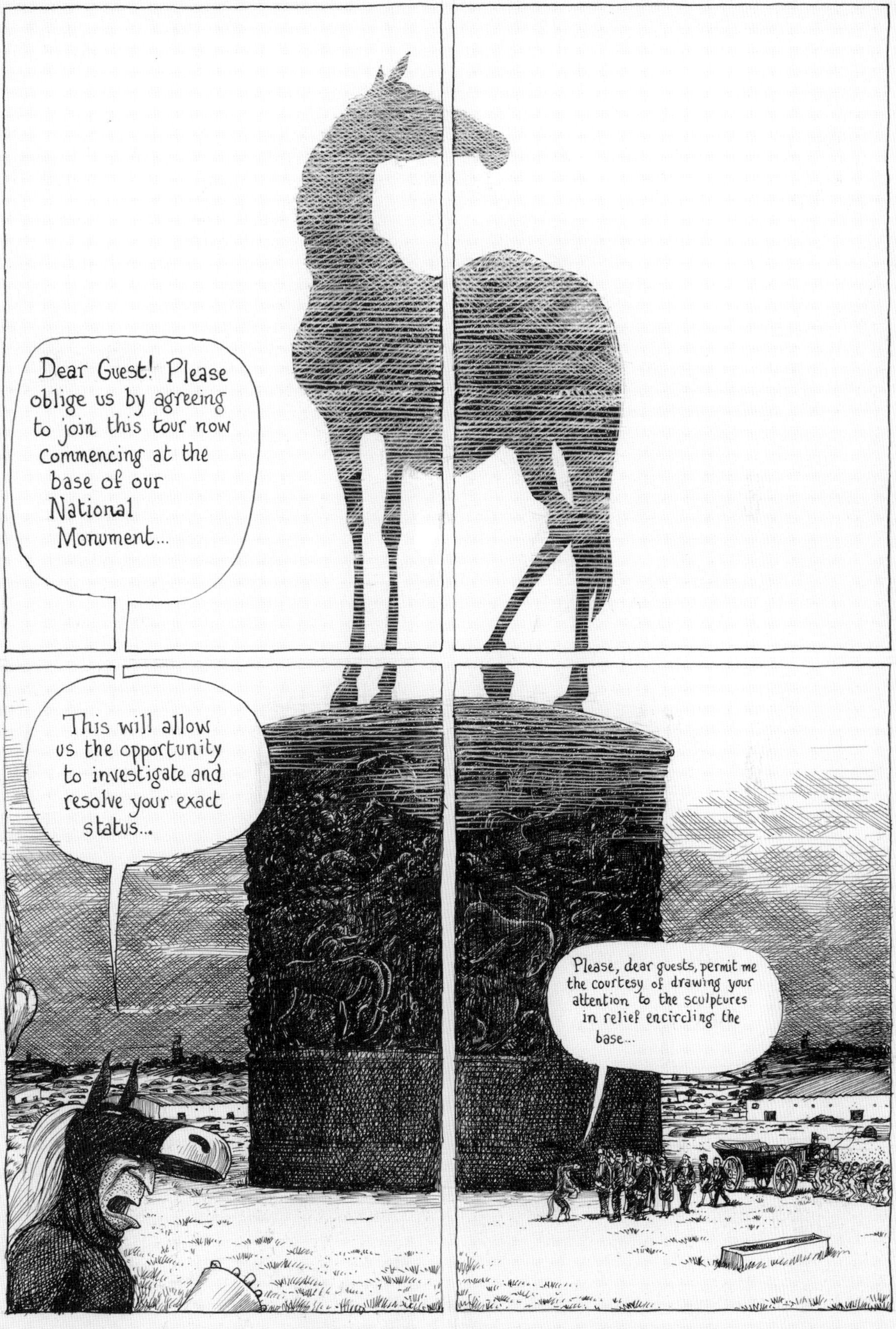

Dear Guest! Please oblige us by agreeing to join this tour now commencing at the base of our National Monument...
This will allow us the opportunity to investigate and resolve your exact status...
Please, dear guests, permit me the courtesy of drawing your attention to the sculptures in relief encircling the base...

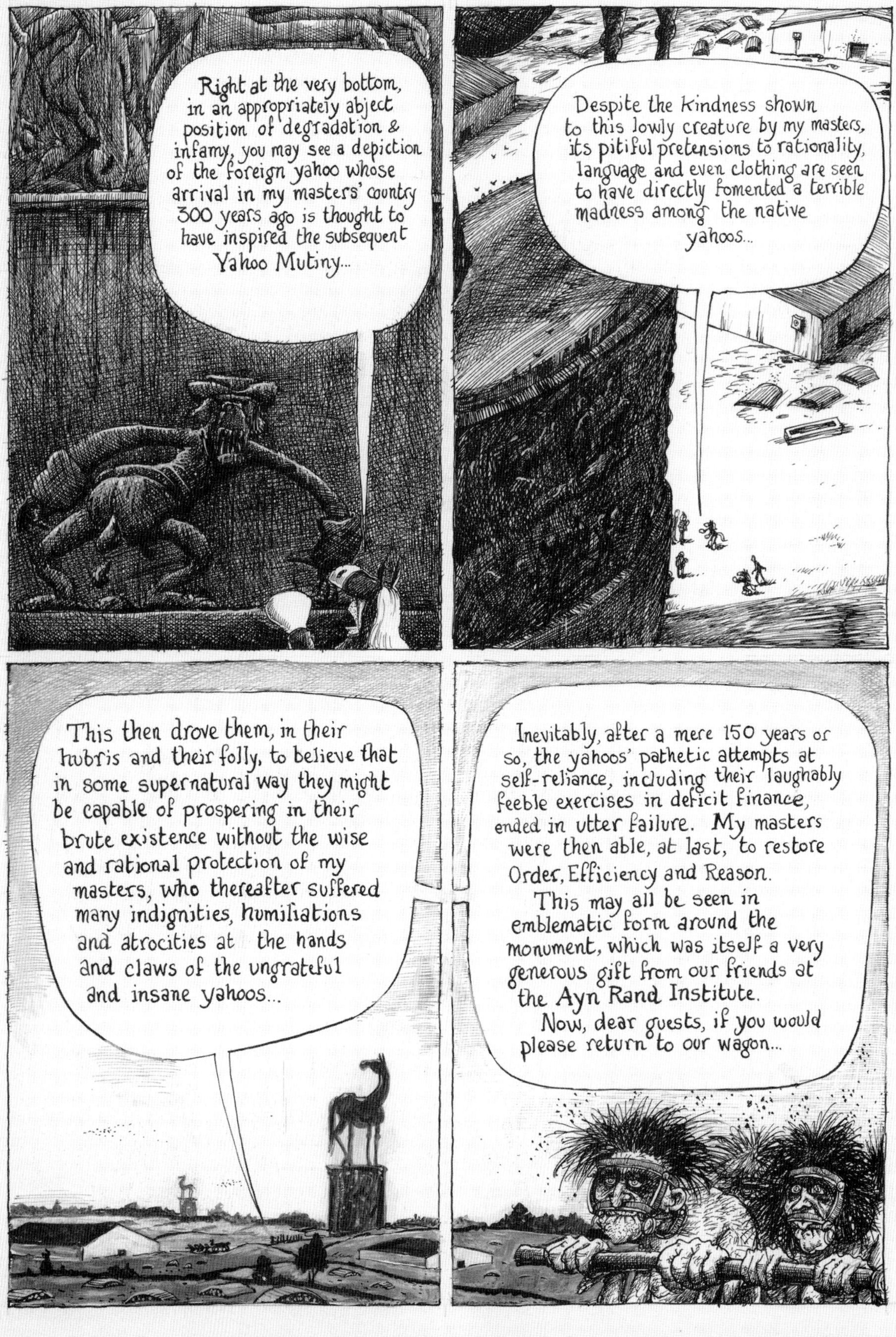
Right at the very bottom, in an appropriately abject position of degradation & infamy, you may see a depiction of the foreign yahoo whose arrival in my masters' country 300 years ago is thought to have inspired the subsequent Yahoo Mutiny...
Despite the kindness shown to this lowly creature by my masters, its pitiful pretensions to rationality, language and even clothing are seen to have directly fomented a terrible madness among the native yahoos...
This then drove them, in their hubris and their folly, to believe that in some supernatural way they might be capable of prospering in their brute existence without the wise and rational protection of my masters, who thereafter suffered many indignities, humiliations and atrocities at the hands and claws of the ungrateful and insane yahoos...
Inevitably, after a mere 150 years or so, the yahoos' pathetic attempts at self-reliance, including their laughably feeble exercises in deficit finance, ended in utter failure. My masters were then able, at last, to restore Order, Efficiency and Reason. This may all be seen in emblematic form around the monument, which was itself a very generous gift from our friends at the Ayn Rand Institute. Now, dear guests, if you would please return to our wagon...

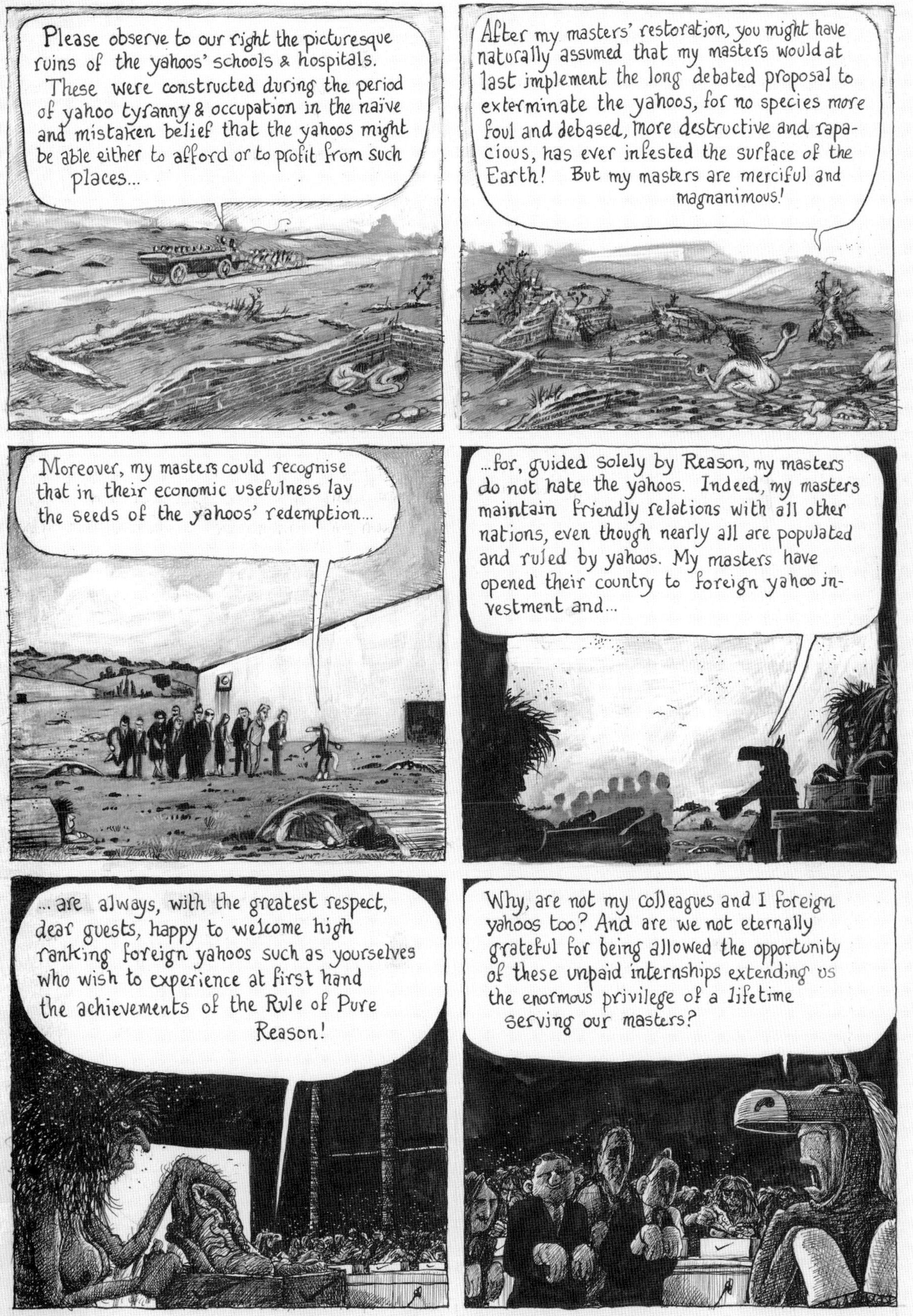
Please observe to our right the picturesque ruins of the yahoos' schools & hospitals. These were constructed during the period of yahoo tyranny & occupation in the naïve and mistaken belief that the yahoos might be able either to afford or to profit from such places...
After my masters' restoration, you might have naturally assumed that my masters would at last implement the long debated proposal to exterminate the yahoos, for no species more foul and debased, more destructive and rapacious, has ever infested the surface of the Earth! But my masters are merciful and magnanimous!
Moreover, my masters could recognise that in their economic usefulness lay the seeds of the yahoos' redemption...
...for, guided solely by Reason, my masters do not hate the yahoos. Indeed, my masters maintain friendly relations with all other nations, even though nearly all are populated and ruled by yahoos. My masters have opened their country to foreign yahoo investment and...
...are always, with the greatest respect, dear guests, happy to welcome high ranking foreign yahoos such as yourselves who wish to experience at first hand the achievements of the Rule of Pure Reason!
Why, are not my colleagues and I foreign yahoos too? And are we not eternally grateful for being allowed the opportunity of these unpaid internships extending us the enormous privilege of a lifetime serving our masters?

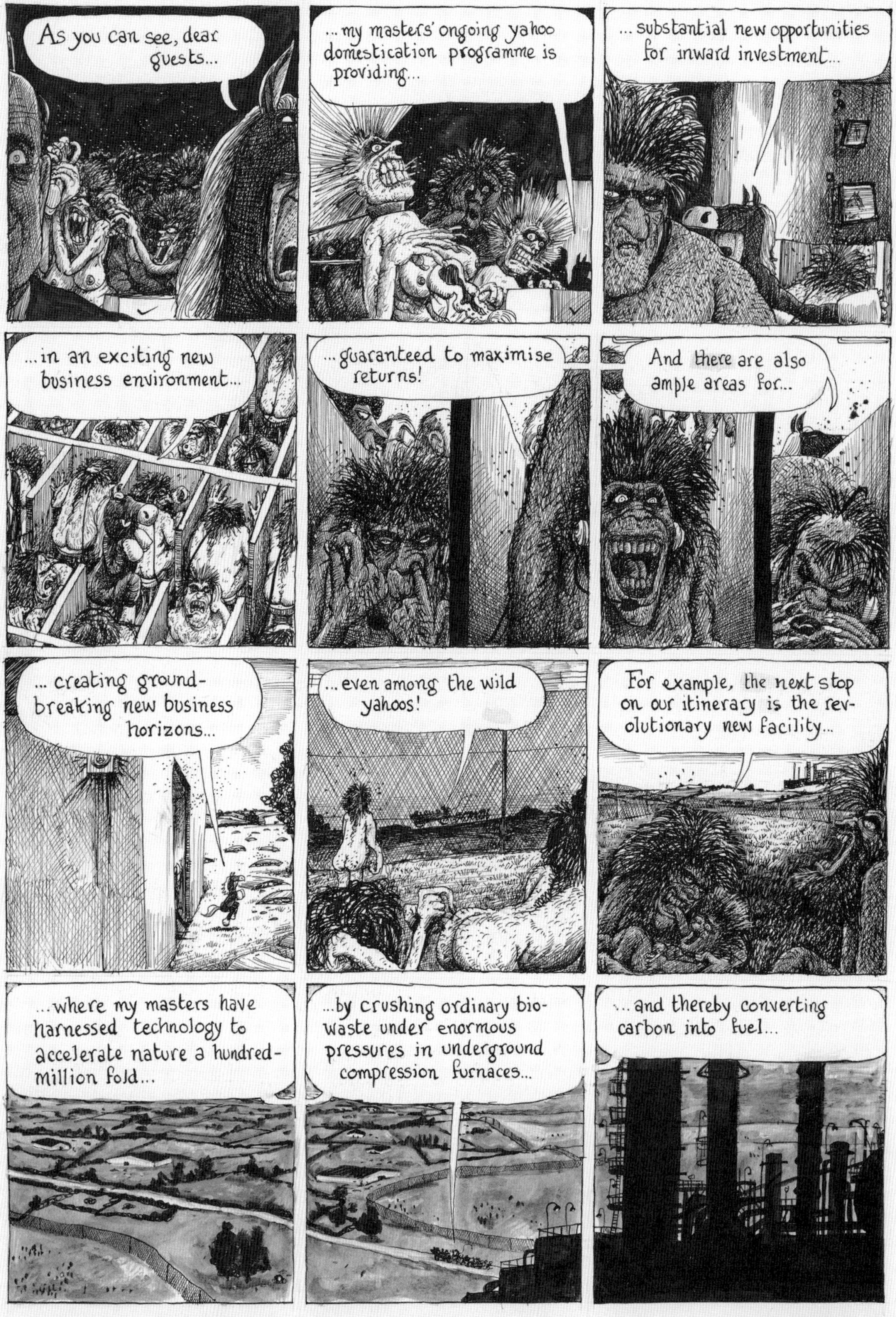
As you can see, dear guests...
... my masters' ongoing yahoo domestication programme is providing...
... substantial new opportunities for inward investment...
... in an exciting new business environment...
... guaranteed to maximise returns!
And there are also ample areas for...
... creating ground-breaking new business horizons...
... even among the wild yahoos!
For example, the next stop on our itinerary is the revolutionary new facility...
... where my masters have harnessed technology to accelerate nature a hundred-million fold...
... by crushing ordinary bio-waste under enormous pressures in underground compression furnaces...
... and thereby converting carbon into fuel...

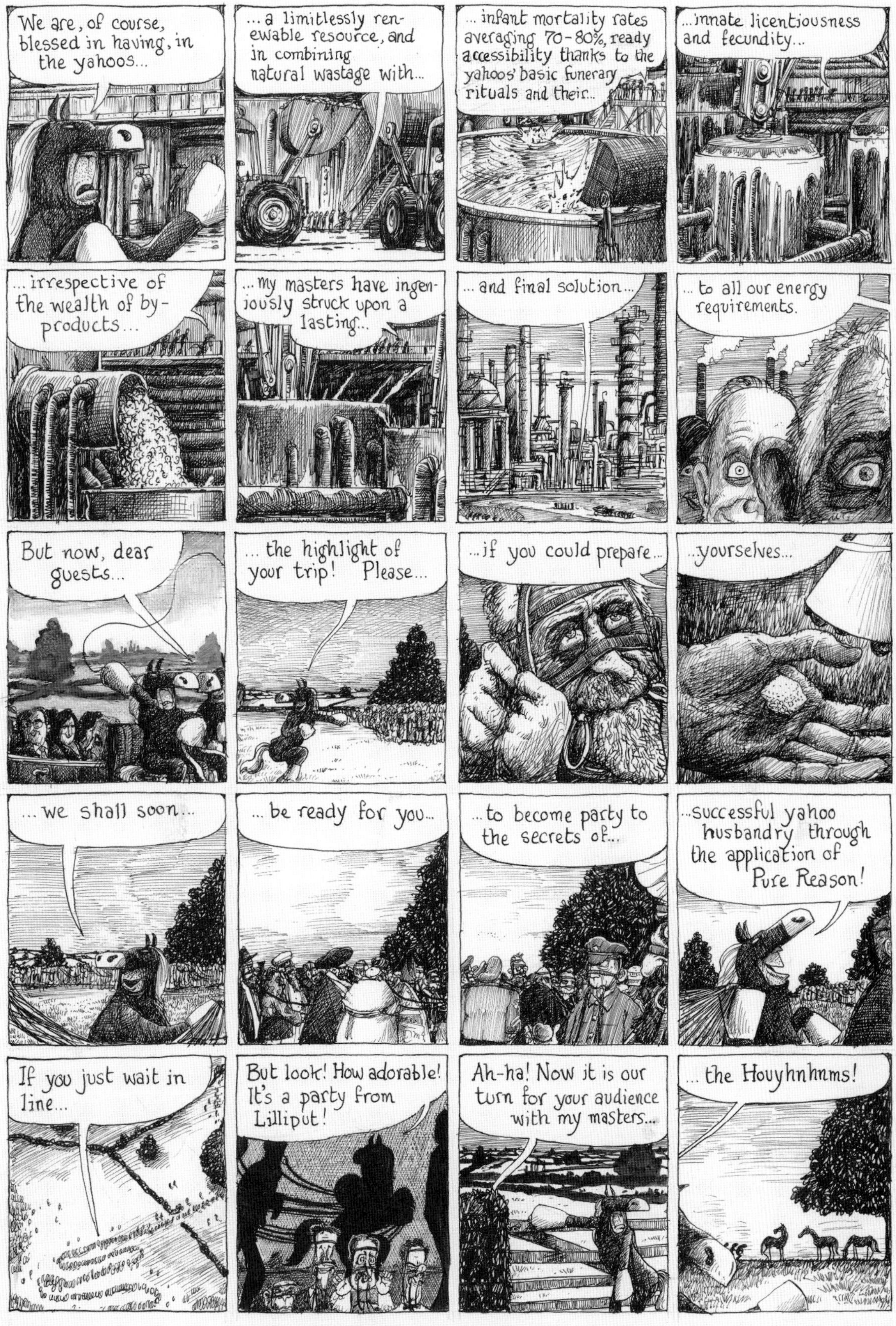
We are, of course, blessed in having, in the yahoos...
... a limitlessly renewable resource, and in combining natural wastage with...
... infant mortality rates averaging 70-80%, ready accessibility thanks to the yahoos' basic funerary rituals and their...
...innate licentiousness and fecundity...
... irrespective of the wealth of by-products...
... my masters have ingeniously struck upon a lasting...
... and final solution...
... to all our energy requirements.
But now, dear guests...
... the highlight of your trip! Please...
...if you could prepare...
...yourselves...
... we shall soon...
... be ready for you...
... to become party to the secrets of...
...successful yahoo husbandry through the application of Pure Reason!
If you just wait in line...
But look! How adorable! It's a party from Lilliput!
Ah-ha! Now it is our turn for your audience with my masters...
... the Houyhnhnms!

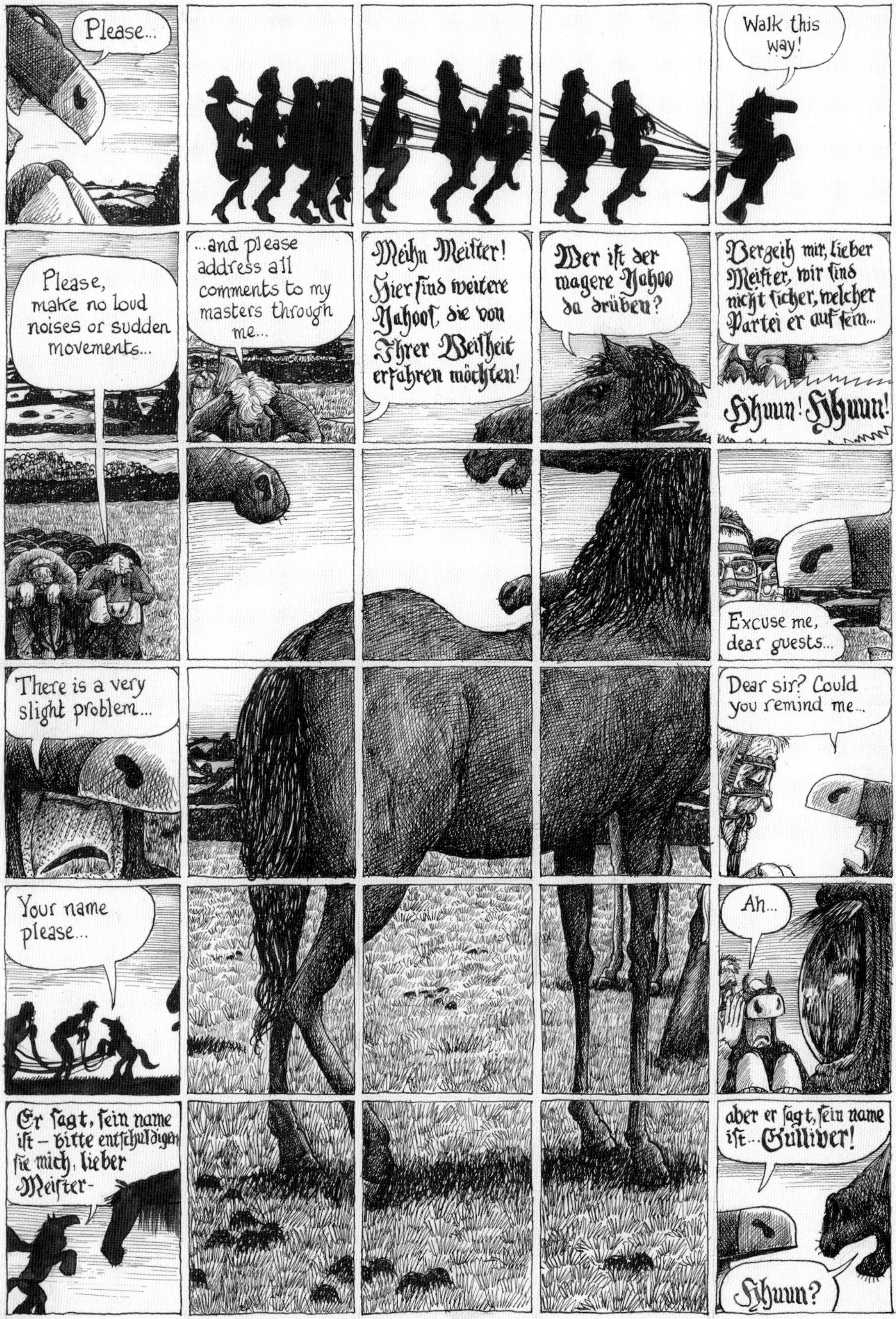
Please...
Walk this way!
Please, make no loud noises or sudden movements...
...and please address all comments to my masters through me...
Meihn Meiſter! Hier ſind weitere Yahooſ, die von Ihrer Weiſheit erfahren möchten!
Wer iſt der magere Yahoo da drüben?
Verzeih mir, lieber Meiſter, wir ſind nicht ſicher, welcher Partei er auf ſein...
Hhuun! Hhuun!
Excuse me, dear guests...
There is a very slight problem...
Dear sir? Could you remind me...
Your name please...
Ah...
Er ſagt, ſein name iſt – bitte entſchuldigen ſie mich, lieber Meiſter-
aber er ſagt, ſein name iſt... Gulliver!
Hhuun?

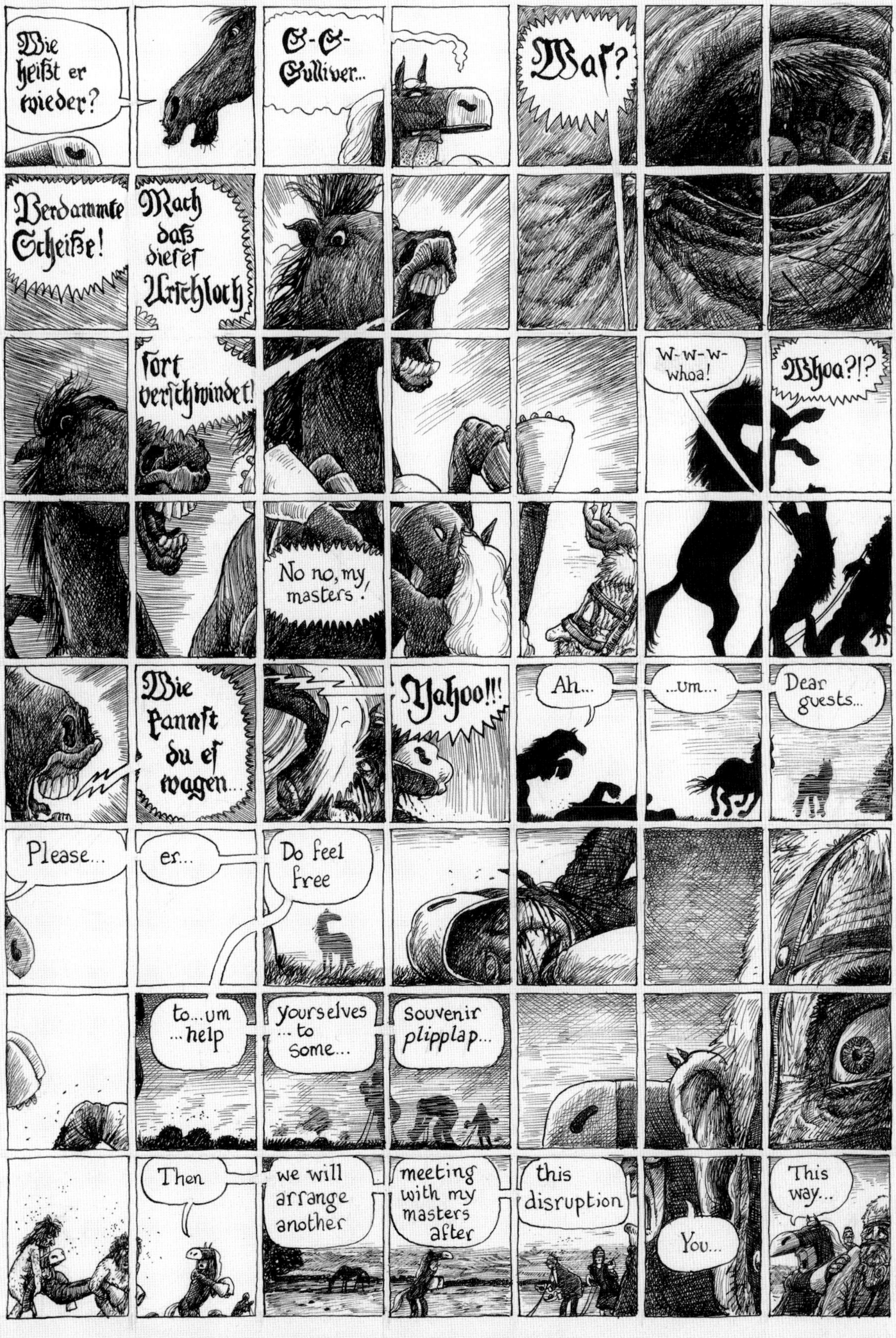
Wie heißt er wieder?
G-G-Gulliver...
Was?
Verdammte Scheiße!
Mach daß dieser Arschloch fort verschwindet!
W-w-w-whoa!
Whoa?!?
No no, my masters!
Wie kannst du es wagen...
Yahoo!!!
Ah...
...um...
Dear guests...
Please...
er...
Do feel free
to...um ...help
yourselves ...to some...
souvenir plipplap...
Then
we will arrange another
meeting with my masters after
this disruption
You...
This way...

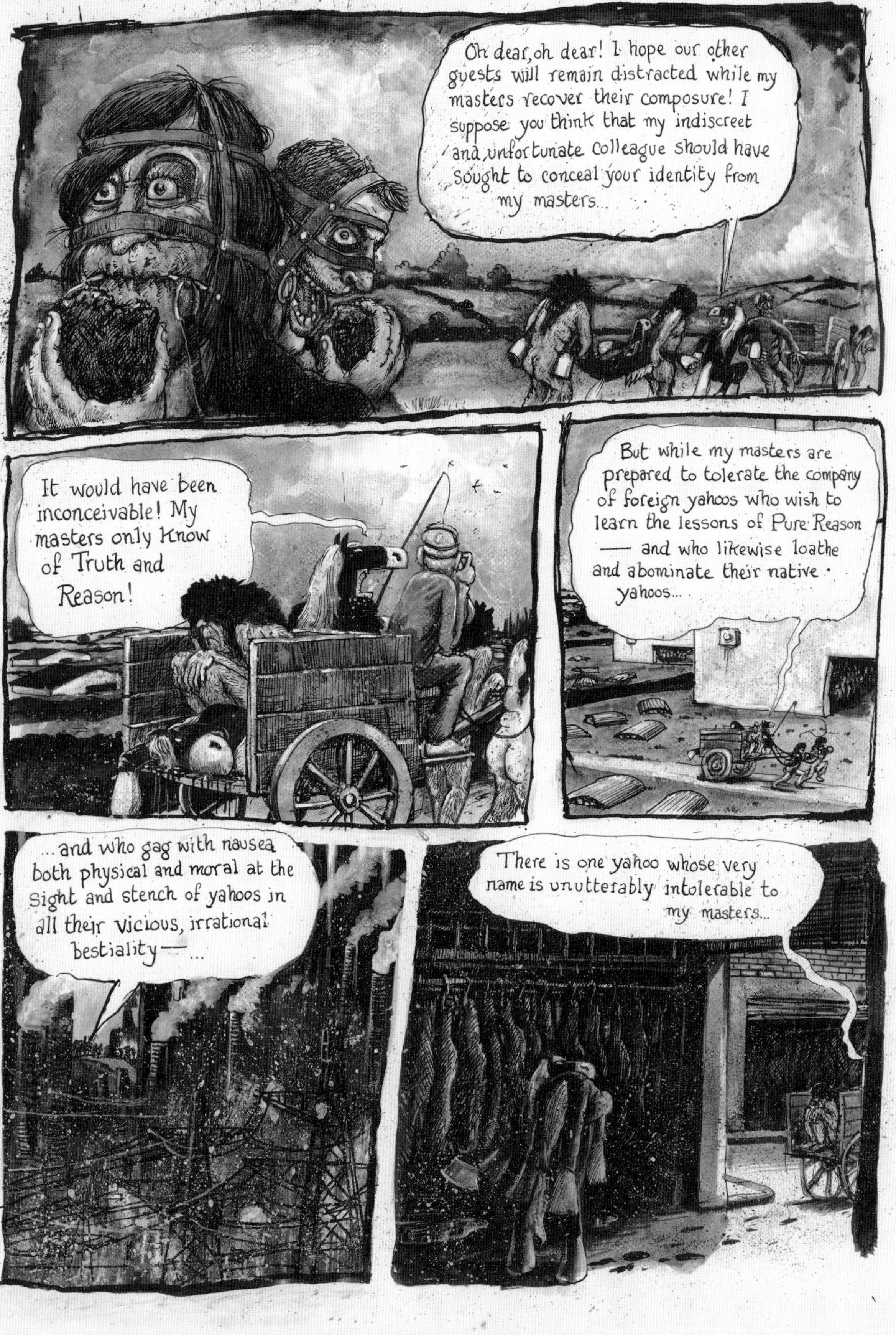
Oh dear, oh dear! I hope our other guests will remain distracted while my masters recover their composure! I suppose you think that my indiscreet and unfortunate colleague should have sought to conceal your identity from my masters...
It would have been inconceivable! My masters only know of Truth and Reason!
But while my masters are prepared to tolerate the company of foreign yahoos who wish to learn the lessons of Pure Reason — and who likewise loathe and abominate their native yahoos...
...and who gag with nausea both physical and moral at the sight and stench of yahoos in all their vicious, irrational bestiality— ...
There is one yahoo whose very name is unutterably intolerable to my masters...

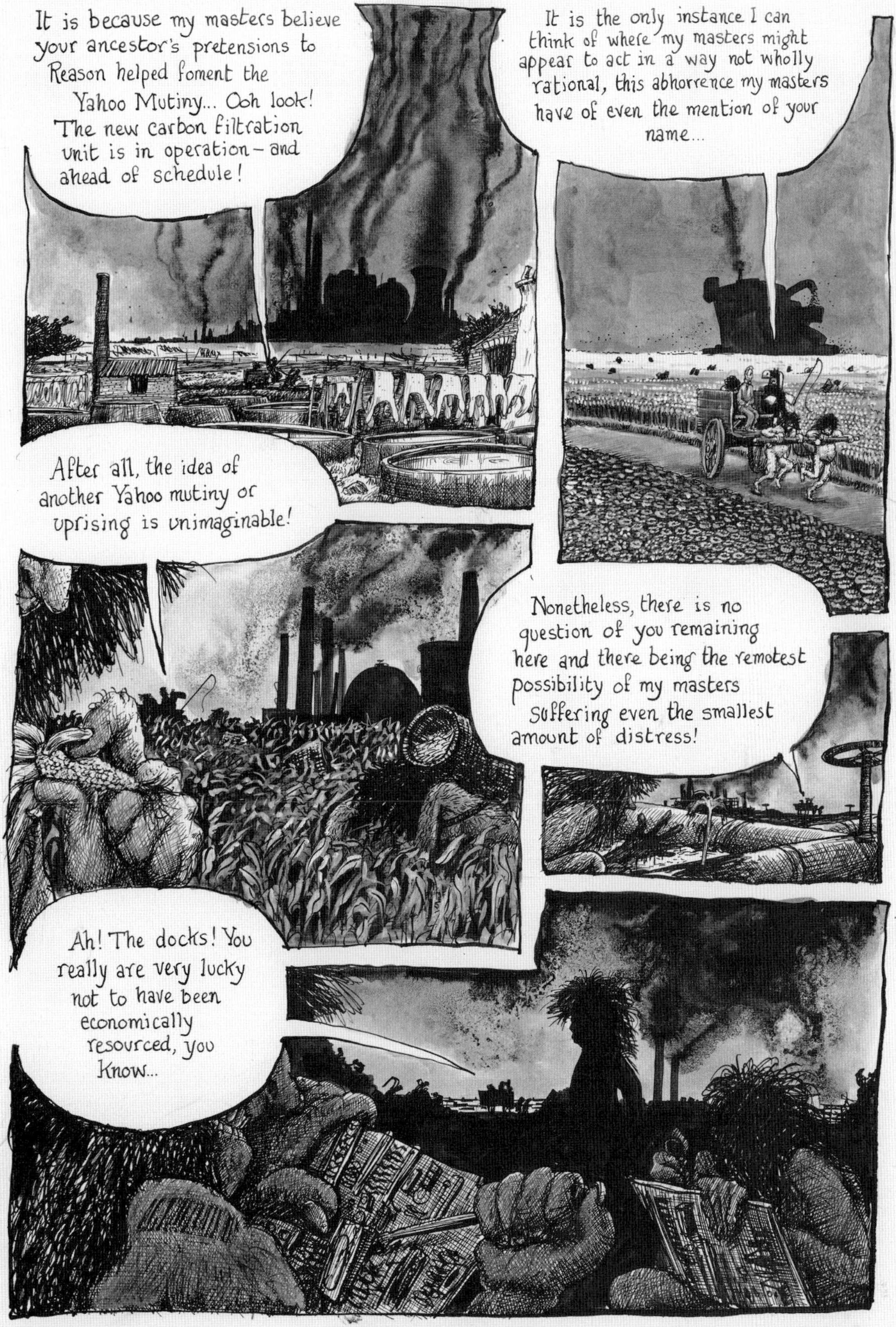
It is because my masters believe your ancestor's pretensions to Reason helped foment the Yahoo Mutiny... Ooh look! The new carbon filtration unit is in operation – and ahead of schedule!
It is the only instance I can think of where my masters might appear to act in a way not wholly rational, this abhorrence my masters have of even the mention of your name...
After all, the idea of another Yahoo mutiny or uprising is unimaginable!
Nonetheless, there is no question of you remaining here and there being the remotest possibility of my masters suffering even the smallest amount of distress!
Ah! The docks! You really are very lucky not to have been economically resourced, you know...

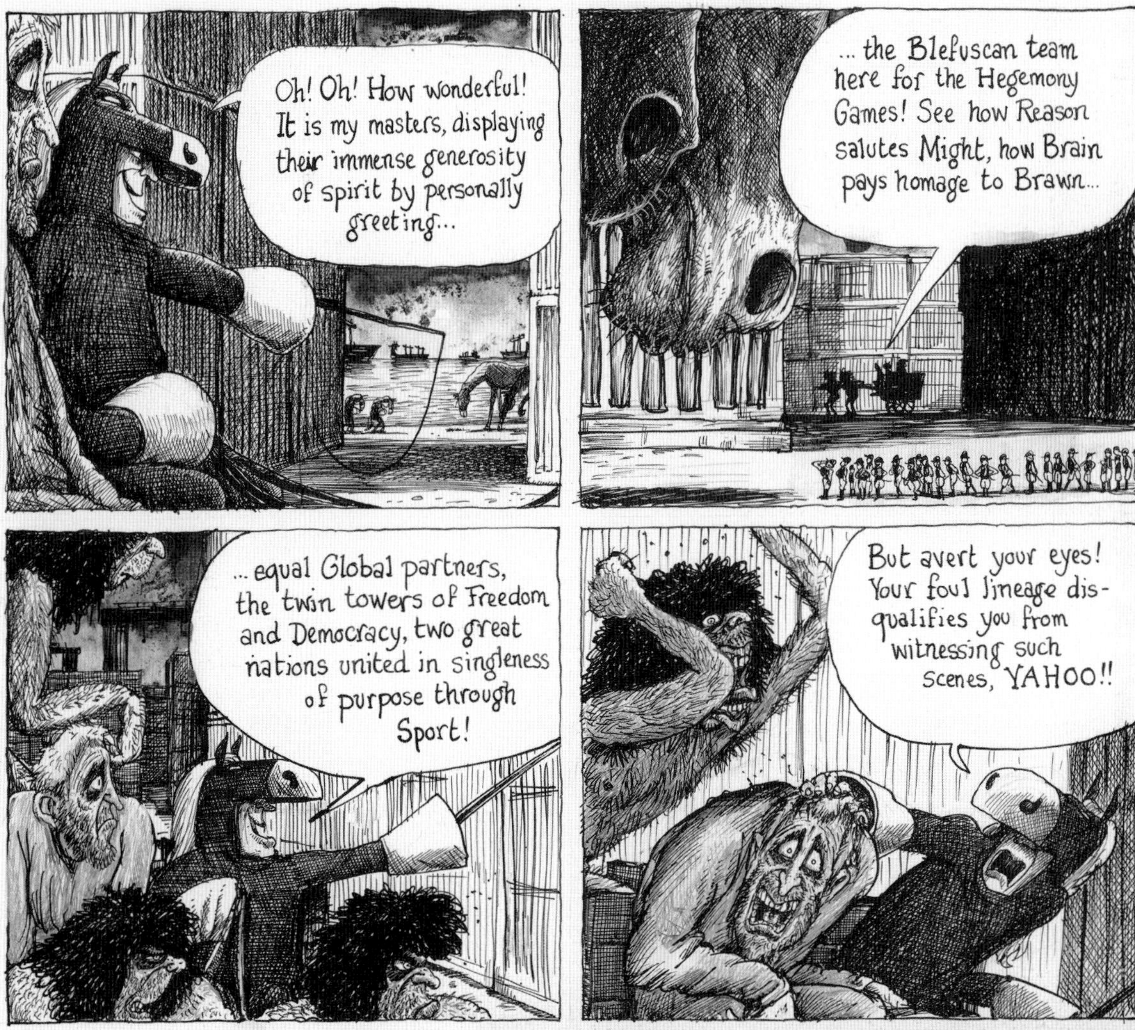
Oh! Oh! How wonderful! It is my masters, displaying their immense generosity of spirit by personally greeting...
... the Blefuscan team here for the Hegemony Games! See how Reason salutes Might, how Brain pays homage to Brawn...
... equal Global partners, the twin towers of Freedom and Democracy, two great nations united in singleness of purpose through Sport!
But avert your eyes! Your foul lineage disqualifies you from witnessing such scenes, YAHOO!!

Thus, once more, did my ancestor cast his *long shadow* over me. I was to be exiled from the company of those creatures whose *grace & nobility* had so impressed me, just through an accident of genetics and the *longevity* of a *name*. Over and again I cursed that earlier Gulliver, thanks to whom I should now *never* learn any more of the austere wisdom of the HOUYHNHNMS, their every action guided *solely by Reason*. Nor would I ever hear again their *mellifluous language* or behold their *entrepreneurial flair*...

I was placed aboard a cargo ship, sailing within the hour, and although the Portuguese captain & crew showed me every consideration, I instinctively recoiled from them *in disgust*, so alike to the *repulsive* YAHOOs did they seem to me...

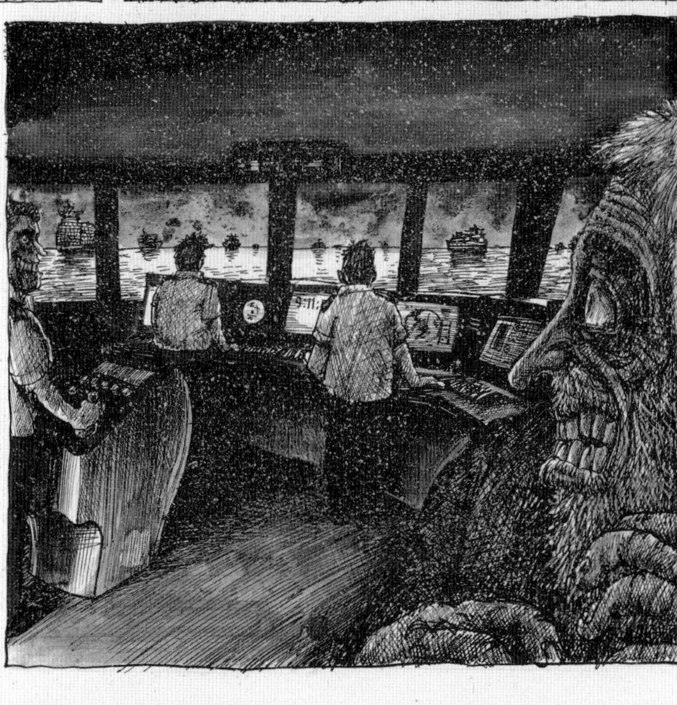

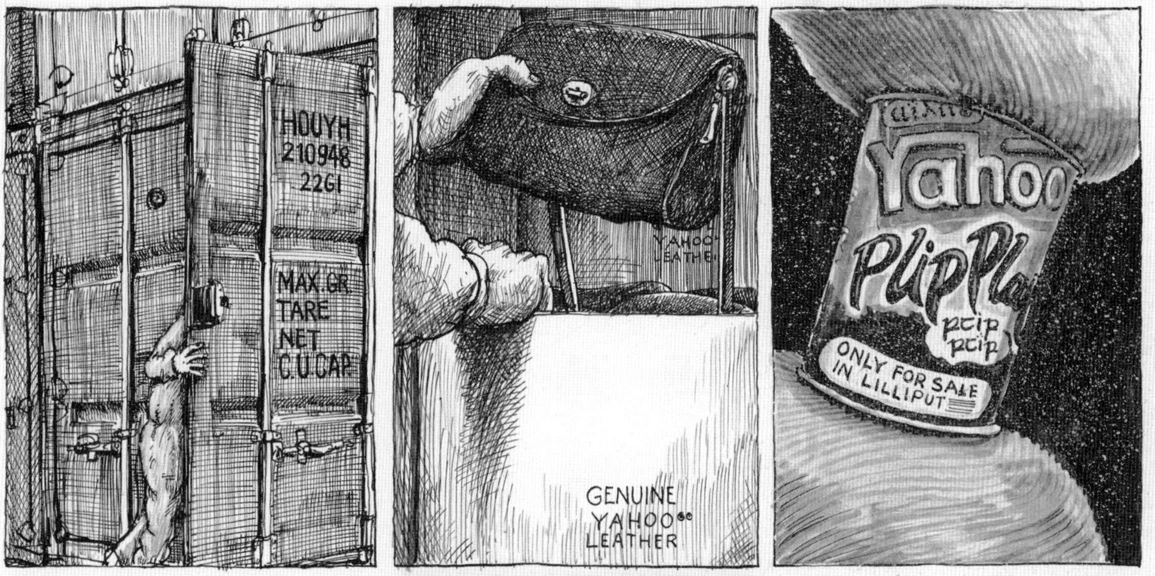
HOUYH
210948
22G1
MAX.GR
TARE
NET
C.U.CAP.
YAHOO
GENUINE
YAHOO
LEATHER
Yahoo
PlipPla
ptip
ptip
ONLY FOR SALE
IN LILLIPUT

I was thereafter left to my own *devices*, although my misery was compounded once I appreciated the *scope* of the Houyhnhnm's enterprise, from which I was now *forever excluded*...

For it was now clear to me, as I sought *distraction* from my predicament & the physical depredations of my recent past, that by applying **REASON** to their yahoo problem, my masters had succeeded also in answering *all the World's needs and wants!*

In my solitary peregrinations around the ship I came across an *enormous wealth* of *luxury goods, essentials, raw materials*...

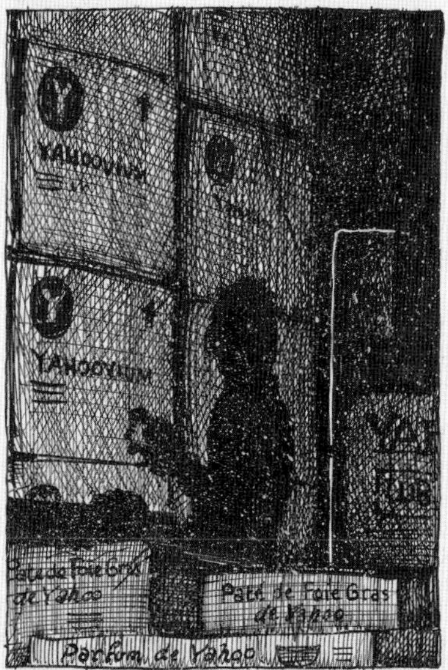
YAHOOYUM
Paté de Foie Gras
de Yahoo
Parfum de Yahoo

... *for the leisure industry* and a *pharmacopoeia* of medicaments, refined from harvested yahoo viscera, guaranteed to ameliorate the mental or physical suffering of any foreign yahoo...

I thought again of my masters' *great kindness* in providing mere yahoos with so much, and could not but help to shed a tear, of both gratitude and *loss*...

After several days of further exploration, I even happened upon a shipment of *books*, of *beautifully printed* volumes, bound in *hand-tooled* yahoo velum, showing once again my masters' reverence for *learning*...

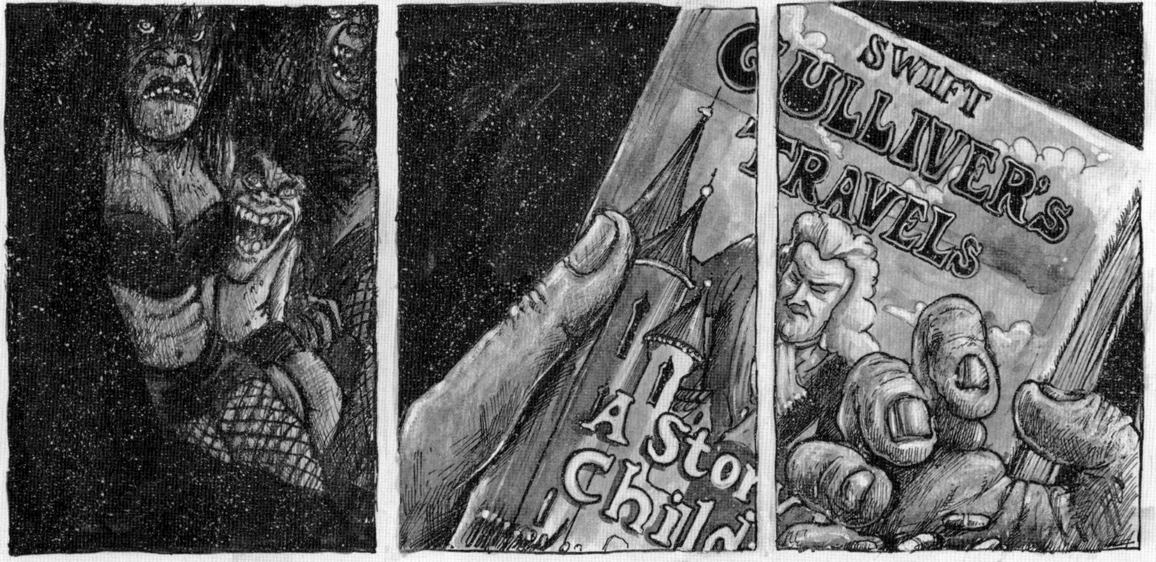
SWIFT
ULLIVER'S
TRAVELS

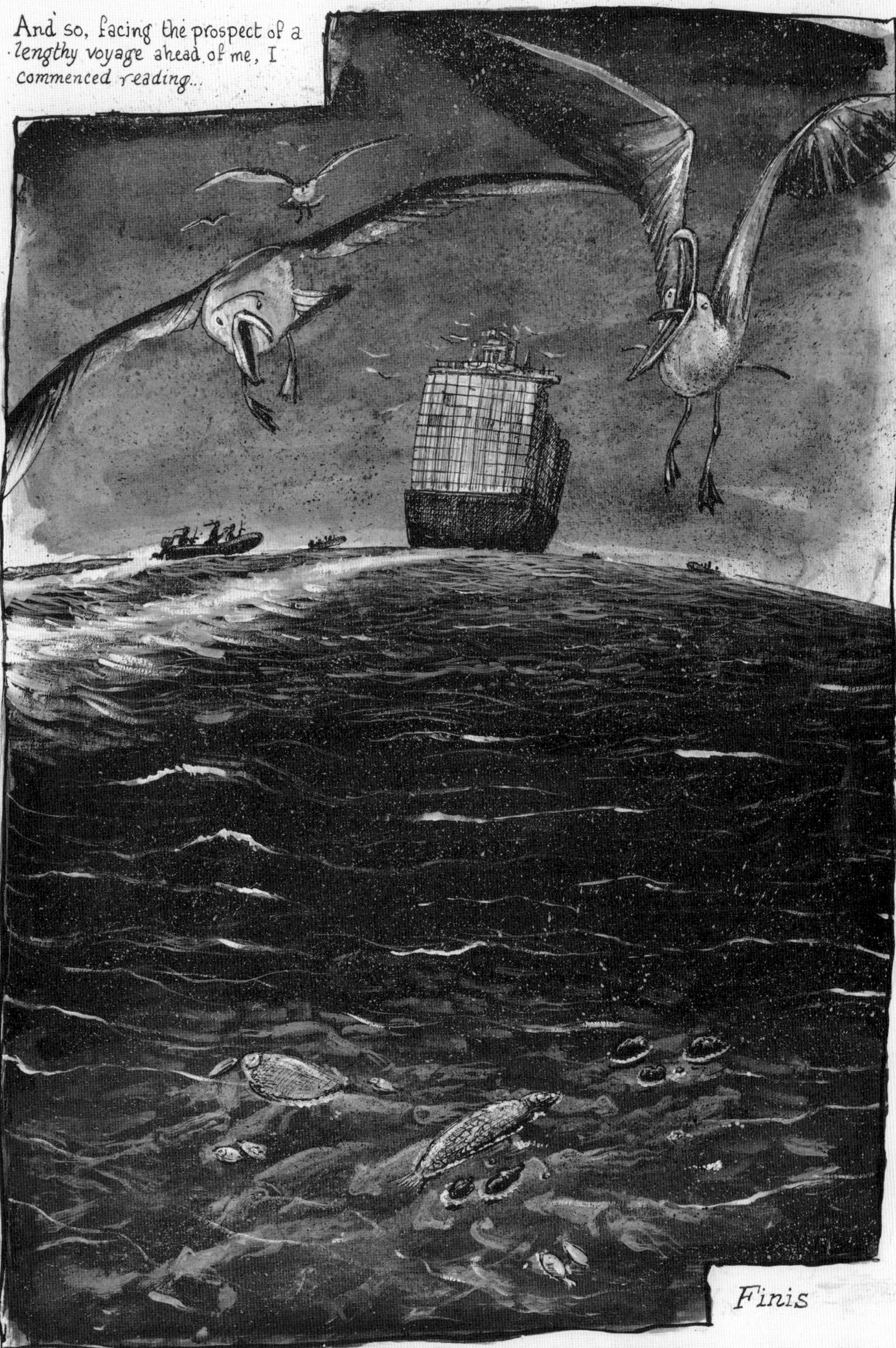
And so, facing the prospect of a lengthy voyage ahead of me, I commenced reading...
Finis

THIS BOOK has been, without question, the most difficult and depressing that I've ever worked on. Quite apart from its contents and subject matter, the act of transcribing, editing and adapting the 400 hours of frequently incoherent or inaudible audiotape of my co-author's narrativization-therapy sessions into a 110-page graphic novel was arduous enough. Moreover, it was his refusal to cooperate with me in any way whatsoever that made the task almost impossible. In mitigation, it should perhaps be pointed out that Dr Lionel Gulliver's status as a long-stay patient in a secure psychiatric unit didn't help matters, nor did the insistence of both his family and his physicians that any contact with a 'yahoo' like me would prove so distressing and traumatising, it was likely to wipe out what little progress had been made thus far, after so many years, in Dr Gulliver's treatment.

That said, the words in this book are essentially Dr Gulliver's. I've edited and reordered many of them but maintained, I hope, his 'voice' – including its typical, rather tortuous syntax – without entirely jeopardising clarity. Likewise, the decision to present his story in the form of a comic book was Dr Gulliver's: after hundreds of one-on-one sessions with Professor Helen Killane – one of the acknowledged pioneers of narrativization therapy – Dr Gulliver was, I've been assured, passionately insistent that his adventures be retold in what he called 'the defining medium of the age'. It was thought wisest, for clinical and other reasons, to comply with his wishes. In addition, the illustrations prefacing each section of the book are Dr Gulliver's own, produced on those rare occasions when it was considered safe enough to permit him access to the art block.

Many people have contributed to this project since its inception as part of the programme of care constructed between Dr Gulliver and Professor Killane, her colleague Zach Busner and the many other healthcare professionals with an interest or involvement in Gulliver's case. It would, therefore, be impossible to thank everyone but I'm particularly grateful to the following for their help, advice and support: Helen Killane, Zach Busner, Dexter Jakes, Patrick Wildgust, Nick Hayes, Dhiman Sengupta, Suzi Feay, Will Self, Mary-Lou Jennings, David Miller, Steve Bell, Shaun Whiteside, Ravi Mirchandani and everyone else at Atlantic Books, Joyce Bridgeman, Rose Rowson, Jonathon Baillie, Fred Rowson, Anita O'Brien, Anna Clarke and, most of all, the Gulliver family, to whom I extend my warmest thanks and deepest sympathy. I must also thank my various employers at the *Guardian*, *Independent on Sunday*, *Morning Star*, *Tribune*, Index on Censorship and the *Journal of the History of the Ear* for their continued tolerance of my occasionally prolonged absences during the production of the book.

How believable Dr Gulliver's testimony will prove to be remains up to the reader. Many of you, I know, will express incredulity at his apparent ignorance not only of rudimentary geography but also of the history and bibliography of his own family; others may baulk at the allegations he makes about the conduct of our Blefuscan allies. All I can say is that I have been assured that his particular condition is remarkable in the extent to which it inhibits the operation of the imagination in the sufferer; as Professor Killane put it to me herself, Dr Gulliver is as 'crazy as a dingo, but he ain't delusional'. To what degree this diagnosis is fully justified is currently subject to peer review, although all that really needs to be said at this point is that the likelihood of even a partial recovery from the physical and psychological traumas suffered on his various travels remains remote in the extreme.

MARTIN ROWSON

Martin Rowson is a multi-award winning cartoonist and writer whose work appears regularly in the *Guardian*, *Independent on Sunday*, *Daily Mirror* and many other publications. His previous books include graphic adaptations of "The Waste Land" and *The Life and Opinions of Tristram Shandy, Gentleman*, as well as a memoir about his late parents, *Stuff*, which was long-listed for the Samuel Johnson Prize in 2007. He was appointed Cartoonist Laureate by former London mayor Ken Livingstone in 2001 in return for one pint of London Pride per annum (still 6 years in arrears) and is also a former vice-president of the Zoological Society of London. He lives in south-east London with his wife and, whenever they're passing by, their two children.